Street Rebellion

Resistance Beyond Violence and Nonviolence

Praise for *Street Rebellion*

"In this significant contribution, Case shows how riots make a difference. Essential reading for anyone who thought that the violence-nonviolence debate was over."
—Lesley Wood, author of *Crisis and Control: The Militarization of Protest Policing*

"For far too long the violence/nonviolence debate has been mired in abstract pontification and muddled terminology. Finally, we have Ben Case's incisive and meticulously researched analysis that captures the contextual utility of violent forms of resistance. *Street Rebellion* is truly a must read for every activist and social movement scholar."
—Mark Bray, author of *Antifa: The Anti-Fascist Handbook*

"*Street Rebellion* strikes a precise blow to the current accepted dichotomy between violence and nonviolence and flips the entire field of civil resistance on its head. Ben Case has eloquently returned riots to their rightful place in the history of modern social movements."
—Akin Olla, contributing writer at *The Guardian* and host of *This is The Revolution* podcast

"Benjamin Case's work is critical for understanding the way that movements for liberation are exploding across the globe, and to counter the misinformation that suggests the only path to change is through strict nonviolence. This is one of the most essential books of the year."
—Shane Burley, editor of *¡No Pasarán!: Antifascist Dispatches from a World in Crisis*

Street Rebellion

Resistance Beyond Violence and Nonviolence

Benjamin S. Case

© 2022 Benjamin S. Case
This edition © AK Press (Chico / Edinburgh)

ISBN: 978-1-84935-486-8
E-ISBN: 978-1-84935-487-5
Library of Congress Control Number: 2022935893

AK Press
370 Ryan Ave. #100
Chico, CA 95973
www.akpress.org
akpress@akpress.org

AK Press
33 Tower St.
Edinburgh EH6 7BN
Scotland
www.akuk.com
akuk@akpress.org

The above addresses would be delighted to provide you with the latest
AK Press distribution catalog, which features books, pamphlets, zines,
and stylish apparel published and/or distributed by AK Press. Alter-
natively, visit our websites for the complete catalog, latest news, and
secure ordering.

Cover Design by Crisis
Cover photo used with permission. SSPL/UIG / Bridgeman Images

Printed in the USA on acid-free paper

To my father, Charlie, for teaching me to think

Contents

List of Tables and Figures

List of Tables

List of Figures

Acknowledgments

This work is the result of innumerable conversations, experiences, and reflections over the course of almost eight years of research and writing. I would not have been able to produce these pages without the direct input, discussion, kindness, critique, and other forms of support from countless individuals and communities. First and foremost, I am indebted to the many movements that have inspired, educated, and motivated me. I have more comrades than I am able to name who have mentored me, talked and argued with me, and struggled alongside me, whose wisdom and experience informs my own. I also have dozens of participants to thank who I cannot name, for their willingness to speak with me about their experiences with riotous protest. I hope I do justice to your words.

For the years of formal education and feedback, I am grateful to John Markoff, Mohammed Bamyeh, Tarun Banerjee, and Michael Goodhart. Also many thanks to Paul Welle, Junia Howell, Stellan Vinthagen, Dana Moss, Ben Manski, Hank Johnston, and AK Thompson, who generously offered their advice and support at different stages of this project.

For various forms of teaching, co-learning, camaraderie, care, and partnership that influenced this work or sustained me as it developed through some very difficult times, more thanks than I am able to express to: James Alex Siebens, Hatem Hassan, Hillary Lazar, Caitlin Schroering, George Weddington, Danny Burridge, Ayşe Alnıaçık, Sebastián Cuéllar, Chie Togami, Ami Weintraub, Dade Lemanski, Eva Westheimer, Daniel Grover, Jess Gold, Ren Finkel, Jenni Walkup Jayes, Hallie Boas, Angela Wiley, Nicole Coffineau, Gillian Goldberg, Gabriel Hernández, Rachel

Elmer, Eric Eingold, Yotam Marom, Zoë West, Melanie Brazzell, Britt Lawson (and their cat, Elmo), Pádraig Korte, Diana Sierra Becerra, Kevin Young, Jonathan Stribling-Uss, Dennis Webster, and Bhavna Ramji. There are certainly more—I hope you know who you are.

Appreciation to Zach and Lorna, the editors at AK Press who helped me improve this manuscript and get it ready for publication, as well as the editors and peer reviewers at *Mobilization*, *Journal of Resistance Studies*, and *Theory in Action*, who aided me in articulating a lot of the ideas that appear in this book.

I have Cindy Crabb to thank for many things, possibly including my sanity, but here I will just say thank you for being such an amazing therapist. Much gratitude to my mother, Linda, and my stepfather, Doug, for the steadfast and appropriately critical support; to my father, Charlie, of blessed memory, for the lifetime of instruction and debate; and to my stepmother, Diana, for going through a lot with me.

And finally, Cat, thank you for offering to change that bathroom lightbulb. My life has been brighter ever since.

1.

Riots and Resistance

As long as there has been private property, there have been angry crowds setting it on fire. Riots have rocked cities throughout modern history in every region of the world, altering the course of political events and generating powerful images of resistance. It is arguably the oldest and most recognizable manifestation of social struggle from below. States have consolidated, technologies have advanced, and the landscape of the Earth is transforming, yet violent protests are no less significant today than they were a century ago. If anything, they are more so. In recent decades, mass civil uprisings have threatened or overthrown governments across the globe, and most of these revolts have included fiery street barricades, property destruction, and physical confrontations between protesters and security forces.

Political demonstrations are increasing worldwide, becoming more intense, and instances of violent protest have grown and spread.[1] Urban police forces undergo focused riot suppression training and keep specialized equipment on hand at all times in case a riot should break out. Amidst the COVID-19 pandemic, when people were directed to stay inside and avoid contact, police departments across the United States stocked up on riot gear.[2] Yet we remain stuck in the same arguments over violence and nonviolence, over peaceful protests versus riots. As we move into what is shaping up to be a new global era of street rebellion, it is time to re-assess the ways we understand social movement tactics and strategy.

The dictionary defines a riot as a violent disturbance of the peace by a crowd—a telling definition that assumes "peace" is the status quo. We will instead explore riots as crowd disturbances

that violate the façade of peace concealing an underlying condition of injustice. Around the world, riots occur in response
to similar repeated offenses: political corruption, displacement,
deprivation, and most of all, police violence. Across countries
and contexts, rioters exhibit patterned behavior—for example
defacing property, smashing windows, attacking buildings associated with political foes, throwing projectiles at police, and
burning vehicles, often involving repeated rituals and unspoken
rules.[3] The riot is a familiar event—we know it when we see it—
making the characters involved appear almost interchangeable
across time and space. Central to uprisings around the world
and throughout history, riots are among the most important and
under-studied aspects of social and political struggle.

Riots play a significant role in our imaginations as well. In
popular culture, from movies and novels to popular art and music
videos, the riot is a favorite narrative mechanism for conveying
chaos, disorder, and popular anger. The rioter has been both
demonized and romanticized, with their images now widely and
rapidly spread via social media. Ever-present in popular culture,
riots have received a resurgence of attention following recent
uprisings, particularly the global waves of anti-regime protests,
racial justice uprisings, and revolutions of the twenty-first century's opening decades. In the country called the United States, the
past few years have seen riots make headline news in New York
City, Oakland, St. Louis, Baltimore, Philadelphia, Minneapolis,
Atlanta, Portland, and in cities and towns across the country.
Riots draw media attention, spark strong and polarizing reactions
in the public, and are the subject of stubbornly recurring arguments about their legitimacy and appropriateness.

Nearly all mass movements that challenge power involve
physically confrontational street actions. However, listening to
most public voices today, you wouldn't know it. The term "nonviolent" is commonly used to designate protests as good, while
"violent" is used to disparage them. When commentators in the
media are describing a protest, you can reliably tell which side the
talking heads are on based on whether or not they refer to the
protest in question as nonviolent. However, many activists and

commentators mistake this rhetorical wordplay for material conflict. Those who insist on strict nonviolent discipline argue that protesters will be able to break through their opponents' negative portrayals if they strictly and incontrovertibly adhere to the principles of nonviolence, thereby appealing to the broader public with a movement that is clearly legitimate. Yet media that is committed to presenting news through a law-and-order framework are likely to describe serious protests with violent language regardless of what protesters do, and demonstrations by racial minorities tend to be viewed as violent by dominant groups no matter how nonviolent they are.[4] And anyone who has experience in contentious protests knows that police can be just as brutal with nonviolent protesters.

A great deal of the confusion comes from social science research claiming that protest tactics that refrain from any type of violence are categorically more effective. Whereas pacifist ideology once centered around the moral claim that it is wrong to be violent no matter what, one of the core tenants of contemporary nonviolence is: *it works better*. This assertion relies on academic studies that claim to show that nonviolent strategies for political change are more effective than violent ones. However, when we look more closely, these studies do not say what many people think they do. The most prominent scholarly research that informs activists and public opinion today applies the term "nonviolent" loosely, specifically ignoring violent actions that fall short of full-scale warfare. That article you read that says nonviolent resistance works better cites studies that quietly include the effects of riots within the category of "nonviolent resistance." This same research then gets turned around and used to argue that riots hurt movements on the basis that they are not nonviolent. For political action to have a chance at success, for organizing to be productive, they say, all actions must adhere to a strict code of nonviolent discipline. The research underlying these claims says no such thing.

The story of strategic nonviolence has misled us. It has misled us into viewing social movement actions in an unrealistic binary of violence and nonviolence that constrains our view of resistance and limits our horizon of liberation. The notion that purely nonviolent revolution is not only possible but is the best or only chance we have to resist domination and build a better world is a counterproductive idea that sets up activists to turn on one another rather than build momentum on each other's actions. Not only are riots a commonplace part of movements from below, they are often intertwined with nonviolent actions during moments of uprising—a connection that is impossible to ignore if we simply observe the uprisings all around us, but *impossible to see* if we approach movements with a starting assumption that violence and nonviolence are mutually exclusive and inherently opposing forms of action. In fact, as research in this book shows, riots often correspond with increased levels of nonviolent protest, riots communicate important political messages, and rioting can have empowering impacts on participants, all making riotous moments crucial aspects of rebellions and resistance movements. If we are to understand social movement contention, if we are to build social-political power from below, it is essential that we grapple with riots.

✵✵✵

I initially wrote these words after returning from what would be called a riot after the fact, a racial justice protest in Pittsburgh, PA, in which police dispersed protesters with rubber bullets and tear gas, and some demonstrators responded by throwing bottles.[5] The potential for police violence against demonstrators is all but taken for granted. But for many organizers and activists, the nonviolence frame has become standardized in a manner that is undermining our ability to understand social power. We now judge protests against a purist rubric of nonviolence, which is to say, based on what is or is not nonviolent. In the media, protests are often discussed as either "remaining" nonviolent or "turning" violent, the assumption being that legitimate protest is nonviolent at baseline. Like the initial wave of Black Lives Matter protests in 2014, the summer 2020 uprising was accompanied by a chorus of heated arguments and handwringing over relatively minor property damage by protesters on the basis that it was *not nonviolent*.

In a political climate marked by barefaced extra-legal violence by police and white supremacist gangs, a 2020 poll in the aftermath of George Floyd's murder under the knee of then-officer Derek Chauvin found that 54 percent of U.S. Americans felt that the burning of Minneapolis's 3rd Precinct by protesters was a justified response. Yet even in this context, countless pundits, otherwise supportive of the movement, and even activists themselves rushed to defend the essential nonviolence of protests.[6] As the argument went, the protests were nonviolent and legitimate, while the property destruction that accompanied some of them was the fault of illegitimate interlopers—anarchists, outside agitators, or *provocateurs*—even, in many cases, in the face of eye witness and video footage to the contrary. During that moment, I witnessed some of the same activists and organizations celebrate images of flaming police cars in one social media post and then turn around and eviscerate the people who actually set police cars on fire in another. Riots raise our collective pulse, but many of us do not have a coherent understanding of the relationship between rioting and social change.

There are two broad approaches to movement strategy. One centers on petitional actions to persuade the powerful to solve social problems. These can include marches, demonstrations, and forms of protest designed to legitimate grievances and bring them to the attention of authorities. The second centers on political conflict, understanding that social problems exist *because* of authorities—because powerful people create and benefit from the problems of others, and will fight to defend those benefits. Here strategies are based on disrupting the status quo, building leverage over authorities, and bringing about solutions directly. In many movements' approaches to power there is ambiguity and overlap between the two (and many protests today are not well situated to accomplish either), but broadly speaking, one set of movement strategies revolves around persuading the powerful to make change, the other around building power to make change.

Nonviolent strategies can fall into either category. However, the typical nonviolent protest functions as an embodied petition to authorities, asking to be recognized and for claims to be taken up by the powerful. Disruptive actions can take many forms, including those we would call nonviolent—though the more materially disruptive a protest gets, the more is it liable to be labeled violent by authorities no matter what it does—but a riot is the most iconic. Rioting is an old phenomenon—there were riots in the ancient world—and yet as the state has consolidated, and populations around the world have urbanized, it has re-emerged in our era as a core challenge to oppression and exploitation. There are few actions that represent corrosion of authority as unmistakably and as powerfully as the riot.

There is another story of twenty-first century uprisings. Whereas the norm for revolutionary struggle in the previous century took the form of armed, martial contests for state power, now we see a proliferation of unarmed, civilian conflict in the streets: civil resistance. To some, this indicates a turn in movements away from violence and toward nonviolence. The field of nonviolence studies, also called "civil resistance studies" and the study of nonviolent action, has taken center stage in both interpreting and promoting movement strategy, sponsoring the notion that what makes uprisings successful is their use of specifically nonviolent methods. The escalating series of civilian revolts across the world in the twenty-first century has thus been described in terms of a global wave of nonviolent revolutions.[7] Central to this framing is the concept of *strategic nonviolence*, the idea that nonviolent methods are the most effective or only way for movements to achieve their goals.

Indeed, the popular uprisings of today, by and large, do not involve armed conflict in the twentieth-century revolutionary-guerrilla model of China, Algeria, Vietnam, and Cuba. Outside of sparse pockets in the world, forces of the Left no longer exchange live fire with state forces the way they did in the previous century. Today, mass protests compose the majority of movements' disruptive toolbox, many of these adhering to the tenets of nonviolence, others involving thrown projectiles, burning barricades, defacement of property, sabotage, pushing, shoving, and fistfights. These actions are indeed *less* violent than warfare, but they are not nonviolent. The binary terms "violence" and "nonviolence" are a central problem; they simply are not equipped to capture relevant categories of movement tactics and strategies. Arguments for strict nonviolence, whether knowingly or not, exploit this conceptual slippage by leaning on research that compares warfare to street rebellion.

This problem is coded directly into the most influential research informing movements today. In 2011, political scientists Erica Chenoweth and Maria Stephan published *Why Civil Resistance Works: The Strategic Logic of Nonviolent Conflict*, a comparative study of violent and nonviolent political campaign success.[8] Based on the dataset that Chenoweth and their co-researchers constructed, Chenoweth and Stephan conclude that nonviolent campaigns are around twice as likely to overthrow a government as violent campaigns, with the trend line moving toward nonviolence being even more comparatively successful. This research has been widely interpreted as closing the door once and for all on the violence/nonviolence debate, proving the superior efficacy of nonviolence and validating the strategic nonviolent approach to movement building. The book won overwhelming praise and numerous prestigious awards, and quickly rose to ubiquity in activist scenes and in popular understandings of protest. More sophisticated nonviolence research since then largely stands on the shoulders of that initial study, assuming its findings as a starting point. The arguments of strategic nonviolence have become conventional wisdom.

However, as chapter three of this book shows, most of the movements that get labeled "nonviolent" involve major riots. The presence of unarmed violent tactics is frequently ignored or sidelined in movement histories and academic literature to make room for a cleaner concept of nonviolent struggle.

Nonviolence research typically compares armed struggle to civilian uprisings, but for decades in the U.S. and in many countries around the world, the violence/nonviolence debate on the ground has been primarily over street rebellion—actions like disruptive protests, rioting, vandalism, and sabotage. The slippage in the operational definitions between academics and activists would not matter so much, except that academic research in the field of nonviolence studies is the main pillar of support for the strategic nonviolence argument on the ground and in public consciousness.

When push comes to shove, so to speak, advocates of nonviolence fall back on the academic research that tells them that nonviolent tactics and strategy are categorically more effective. Movements are being equipped with a blueprint that does not match their tools, leading to drastic misunderstandings of how people build power from below.

We look around us and everywhere we see either riots or their seemingly imminent potential. Many protests now begin with leaders asking, demanding, imploring, or shaming participants *not* to riot. When videos expose racist violence and murder by police officers, and communities gather in outrage, the police invariably release a statement calling for protests to remain peaceful. When protests spread, government officials will affirm the right to peaceful protest—and remind the public that rioting is unacceptable. Even more common than their actual occurrence is reference to riots by politicians and political influencers as a bogeyman. For conservatives, riots are what happen when society gets of out of control; for liberals and progressives, riots are what happen when protest goes too far, gets it wrong, or is exploited by the wrong elements. Riots are a recurring feature of our political landscape, and it is time we explore them on their own terms.

What I present in this book directly contradicts prominent claims around nonviolence, understandings of social conflict that are not only widely believed, but that I think many of us *want* to believe. As the chair of my dissertation committee put it to me when I introduced the research proposal that would lead to this book: we would all prefer it if Chenoweth was right. It would indeed be comforting to know that peaceful protest is the most effective way we can engage in political struggle. Many people are deeply attached to believing that nonviolence works better and do not want to see that view challenged. But if the field of research that dominates study and circulation of movement strategy is getting it wrong, that is a problem worth pushing through discomfort to address. Arguments for the superior efficacy of nonviolence are simply not supported by evidence and ignoring the recurring reality of riots in our analyses seriously inhibits our understanding of movements collectively bringing about change.

Just because the data does not support the claim that nonviolent tactics are categorically more effective does not imply that nonviolent tactics are irrelevant. Far from it. Nonviolent actions can be powerful and effective and are a necessary aspect of struggle. There are certainly times and places where actions that do not physically confront opponents or threaten to destroy property are appropriate and strategic. The mistake is imagining civilian movements to be wholly nonviolent, and imagining violent tactics to be wholly detrimental to political struggle. Here the field of nonviolence studies is implicated, though not (necessarily) the practice of nonviolent action.

Calling attention to real-world collective actions and tactics is not only an empirical question, but also brings up the question of what story we are telling about movements. Resistance in itself requires only a defensive posture, an organic distaste for oppressive authority, but it is strongest when it is collectivized, organized, and geared *toward* something. That positive construction requires narrative, a story of the world and of ourselves. Sociologists have similarly described the *framing* tools that movement participants use to make meaning of political struggles and communicate to each other and the public. While some frames are specific to one group or issue, there are those that serve as "a kind of master algorithm that colors and constrains the orientations and activities" of movements in general.[9] This "master frame" is the grand story of struggle we tell in which our political forces are the protagonist.

The idea of nonviolent struggle has become a master frame, a story of political contention based on a constructed conception of the world. At its core, this story involves three premises: 1) violence is bad; 2) our enemies are violent; 3) we are nonviolent. Identification with this story informs strategy, but it also serves as a collective identity within movements, allowing activists to locate and connect with others who they associate with the same principles.

Because a story of change is resonant for some people does not mean that it accurately reflects what goes on in the contentious politics that actually fuel social change. The research presented in chapters three and four shows that riots are an important part of civil uprisings; interviews presented in chapters five and six demonstrate that a certain type and limited amount of collective violence has its own story of resistance and revolution. To really engage with riotous moments, we must be ready to open our minds to a different master frame—one that is less comfortable than the nonviolence story, but just as powerful, and far more holistic. But regardless of the story one prefers, providing people with empirical research based on idealizations of movements is unhelpful; organizers and activists should be armed with research that accurately addresses movement realities on the ground. Even if you want to believe that nonviolence is the only way to create positive change, you are still not served by researchers drawing you a false blueprint of struggle.

A lot of people who pay attention to movements know that there are problems with a purist framing of nonviolence, too often they just don't know what to do with it. The primary path has been to ignore the problem. Despite riots being common occurrences—in fact appearing central to a series of uprisings in the U.S. and across the world in recent decades—there is surprisingly little existing research on the topic. Rioting is in our faces, and yet those actions as part of movements remain largely under studied, with opinions in whatever direction based more often on assumption than analysis. Unarmed violence within movements has become *"familiarly unknown*: a semi-legitimate cognitive gap, a new 'black box' to which we are increasingly becoming accustomed to acquiesce."[10] Specifically, there is very little research that investigates interactions between more and less violent forms of unarmed action within movements, and even fewer studies have explored the experiences of rioters themselves. This book makes a foray into both. In doing so, my goal is to help clear the air of popular misconceptions about nonviolence that cloud our vision of movements' strategy, to center for a moment rioters as agents of social struggle, and to begin to integrate riots into our theories of change. Sociologist Paul Gilje begins his 1996 book, *Rioting in America,* by saying we should study riots "because they're there." When I first read this opening, as a relatively experienced organizer and relatively inexperienced sociologist, it struck me as a remarkably banal introduction. After all, simply because something is there does not make it interesting. As my research progressed, however, I realized how difficult it was to even point out gaps in understandings around riots, much less try to fill them in. When it comes to protester violence, many people simply don't want to hear it. Years later, it would dawn on me that my first published article on the subject would be little more than an attempt to quantitatively prove that riots are there.[11] And it was not easy to get that simple intervention published—among numerous rejections, I received one in which an anonymous reviewer attached a comment almost as long as the article itself lecturing me about Gandhi and the correctness of nonviolence. When one considers the degree of attention that riots attract in media and popular culture, and compares this with the overall lack of research on riots by movement scholars, and in fact the degree to which the serious study of the topic is discouraged, Gilje's opening line starts to make more sense.

It is not just researchers who have overlooked riots. By and large, rioting has not received the theoretical analyses that other forms of social and political struggle have.[12] Riots grab attention when they're happening and generate painfully recurring debates over their legitimacy and meaning, but the riots themselves tend to be associated with chaos, mob mentality, and disorganization. Even for many leftists, riots are often viewed as a backdrop against which real politics happen. Riots are not so much as mentioned in canonical texts on revolutionary armed struggle by Mao Zedong, Võ Nguyên Giáp, and Che Guevara, nor do they appear in classic manuals on unarmed activist strategy like Saul Alinsky's *Rules for Radicals.* Lenin had little to say apart from decrying riots when they threatened Soviet Union rule. Sun Tzu's *The Art of War* has no comment on the subject. Gene Sharp's formative volume on nonviolent struggle, which is the subject of chapter two, mentions riots in passing, but only to associate them with other forms of "violent" conflict such as warfare. That riots are missing from famous texts on strategy is not altogether surprising. Strategy is about directing the forces under one's control to the greatest effect in pursuit of a goal, and riots are by definition out of control.

Discussion and theorization of riots does occur in some radical scenes, particularly in insurrectionary anarchist circles, where the riot can take on a celebrated image, sometimes bordering on hallowed. For insurrectionary anarchists, rioting has become a prime form of "propaganda of the deed," or actions that spread radical politics and catalyze revolt by directly attacking authorities.[13] However, even where riots are admired, their actual strategic application and function within broader movements is more often assumed than theorized. Similarly, though conversely, most activists today, as well as the broader public, take the correctness and superior efficacy of nonviolent protest as a given. The "pro-riot" and "nonviolence" positions can appear so far apart, and the argument between them so severe, that the actual dynamics of violent protest are prone to being overlooked. When riots happen, everyone is talking about them, but few are actually looking at them. When they are not happening, riots tend to be discussed in abstraction. In this book, I work toward a social-political theory of the riot, one that places the rioter at the center of the analysis.

***

The intervention I make is innovative, but not unique. There have been an increasing number of studies and publications in recent years specifically calling into question the shortcomings of the violence/nonviolence binary and investigating the unarmed political violence that gets lost in the grey area in between.[14] The work of Frances Fox Piven in particular has been influential to my thinking in this area, both in demystifying protester violence as an area of movement research and in connecting useful scholarly frameworks to activist-centric analyses geared toward informing and building collective action. While my experience and context is based in the U.S., emergent theory from scholar-activists in the Global South, particularly South Africa, helped orient me toward a cutting edge of understandings of contentious politics from below.[15] AK Thompson's theoretical exploration of the black bloc and its conflict with representational politics in the 2010 book *Black Bloc, White Riot* was important for me. My work also shares much in common with Francis Dupuis-Déri's 2014 book, *Who's Afraid of the Black Blocs?* and Shon Meckfessel's 2016 book, *Nonviolence Ain't What It Used to Be*, which both make arguments akin to many that I advance in this book. Chapter five especially could be read as a companion to all three of these volumes, and that my empirical findings cohere so closely with theirs should serve as additional validation of all four studies. Joshua Clover's 2016 book, *Riot. Strike. Riot.*, Vicky Osterweil's 2020 book, *In Defense of Looting,* and Elizabeth Hinton's 2021 book, *America on Fire*, have added much needed historical and critical perspectives to the subject matter at hand.

My approach to the study of riots combines theoretical critique of strategic nonviolence, empirical findings about the prevalence and impact of riots, the voices of rioters, and social-political analysis in service of a more holistic understanding of violent protest. I am indebted to the prior research and polemics on riots that enabled the steps I take, and, of course, this work owes deeply to the experiences that contentious protests have granted me as a participant, as well as to the writers who have influenced my critical social and political thinking more broadly, most notably here Frantz Fanon and Hannah Arendt.

My hope is for this work to serve as a launching point. There are a number of radical critiques of nonviolence out there, but to my knowledge no single work to date presents a thorough, comprehensive, and empirical challenge to strategic nonviolence along with original research on riots and theoretical interventions in pursuit of integrating riots into our understanding of unarmed resistance. There remains much to be expanded upon in this area, and while I believe this work is relevant to many types of non-nonviolent actions that I do not directly address, for example strategic sabotage and community defense, we would greatly benefit from increased attention to those areas as well.

In the remainder of this chapter, I briefly review some of the ways the phenomena I am addressing have been studied and theorized as well as how those approaches bear on our understandings today; I discuss the applied concept of violence; and give an overview of the argument to come.

The Study of Riots, Crowds, Movements, and Strategic Nonviolence

The official designation of the riot as we know it can be traced to King George I's Riot Act of 1714. Whereas "riots" had previously been associated with "debauchery" and "unrestrained revelry and mirth," the Riot Act legally re-defined the term as a physically destructive political assembly, declaring: "persons to the number of twelve or more, being unlawfully, riotously, and tumultuously assembled together, to the disturbance of the publick peace" as related to "the endangering of his Majesty's person and government" should be punished by death "without benefit of clergy."[16] In other words, in the British legal system, which would be formative across the world, this decree made the politicization of the riot official from the standpoint of the state. The Riot Act was later rewritten to specifically forbid property destruction in demonstrations while granting the right to peaceful protest, giving those who have been touched by the British and American empires the distinction between legitimate nonviolent protest and illegitimate violent protest we have until today.[17]

The term "riot" is ambiguous and controversial. To famed sociologist of movements Charles Tilly, the word has been so thoroughly leveraged for rhetorical meaning that it has become nullified as an analytic term, though he acknowledges its usage is both popular and significant.[18] Nevertheless, the types of collective actions associated with the term are surely instances of what social scientists call "contentious politics."

The sociological study of riots has taken different forms and occurred in different phases, often compartmentalizing riots by type, for example the study of food riots.[19] In the U.S., the term *riot* has been deeply entangled with race. At least since the 1965 Watts Riots, the term "race riot" has been applied to Black neighborhoods rising up in response to police violence.[20] Based on this usage and its widely negative connotation, some argue that alternative terms such as "rebellion" are more appropriate for these uprisings.[21] Prior to the mid-twentieth century, however, race riots were more typically associated with white mobs attacking Black neighborhoods, for example the 1921 Tulsa Race Riot, or Greenwood Massacre. Whatever terms we choose, we must be clear that these are not the same phenomena, and referring to them as such can hurt our ability to distinguish between acts of oppression and those of resistance. For the sake of clarity, I will call a dominant racial caste attacking an oppressed group a *pogrom*.[22] In studies outside the U.S., pogroms are sometimes called "ethnic riots," as with anti-Muslim riots in India, or anti-foreigner riots in South Africa. Pogroms and anti-police riots, the latter of which we will call riots, can appear similar from a distance, but they represent different sides of collective violence and are manifested by different tactics, targets, and scope of violence. The sports riot, meanwhile, has its own history and dynamics, which at times, crosses over into explicitly political violence as either riots or pogroms.

Many scholars who choose to deploy the word "riot" do not define it based on abstract criteria but rather based on constituent examples of collective behavior such as smashing windows, attacking buildings associated with political foes, throwing projectiles at police, burning cars, and so forth. This approach makes particular sense considering the patterned behavior rioters often exhibit.[23] Some have gone even further, defining the riot based on its "open-ended" collective potential to experiment with violence, or in essence, its non-nonviolence.[24] Crucially, violent protests are common events in the context of social movement uprisings, and the word *riot* is highly recognizable in this context. While the use of this term to subsume unarmed collective political violence against authorities is fraught and perhaps lacking in precision, I believe it is nevertheless important to grapple with based on its presence and power in the popular consciousness. I use "riot" to indicate collective, unarmed political action by a group of civilians against authorities that involves destruction of property and/or harm to people. In other words, I use "riot" and "violent protest" synonymously to denote public collective actions that are not nonviolent, and are targeting forces or symbols of domination, oppression, or exploitation, acknowledging that all of these terms are imperfect and there are types of riots that may not fit this analysis.

Studies of riots as part of social movements may have been overlooked in recent decades, but the study of riotous crowds was formative for modern social theory. The earliest treatments of riots largely conflated them with crowd behavior in general— which should tell us something about the ways that elites viewed large, uncontrolled groups of common people. Indeed, crowds under control are a great asset to totalitarian governments, while crowds out of control can constitute the gravest threat. However, the idea of mob mentality came to dominate theories of riotous crowds. The myth that crowds drive individuals who join them to madness and violence has since been critiqued to the point of debunking, but it nevertheless continues to influence popular and scholarly understandings of crowd behavior.[25]

Gustave Le Bon's 1895 essay, *The Crowd*, is most famous for laying out a theory of group behavior as *crowd hysteria*, that is, as an irrational, mindless, and violent phenomenon. To Le Bon, the crowd is "perpetually hovering on the borderland of unconsciousness, readily yielding to all suggestions, having all the violence of feeling peculiar to beings who cannot appeal to the influence of reason, deprived of all critical faculty."[26] In addition to impulsiveness, irritability, irrationality, and lack of judgment, Le Bon focuses on the suggestibility of crowds, drawing analogies to hypnosis, where those who are elsewhere autonomous individuals become in a crowd utterly open to the implanted ideas of the mob the way a patient is (imagined to be) by a hypnotist.

Le Bon's analysis of the crowd would go on to be one of the most influential works in social psychology, but in his day he was not taken very seriously in professional circles. Gabriel Tarde, who Le Bon drew from, was much more important to scholarly debates, among other things through the idea of *crowd semantics*— the idea that crowds lower individuals' intelligence and awareness, making them more susceptible to deviant influences and criminal behaviors. Many who drew from these analyses, Le Bon in particular, lean so heavily on racialism and misogyny that it can be difficult to disentangle useful observations they might have had from the rest. For example, Le Bon connects the crowd's lack of reason and violent impulses to that which he says is typical of Latin races, and ascribes the crowd's impulsiveness and tendency to be influenced by strong leaders to its inherent femininity.

Arguments over the nature of the crowd became formative for the boundaries of the congealing field of sociology.[27] Émile Durkheim attacked the foundations of crowd semantics and group opinions in general for their lack of methodological rigor, going so far as to label the conclusions of crowd hysterics "imaginary."[28] These attacks effectively undermined Tarde's and Le Bon's positions in academia, though there has been some effort to rehabilitate both in recent years.[29] However, later in his career, Durkheim would soften some of his previous attacks and actually incorporate points very similar to those of his previous opponents into his own work. Durkheim used the term *effervescence* to describe in crowds a temporary but profound state of exhilaration and susceptibility to influence similar to what Tarde and Le Bon had described. The feeling associated with this phenomenon is so powerful that Durkheim suggests that it is the social birthplace of religion. Something like the effervescent experience appears to be present in riots, as we will see in chapters five and six, though in both more nuanced and political ways.

Outside the academic debates, Le Bon was widely read in lay society, and common characterizations of riots as random or wanton violence often resort to derivations of crowd hysteria. Other similarly negative views of riots derive from much older sources. When the riot is not viewed as weak-minded individuals succumbing to a crowd's will for irrational destruction, it can be seen as a deeper window into the ugliness of humanity. The rioter is often portrayed as an embodiment of Thomas Hobbes's "state of nature," the chaotic war of everyone against everyone else, which was imagined by Western philosophers to be the natural human condition prior to the creation of the state—a war that is supposed to resume if the state were ever to collapse.[30] Here the rioter is a participant in the wanton chaos that results from lack of proper authority; not the precipitator of the state's decline, but the result of it. Either way, the importance elites placed on studying the crowd had everything to do with the capacity of the riotous collective to upend society. According to philosopher Elias Canetti in his work, *Crowds and Power*: "To the crowd in its nakedness everything seems a Bastille."[31] Or at least it seems so from the perspective of the Bastille.

"The long history of protest movements is in fact mainly the history of mobs and riots."[32] Sociological studies of movements in many ways emerged directly from attention to raucous crowds via the study of the French Revolution.[33] According to historian George Rudé, the phenomenon of utilizing the term "riot" as an epithet to delegitimize popular protest also dates back to this episode—though as frightening as it was for European elites, I think the deep-seated fear of riotous crowds in the West can be more accurately located in the Haitian Revolution.[34] Riots again became an acute topic of study for twentieth-century social scientists during the urban rebellions of the 1960s. However, as sociologists came to take social movements seriously as a topic of study, riots were largely left by the wayside as researchers focused on legitimizing protest and examining organizations and formal processes.[35] But if social movements are a continuation of the political process via disorderly means, as a famous sociologist once said, then riots ought to fit perhaps even better than "orderly" social movement protest—especially in an era when many formal protest forms have become more performative than disruptive.[36] For academic studies of movements, riots fell into the gap at the intersection of two systemic failures: the dismissal of actions that appear to be disorganized or apolitical, and the false dichotomy of violence/nonviolence.

Nonviolence studies developed as its own field in the 1970s, largely separate from other research on social movements.[37] Not only did nonviolence studies grow independently of the sociological study of movements, until fairly recently it was also distinct from the political Left (discussed further in chapter two). Nonviolence studies, or civil resistance studies, continues to function largely as an independent field of study, with its own canons, references, and internal debates. As a school of thought, it now spans academic departments of sociology, political science, and peace and conflict studies, with practitioner audiences among both security specialists and social justice activists. The field produces a variety of research aimed at understanding the particular mechanisms of nonviolent methods, and spans political ideologies from liberal to radical to religious. Nonviolence studies begins with Gene Sharp, a political theorist who sought to disentangle Gandhi's nonviolent *morality* from his nonviolent *strategy*. There has been a more recent reintegration of moral considerations in more holistic treatments of political nonviolence, but the distinction between strategic or practical nonviolence on the one side, and moral or principled nonviolence on the other remains the basis for the bulk of the field. This approach became known as *strategic nonviolence*.

At the core of the strategic nonviolence framing is a binary understanding of movement actions: "violent" and "nonviolent." This view not only muddies the difference between disruptive and non-disruptive nonviolent actions, but also obscures the vast and varied spectrum of collective actions that are *not* nonviolent and therefore fall under the umbrella of violence—everything from a brick thrown through a corporate window to a bomb killing hundreds of civilians to full-scale warfare with millions of casualties. This problem is especially important to unpack because, unlike many other academic studies of movements, nonviolence studies has, to its credit, largely been oriented toward application in recent years. Large think tanks like the International Center on Nonviolent Conflict and the Albert Einstein Institution routinely sponsor public lectures, trainings, and accessible publications, many of them specifically oriented toward activists. The strategic nonviolence framework has become dominant in activist understandings of power in the U.S., and Chenoweth and Stephan's research in particular continues to be reiterated and reinforced as definitive proof of the superiority of strict nonviolence. However, while many social scientists have noted the "troublesome" violence/nonviolence dichotomy in describing social movements, most have adopted it anyway.[38]

There have been a number of blistering critiques of nonviolence from the Left—most notably from Ward Churchill, Peter Gelderloos, and Vicky Osterweil—which have been influential primarily in certain radical Left and anarchist *milieus*.[39] While many of the critiques these authors levy are solid, their apparent frustration with the dominant insistence on nonviolent discipline at times leads them to favor vitriol over persuasion. When it comes to the issues at hand, sometimes such venom is called for, but it is also prone to mute the resonant power of the strategic nonviolent message, which can make large-scale social change seem approachable and achievable. For example, Gelderloos is correct that we should not be "trying to offer easy solutions, cheap hopes, or false promises to anyone," and yet to present movement victories as accessible and achievable, as the strategic nonviolence approach tends to, is not necessarily to offer false hope.[40] As the characters Cassian Andor and Jyn Urso remind us in the *Star Wars* film *Rogue One*: rebellions are built on hope.

On the back of Gelderloos's 2007 book, *How Nonviolence Protects the State*, CrimethInc Ex-Workers' Collective writes: "It will be a shame if *How Nonviolence Protects the State* isn't read and discussed by people who disagree with it."[41] But if we want constructive discussions by those who disagree, it is best to open the conversation in a way that makes that possible. Those of the Left who defend rioting have a tendency to flatten adherents of nonviolence into a category of less-than-radical, and thereby miss opportunities to inform and learn from this legacy of struggle. And, of course, there are many instances when violent tactics are infeasible or are highly likely to backfire, in which case the nonviolence playbook is crucial. Most importantly, it is less a matter of choosing one approach or the other and more about understanding that elements of both are part and parcel of real-world resistance. Many critics of nonviolence acknowledge as much, but then go on to approach the debate in such a way as to reify the violence-vs.-nonviolence split and undervalue the massive potential of nonviolent methods as components of political struggle. In my approach, I take CrimethInc's comment to heart, and attempt to go step-by-step through a critique of nonviolence studies in service of advocating for a more productive working definition of civil resistance.

A Discussion about Violence

Terminology has been one significant barrier in meaningfully discussing unarmed violence. Social movement strategy has long been divided into distinct and opposing conceptual categories of "violent" and "nonviolent" by scholars and practitioners alike. Historically, proponents of political violence in social movements have argued that radical change requires armed struggle, while advocates of nonviolence believe true change can only be achieved without threatening or harming opponents. Diametrically opposing theoretical categories of "violent" and "nonviolent" is a central problem; these concepts do not readily lend themselves to dichotomous thinking, particularly around social and political resistance.

Movements are deeply emotional processes. Engaging in social struggle necessarily impacts, draws from, and intertwines complex human lives, memories, relationships, traumas, and aspirations. In addition to material struggle, as I will argue, in order to really know in our bodies that politics is a struggle between opposing forces, and to believe something can be done about it, at some point partisans need to *feel* like we are in a fight. The word "violence" is often used for some of the actions that manifest this kind of contentious action.

What constitutes violence is deeply contested—a discussion that emerges in activists' words in chapters five and six. First, "there is no consensus in the literature about what is violence."[42] Various thinkers and fields have conceived of violence as a moral wrong, as necessary for social progress, as an extension of politics by other means, as structurally or symbolically imbedded in the systems of the status quo, as a form of interpersonal communication, and more. Some discuss violence as a simple descriptor for actions that involve physical harm to people or property, while others apply the term as an ethical judgment. Meanwhile, nonviolence as a concept has suffered from the widespread notion that it is defined based on the absence of something, presupposing both a consensus on and a rejection of what that thing actually is. The term *non-nonviolence* would be absurd, but it is essentially the standard by which we judge movement actions today—based on what is and is not acceptably nonviolent, grounded in fuzzy and shifting understandings of what constitutes violence. Not to mention that commonsense definitions of violence and nonviolence are culture-dependent, and it is unclear where the terms begin and end with any given action, since seemingly nonviolent actions can end up reproducing violent structures.

In terms of clinical definitions of violence for the purposes of studying movements, it is difficult to beat Tilly's: "episodic social interaction that immediately inflicts physical damage on persons and/or objects."[43] However, this excludes systemic violence, which is of course deeply connected to motivations for, and perceptions of, the direct application of violent tactics in social justice movements. Among the most difficult elements of violence to grapple with is balancing the word to simultaneously describe actions by movements from below and also to describe systems of oppression. On the one hand, we want to be able to call what appear to be materially violent protest actions like riots "violent" on the face of it, while on the other hand taking seriously the vastly more destructive and harmful forms of systemic violence that those riots are resisting or reacting to. An activist I interviewed, quoted in chapter six, refers to these categories respectively as "little violence" and "big violence." The fact that we use the same word for both—violence—can muddy understandings of either. Yet this is an area of tension we should lean into, as the two are inherently connected. In Paolo Freire's words: "Never in history has violence been initiated by the oppressed.

How could they be the initiators, if they themselves are the result of violence? ... There would be no oppressed had there been no prior situation of violence to establish their subjugation."[44]

Media narratives that present violent protest actions in isolation from historical context are reinforcing current power structures. As James Baldwin put it, describing a rioter confiscating a television from a local store: "How would you define somebody who puts a cat where he is and takes all the money out of the ghetto where he makes it? Who is looting whom? Grabbing off the TV set? He doesn't really want the TV set. He's saying screw you. It's just judgment, by the way, on the value of the TV set... After all, you're accusing a captive population who has been robbed of everything of looting. I think it's obscene."[45]

Violence cannot be meaningfully discussed without political context, which is to say, without an understanding of power. But even in context, violence is an unwieldy term, prone to misinterpretation through its expansive association with so many different types of actions. Additionally, as I will discuss in later chapters, violence is often viewed as purely *instrumental*, as a tool to accomplish something tangible when other means will not do. This has been the predominant approach to understanding the use of violence by movements as well. In other words, whether it's "the strategic logic of nonviolence" or "by whatever means necessary," both violence and nonviolence by movements are widely understood in instrumental terms. While measurable outcomes are no doubt important, there is deeper symbolic power to different kinds of resistance that can end up being just as important in the long history of revolutionary struggle. There can certainly be tangible goals for some unarmed violent protest actions, for example looting and de-arresting, but to the extent that rioting is instrumental, it is primarily via its semiotics. In other words, it is often just as much about what violent protest actions *say* as what they *do*. Violent protests of the kind examined in this book are typically not meant to materially defeat enemy forces or redistribute enough wealth to make a difference in the long run, and few of them escalate to the kinds of large-scale rebellions that threaten to topple regimes. Rather, these actions engage in the kind of fight that acknowledges unacceptable conditions and signals seriousness of dissent.

The term "symbolic violence" is often associated with the social theory of Pierre Bourdieu. In my discussion of violence, I use the word "symbolic" differently, though Bourdieu's usage will still be important. For Bourdieu, symbolic violence refers to systemic domination in society: "Symbolic violence is the coercion which is set up only through the consent that the dominated cannot fail to give to the dominator (and therefore to the domination) when their understanding of the situation and relation can only use instruments of knowledge that they have in common with the dominator, which, being merely the incorporated form of the structure of the relation of domination, make this relation appear as natural."[46]

Bourdieu's symbolic violence flows from the dominator to the dominated and is primarily non-physical, based in institutions, knowledge, and norms; it is the way that systemic domination is infused in our lives and perpetuates itself through mindsets and behaviors. It is, for example, how many textbooks gloss over genocide and slavery in the Americas, and it is the backlash against attempts to teach these histories in our schools. It is the "obscene" view of looting that Baldwin describes. At the same time, there is a "close connection between symbolic violence and physical violence in the making and contesting of social order," and as such, resistance to symbolic violence "not infrequently involves physical violence."[47] It is a form of this resistance that I explore in this work. As we will see, the symbolism of violent protest is intimately connected with a rupturing of what Bourdieu calls symbolic violence. I use the term "symbolic" not in Bourdieu's sense, nor to imply that the materiality of the riot is somehow not real or not significant, but rather I use the term in its more common meaning: to describe a material thing that represents a larger abstract idea. My goal is to distinguish the physical transgression of the riot from purely instrumentalist views of both violence and nonviolence.

In order to further articulate the particular type of collective actions I study here, I borrow Michael Schwartz's articulation of the *institutional* power that landlords wield over tenants (power that depends on the state), and the *noninstitutional* power that organized tenants can attempt to exert on landlords (power lying outside the state), and likewise distinguish between *institutional* violence and *noninstitutional* violence, and, for our purposes, *anti-institutional* violence.[48] When it comes to violence, of which the state is usually looking to shore up its aspirational monopoly, all forms of violence that are not institutionally sanctioned are potentially a threat. Nevertheless, there is a difference between the noninstitutional violence of a sports riot and the anti-institutional violence of an anti-police riot. The first is extra-legal violence, but with a coincidental rather than a political stake in opposing authority.

Whereas some social scientists have approached white lynch mobs and Black anti-police riots as comparable instances of extra-legal violence, we must draw a distinction that makes it clear how the white mob is enacting the institutional violence of systemic anti-Black racism, even if technically doing so in an extra-legal way, whereas the Black-led rebellion is enacting anti-institutional violence in resistance to the institutional violence of systemic racism. Anyone who is confused about how the state views this distinction need only examine the police and military responses to the peaceful Black Lives Matter march in Washington, DC, in July 2020 and to the pro-Trump assault on the U.S. Capitol six months later on January 6, 2021. The first was met with militarized police and National Guard; the second was practically invited into the Capitol by DC police, some of whom fraternized comfortably with protesters even while elements of the crowd were physically threatening and fatally injuring other officers.[49] Or look at physical confrontations between fascists and antifascists in the U.S. and elsewhere, where the police reliably defend the former. The state, as well as its agents and beneficiaries, feels far more threatened by some crowds than others, and this has at least as much to do with who is in the crowd and why as it has to do with what the crowd is doing.

The riot as a form of collective action is by no means inherently liberatory; it depends on the dynamics of the assembly *vis-à-vis* systemic power. Riots might generally be extra-legal forms of collective action, and they might bear tactical similarity from a bird's eye view, but where the anti-police riot relies on anti-institutional power, the pogrom relies on institutional or noninstitutional power, depending on the posture of the state toward the groups involved. Nevertheless, the dynamics of the anti-police riot and the pogrom are not completely disconnected. In at least some cases, pogroms can be understood as deriving from the same social, political, and economic frustrations as anti-police riots, but mis-applied and targeting the wrong people. Likewise, in addition to the anti-institutional student riots described in chapter six, South Africa has seen a surge in noninstitutional ethnic and anti-immigrant riots against Zimbabweans and other foreigners in recent years.

The theory of decolonization, primarily associated with Frantz Fanon, will be important to this analysis. Fanon has become famous for his advocacy of revolutionary violence, though his endorsement is sometimes misread in overzealous ways.[50] Decolonization at its core is about remaking oneself and one's people through struggle. Put another way, it is about the ways in which revolutionaries *become* through resistance. Through the process of struggle, the oppressed can become a new type of person, not a product molded by oppression but a liberated subject. According to Fanon, post-colonial politics that do not deal directly with decolonization can end up becoming twisted into racism in the mentality of the former colonizers, particularly concerning the deployment of violence: "Whereas the national bourgeoisie competes with the Europeans, the artisans and small traders pick fights with Africans of other nationalities. In the Ivory Coast, outright race riots were directed against the Dahomeans and Upper Voltans who controlled much of the business sector and were the target of hostile demonstrations by the Ivorians following independence. We have switched from nationalism to ultranationalism, chauvinism, and racism."[51]

This difference between riots as anti-institutional violence and riots as institutional violence correlates to a common disparity between violence against property and violence against people in anti-police riots and pogroms, respectively. For example, the "long hot summer" of 1967, the most violent national outburst of urban rebellions in modern U.S. history (so far), overwhelmingly targeted property, with most fatalities resulting from police or National Guard bullets. Conversely, in the Tulsa Race Riot of 1921, the vast majority of fatalities were caused by white assailants targeting Black bodies as well as homes and businesses. These kinds of pogroms across the world are typically associated with mass atrocities and a large numbers of casualties, whereas the type of protester violence I am examining, in which participants attack symbols of state and capital, is far more limited in terms of the scope of violence, especially against bodies, and often more selective in terms of target, speaking to underlying political claims and ideology.

This leads to the last important point to note about the use of the term violence. Not only are we talking about unarmed anti-institutional violence, but we are talking about extremely low-level violence at that. If it makes sense to put violence on a spectrum, the types of protest violence relevant to the interview studies in this book are about as close as you can get to nonviolence; relatively minor property damage, and the potential for bodily harm from thrown projectiles or accidental injury as a result of arson, pushing and shoving, and perhaps a punch or two. The quantitative analysis involves data on major riots, but even then the criteria is property destruction and many data points are not associated with fatalities at the hands of rioters.

I have at times been challenged by those who claim to not believe that property destruction is violence, arguing that when I talk about these kinds of riots, I am not really discussing violent protest. However, I have yet to see this opinion manifest in those who enforce nonviolent discipline during a protest where someone throws a brick through a window or sets a car on fire. One way or another, the aura around the spaces in which these kinds of actions take place certainly *feels* violent. This kind of ambiguity is present throughout this work. Those who are seeking a definitive answer to the question, "do riots work?" will likely be disappointed. To ask whether or not riots work in the abstract is the wrong question, because the level of simplicity it requires cannot account for the realities of social-political struggle. The tension between appropriately strategic visions for movements and the reality that radical social change is messy, unpredictable, and emotionally fueled—not least by righteous anger—as well as the ways in which the forms of resistance we embody change us, will be recurring themes.

The Argument Ahead

As I developed the research project that led to this book, I began to notice a trend. Whether at a conference, activist scene, or a social gathering, whenever I would tell someone that I studied riots, they would light up—it is interesting material, and timely, they would always say—and then, without letting me get another word in, they would proceed to tell me my conclusions. Whether they were close to the mark or not, the reaction itself became a noticeable phenomenon. Riots are undeniably there, but most of us already think we understand them. Riots are destructive; they ruin movements. Or they are necessary; nothing gets done without violence. Or the word itself is just an epithet to vilify protest. Or riots are sheer chaos, the inevitable face of human nature in a society unable to constrain its impulses. Or they are the sort of thing you would expect from the French (or whoever). Or they are the byproduct of late capitalism, whatever that means. One way or another, riots are a spectacle, but are often dismissed for further analysis because we assume we already know what they are. And, as Hannah Arendt observed in her work, *On Violence*, "no one questions or examines what is obvious to all."[52] This book attempts to push through these assumptions and explore the riot as a form of political action on its own terms.

The rest of this book can be broken down into two broad interventions: First, I argue that dominant theories about violent protest get it wrong; second, I explore the phenomenon of violent protest through the experiences of participants. The first part is presented in chapters two, three, and four, where I challenge foundational arguments around strategic nonviolence on theoretical and empirical bases, demonstrate the catalyzing and mobilizing effect that riots can have, and argue for the possibilities of integrating the riot into analyses of civil resistance uprisings. In chapters five and six, I explore the dynamics of violent protests through the experiences of rioters themselves in two qualitative interview studies, and develop on theories emergent in the words of interviewees.[53] In chapter seven, I conclude and offer a political analysis of the riot. An appendix discusses the research that went into this book, including parameters and limitations of the empirical studies, and offers a few thoughts on avenues that, for various reasons, I did not pursue in the body of this text. Many components of the book also draw heavily from previously published essays.[54]

The language of violence and nonviolence is present throughout this book—there is nothing inherent in these terms that makes them problematic, any more than any words for any political actions are problematic. The problem lies in approaching these terms as preconceived moral claims or as totalizing, mutually exclusive, and necessarily oppositional concepts. As scholars of movements, we are hungry for understanding, and as organizers and activists, we are thirsty for knowledge and tools we can use to change the world; in both cases, we can no longer afford the illusion that a narrowly constructed nonviolent playbook is the only means by which movements build power. The aspiration is to be able to discuss civil resistance—that is, uprisings by and of civilians—without having to argue over violence-vs-nonviolence as such, but rather to focus on what actions are appropriate at what times, what the effects and consequences of different tactics are likely to be, and ultimately, how we understand ourselves as we struggle toward liberation. Sometimes the types of non-physical techniques that get labeled nonviolent are sufficient to the task at hand; sometimes they are not. It is the latter times that are the inspiration for and subject of this work.

2.

A Sharp Critique of Strategic Nonviolence

"The smart way to keep people passive and obedient is to strictly limit the spectrum of acceptable opinion but to allow very lively debate within that spectrum…"

—NOAM CHOMSKY

I was formally introduced to the idea of strategic nonviolence ten years ago. Someone I wanted to impress was impressed with Erica Chenoweth and Maria Stephan's now-famous book, *Why Civil Resistance Works: The Strategic Logic of Nonviolent Conflict*, and insisted I check it out. Reading that book was a puzzling experience, and my quest for understanding ultimately led to the research projects that would become this book. As someone who had been trained in militant organizing and radical activism, I associated movement strategy with revolutionary praxis, community and labor organizing, dual power, and guerrilla war theory. This book was different. It claimed to be about movement strategy, but it situated itself in security studies literature and presented neither an analysis of tyranny nor a vision of liberation. The book was geared toward a single point: that nonviolent methods are more effective than violent methods in overthrowing governments.

Nevertheless, the quantitative findings that the authors presented—that nonviolent movements have been about twice as effective as violent movements in overthrowing governments—demanded serious attention. *Why Civil Resistance Works* was popping up all over commentaries on protest, Chenoweth gave a TEDx Talk, and the book's findings were quickly picked up by organizers, movement trainers, non-profits, and the media. Shortly after its publication, the book was on everyone's tongues in activist scenes, and not long after that, Chenoweth and Stephan's central claim that nonviolent tactics are decidedly more effective had become gospel.

As it turns out, the research underlying *Why Civil Resistance Works* has massive limitations, which render its findings all but meaningless for contemporary movements. Few seemed to notice. For many scholars, activists, and pundits, that book closed the age-old argument between violence and nonviolence, validating once and for all the strategic logic of nonviolence. I will address these problems in detail in the following chapter, but first, let us take a step back and ask: where did the strategic logic of nonviolent conflict come from? To answer, we have to look at the theoretical origins of strategic nonviolent power as presented in its foundational document, Gene Sharp's three-volume 1973 work, *The Politics of Nonviolent Action*.

Proponents like to call it a theory of power, or more recently, *a theory of change*. Really, it is a theory of leverage. The difference is significant. Strategic nonviolence as outlined in *The Politics of Nonviolent Action* is a toolkit for creating civilian leverage against governments. The concept of social change is barely present at all, and when it arises it is discussed only in the narrowest sense. In other words, it is a car manual, not a roadmap. Sharp devotes his attention entirely to the *how*; he assumes the *who*, *where*, and *when* are basically interchangeable, and, most importantly, he explicitly ignores the *why*. The study of strategic nonviolence, or civil resistance studies, does not originate from sociological research of movements, and neither does it grow out of the political Left. It is a parallel field of theory and practice of its own, at least until recent decades when it began to dovetail with both social movement studies and leftist practitioners. We'll come back to that.

Chenoweth and Stephan have become the standard-bearers of nonviolence studies due to their quantitative methods, which are specially prized in academia and mainstream media, but the conclusions in *Why Civil Resistance Works* essentially just empirically validate and re-state Gene Sharp's arguments from four decades prior. Sharp's ideas have been reiterated, developed, and fleshed out by a number of authors, and they underlie just about all works in nonviolence studies, remaining largely unchanged. In order to understand the arguments for nonviolent strategy, Sharp's inaugural theory is still the most complete source, serving as the theoretical underpinning of nonviolent actions by social activists since the 1980s.[1]

Sharp is credited with founding the field of civil resistance studies based on his study of Gandhi's thought and practice. The field grows from Sharp's distinction between Gandhi's use of nonviolence as a political strategy and Gandhi's spiritual beliefs in pacifism, or in other words, from the parsing of *strategic* nonviolence from *moral* nonviolence.[2] Sharp claims to leave morality aside and focus on the strategic part of nonviolence, developing a social-political theory of power oriented exclusively toward the practice of nonviolent action. In his three-volume magnum opus, *The Politics of Nonviolent Action*, Sharp lays out the social and political theory that has served as the foundation of the field of study of nonviolent action ever since. The second volume of this work is also the source of Sharp's famous "198 Methods of Nonviolent Action," which anyone who has participated in a nonviolent direct action training has likely encountered.[3]

Sharp's Politics of Nonviolent Action

When *The Politics of Nonviolent Action* was published, Gandhi's theory and practice of nonviolent struggle in the Indian movement against British colonial government was the main reference point for the concept of nonviolence worldwide. Through nonviolent struggle, the story went, Gandhi had led an uprising to liberate the most populous colony in the world from European rule, accomplishing what many believed was only possible through armed struggle. This revolt appeared to present an inspiring alternative to bloody anti-colonial wars and insurrections. It is no surprise then that Sharp's career began with Gandhi. Sharp had been a committed pacifist; he refused induction into the

U.S. Army during the Korean War, edited a prominent pacifist newspaper, and wrote two books on Gandhi before distilling his dissertation (in Political Theory at Oxford) into *The Politics of Nonviolent Action*. Gandhi was clear that he believed in nonviolence as a practice of life, and for him its use in political struggle was inherently connected to nonviolent mindset and spirituality.[4] Sharp, on the other hand, claimed to leave aside the belief in pacifism and instead analyzed Gandhi's strategy in terms of material conflict. He identified and explored the power dynamics that made nonviolent methods successful and used those dynamics to compose a universal theory of nonviolent power. The contention is that nonviolent struggle is the most effective method of organizing political power, and that it should be applied on this basis even by those who do not believe in pacifist morality.

The centerpiece of Sharp's theory is the assertion that all political power is ultimately based in the consent of the governed (an observation he shares with many political theorists). Regimes and leaders might appear powerful, but their power is reliant on the material cooperation of their government bureaucracy and the population at large. This cooperation can be revoked by an organized population and thus used to influence or topple regimes. People generally obey rules even against their own interests, Sharp tells us, whether out of habit, fear of punishment, moral or psychological belief in obedience, patriotism, apathy, lack of confidence, or simple ignorance. Regardless of the reason, ordinary people "usually do not realize that they are the source of the ruler's power and that by joint action they could dissolve that power."[5] Power is with the people, and the state's authority evaporates in the face of collective withdrawal of support by its population.

The idea is simple and powerful. Many political thinkers had assumed warfare to be the logical, and in many cases necessary, extension of political conflict, summed up in Clausewitz's famous adage that war is a continuation of politics by other means. Sharp essentially says that this continuation is unnecessary, and in fact is counterproductive. By organizing collective refusal and disobedience, populations can direct or overthrow governments without resorting to the vastly destructive violence of war.

Importantly, Sharp challenges the popular notion that nonviolent struggle relies upon changing the heart of the oppressor. Kwame Ture famously argued in a 1967 speech repudiating King's nonviolence that: "Dr. King's ... major assumption was that if you are nonviolent, if you suffer, your opponent will see your suffering and will be moved to change his heart. That's very good. He only made one fallacious assumption: in order for nonviolence to work, your opponent must have a conscience."[6] On the contrary, Sharp argues that nonviolent action is not about persuading the oppressor, but is an effective mode of political combat. To Sharp, if an opponent changes their mind based on nonviolent action, that might be, as Ture put it, "very good," but the success of nonviolent action does not rely on such a transformation. Nonviolent action can generate powerful material sanctions that can force regimes to capitulate or collapse against their will. Unsurprisingly, once this idea reached movements, it was inspiring to many activists who sought to create social change or revolution but lacked the means, will, or disposition for a physical fight.

Sharp makes a variety of arguments for the use of nonviolent action over violent action, but they all boil down to the central belief that most people find direct violence distasteful. Successful movements require sustained mass participation, and the use of violence alienates supporters and turns away the public at large. The alienating quality of violence cuts both ways, Sharp says, and can be used to the benefit of nonviolent movements. He uses the term "political jiu jitsu" to describe a phenomenon in which violent state repression of nonviolent protesters can generate sympathy for a movement and undermine a government's legitimacy. Nonviolent activists can exploit this dynamic by putting security forces in a position where they must either forcibly attack protesters who refuse to fight back, thereby expanding sympathy for the movement, or disobey orders, which would empower the movement even more. In chess, this situation is called *zugzwang*— the opponent is compelled to act, but any action they take worsens their position.

Sharp discusses a variety of important mechanisms of nonviolent action such as solidarity, discipline, persistence, and public support, but the main argument revolves around nonviolent protesters' ability to generate material sanctions that can pressure or ruin political regimes. Sharp's intervention is potent and has been extremely influential, founding an entire field of study and practice. The argument for nonviolent power is also deeply problematic at the theoretical level.

The Illogic of Strategic Nonviolence

Taking strategic nonviolence theory on its own terms, there are significant conceptual limitations that are borne out in real-world application. Problems with Sharp's theory stem from four interrelated problems: (1) He begins with a starting belief in nonviolence that is exogenous to his theory of power; (2) he defines violence and nonviolence in inconsistent ways; (3) his argument is promoting a method, not a political goal; (4) his approach to power is philosophical, not sociological.

Nonviolence has nothing to do with the underlying theory of power

Sharp makes a partisan argument, meaning he does not merely analyze society but seeks to persuade the reader to a course of action. In other words, rather than exploring the subject of political power and arriving at a conclusion about the importance of nonviolent action, he seeks to promote the use of nonviolent action, and marshals theory and evidence to prove that it can be effective. In and of itself this is not a problem, but in Sharp's case, if we follow the argument, the thing he is suggesting (nonviolent action) is not actually being argued for, but rather is assumed as a starting point from which the line of reasoning proceeds. Beneath Sharp's argument is an unseen claim that nonviolent action, as he defines it, is inherently preferable.

For Sharp, history has been primarily characterized by unchallenged political regimes, and he believes the existence of tyranny in the world is a result of the masses' ignorance of the nature of power dynamics, which he seeks to illuminate for us. He begins with the goal of promoting nonviolent political action and then assembles evidence that such action has at times been effective and that it has even greater potential to be effective in the future. But the dynamics he describes have to do with the fragile nature of political authority, specifically that governments and leaders are only as powerful as their subjects permit them to be via participation in the functioning of society. The mass withdrawal of that participation, Sharp argues, can bring down even the most ostensibly powerful regimes. Notice, however, that this observation has nothing to do with nonviolence. Though they are presented as inseparable, the form of action he promotes does not flow from the substance of his analysis, but rather is tacked onto it.

Many social theorists begin with a partisan argument, but sound models build that argument into the structure of the theory. Marx is credited with pioneering explicitly partisan (as opposed to removed and "objective") political theory in the Western canon. His politics are presented as deriving from a thorough materialist analysis of history, not the other way around. Marx's view that all history is the history of class struggle arises from his understanding of political economy, which he argues for explicitly in his work; he then places himself on the side that he understands to be revolutionary and agitates for change from that standpoint. To take another example, Fanon argues that the legacy of colonialism had not only occupied land, exploited people, and extracted resources, but that the colonial relationship deeply impacts the minds of people subjected to it. His revolutionary resolve may have come from his personal experience at least as much as it did from his study, but his revolutionary argument arises from his social-psychological analysis of the inferiority complexes he saw resulting from French colonialism in Algeria. He then constructs his political vision and strategy based on his experience and analysis.

In Sharp's case, however, the argument for nonviolence is not part of his text, but rather precedes it. The text does not persuade the reader that nonviolence is preferable—this is assumed—but rather argues that nonviolent action can be just as politically effective as violent action. The problem is, elsewhere Sharp claims to be doing the exact opposite: he claims to be arguing for the use of nonviolence on purely strategic terms, specifically as distinguished from a principled belief in nonviolence. Notably, many of the supposedly secular arguments Sharp makes for why strict nonviolent discipline is essential are backed up by citing Gandhi's moral claims.[7] As we will see, in order to foreground nonviolence in his social theory, Sharp has to twist the concepts and misrepresent the historical examples he deploys. This problem matures into a paradox of nonviolent strategy on the ground: those who believe in "strategic nonviolence" are not assessing conditions and selecting nonviolent action because it is the best option in a given instance, but rather are assuming nonviolent tactics are always the most strategic and proceeding from there—literally the opposite of strategic thinking.

The inconsistency of violence-vs.-nonviolence

In presenting potential avenues for the mobilization of popular power, Sharp creates a dichotomy of political action: violent and nonviolent. Strangely, Sharp himself articulates the problem with this approach: "It is widely assumed that all social and political behavior must be clearly either violent or nonviolent. This simple dualism leads only to serious distortions of reality, however, one of the main ones being that some people call 'nonviolent' anything they regard as good and 'violent' anything they dislike."[8]

Here, Sharp is absolutely correct. In fact, through this acknowledgment alone he admits more nuance than many of his disciples. But despite his recognition of the problem, he immediately recreates it. Framing the problem as one of "dualism," Sharp instead presents a six-way breakdown of types of political action:

(1) verbal persuasion, (2) institutional procedures backed by the threat of sanctions, (3) violence against people, (4) violence against people and property, (5) violence against property, and (6) nonviolent action. His main purpose in doing so is to clarify that there are actions that are technically nonviolent, for example verbal persuasion, which he wants to distinguish from the category of struggle he defines as *nonviolent action*. This aggregation is technically not dualistic in that there are six, but there remains an underlying separation between the three actions that involve direct violence (3-5) and the three that do not (1, 2, and 6), and he rejects the ones that involve violence out of hand *because* they involve violence.

Sharp makes ambiguous reference to the difference between destroying property and harming people, and alludes to a potential for property destruction to be nonviolent, but he also categorizes "violence against property" as just that—violence.[9] He groups "riots, assassination, violent revolution, guerrilla warfare, *coup d'état*, civil war and international war" into a single category of political action that is based on "applying superior means of violence."[10] He contrasts this with the nonviolent action approach, which is fundamentally different in that it relies on strategic withdrawal of support. By the nature of this *de facto* dichotomy, Sharp proceeds as though the dynamics of violent struggle and those of nonviolent struggle are inherently distinct and mutually exclusive—precisely the dualism he himself earlier described as a distortion of reality.

Sharp's limited and selective understanding of the power dynamics in both violent and nonviolent force is well represented in the term he uses for a central aspect of nonviolent strategy: "political jiu jitsu." Sharp adapts the term from "moral jiu jitsu," a term Richard Gregg used in 1944 to describe the way that Gandhi's nonviolence could psychologically destabilize agents of repression by using their force against them. Sharp uses "political jiu jitsu" to describe a similar maneuver that throws an opponent off balance using their own force, only in a broader political sense as opposed to having an emotional or spiritual effect.[11] Both usages appear to be based on a tellingly limited (and likely orientalist) misreading of the reference point. Jiu jitsu is a Japanese, and later Brazilian, martial art and combat sport that sometimes involves leveraging an opponent's force against them, enabling a smaller person to subdue a larger adversary, but it also involves the direct application of force as appropriate and based on the technique and strategy being employed. To Sharp, jiu jitsu represents a conceptual framework where the combatant who only uses their opponent's force can knock the opponent off balance and win, the metaphor implying that this is fundamentally different from systems of fighting that rely on the direct use of one's own violent force against an enemy. In fact, all martial arts and combat sports involve a mix of the direct use of one's own force and indirect use of the opponent's force; i.e., both "hard" and "soft" techniques. The irony of Sharp's misreading is that if a person attempted to compete in jiu jitsu without using any physical force of their own, they would surely lose. The very fact that Sharp uses a *martial* art as an analogy for nonviolent power demonstrates his selective vision in terms of where power comes from, as well as the slippages in his theory between meanings of violence and nonviolence.

As organizer and researcher Shon Meckfessel explains it, the argument for strategic nonviolence "deftly exploits ambiguities in the shifting definition of violence, particularly by equating apparently very dissimilar phenomena together as 'violence.'"[12] Sharp lists riots alongside assassinations and conventional warfare as a violent tactic, assumed to be based in wholly different power dynamics from nonviolent action, while elsewhere he classifies uprisings that involved riots as nonviolent struggle without engaging with the apparent contradiction. These shifting definitions allow Sharp to misrepresent the very dynamics he claims to explicate. For example, he repeatedly uses the labor strike as a prime example of nonviolent power, and names the Industrial Revolution-era "trade unionists and other social radicals who sought a means of struggle—largely strikes, general strikes, and boycotts—against what they regarded as an unjust social system and for the improvement of the condition of working men" as instrumental in the development of nonviolent technique.[13] As with the jiu jitsu analogy, Sharp treats the strike as though it has always been a nonviolent tactic. Strikes *do* rely on power dynamics of collective refusal and withdrawal of cooperation, but historically they have not necessarily been nonviolent about it. In precisely the timeframe Sharp discusses, when the labor movement was congealing and growing powerful, organized violence was integrally connected to the power dynamics of the strike. It is worth quoting Voltairine de Cleyre at length from her 1912 essay on direct action:

> Now everybody knows that a strike of any size means violence. No matter what any one's ethical preference for peace may be, he knows it will not be peaceful. If it's a telegraph strike, it means cutting wires and poles, and getting fake scabs in to spoil the instruments. If it is a steel rolling mill strike, it means beating up the scabs, breaking the windows, setting the gauges wrong, and ruining the expensive rollers together with tons and tons of material. If it's a miners' strike, it means destroying tracks and bridges, and blowing up mills. If it is a garment workers' strike, it means having an unaccountable fire, getting a volley of stones through an apparently inaccessible window, or possibly a brickbat on the manufacturer's own head. If it's a street-car strike, it means tracks torn up or barricaded with the contents of ash-carts and slop-carts, with overturned wagons or stolen fences, it means smashed or incinerated cars and turned switches. If it is a system federation strike, it means "dead" engines, wild engines, derailed freights, and stalled trains. If it is a building trades strike, it means dynamited structures. And always, everywhere, all the time, fights between strikebreakers and scabs against strikers and strike-sympathizers, between People and Police.[14]

A labor strike is the most iconic example of withdrawal of support, but in practice that has often meant physically reinforcing the leverage of that withdrawal by sabotaging the means of production or physically fighting with strikebreakers, scabs, and police. Sharp's vision of the strike is based on a theoretical idealization of what it could look like, not a grounded conception of what it has looked like. And his discussion of nonviolent discipline, which specifically boxes out strategic sabotage and use of physical force against bodies, makes his misunderstanding of the historical power dynamics of the strike unmistakable. By using eighteenth- and nineteenth-century strikes as key examples of nonviolent action, Sharp quietly rolls the positive effects of real-world violent action into the narrative of nonviolent power without taking responsibility for the more difficult aspects.

A method without a cause

Sharp's argument is not promoting a political cause, but rather a method of action in the abstract. This is worth focusing on, first, because it starkly differentiates his work from previous theorists of both violent and nonviolent struggle, and second because it is connected to how the theory of change is applied. To Sharp, "there is nothing in nonviolent action to prevent it from being used for both 'good' and 'bad' causes," and while he does not define good and bad, he recommends nonviolent action regardless of the cause as a "good" substitute for "bad" violence.[15] Sharp's work was originally inspired by a material analysis of Gandhi's political strategy, but Gandhi constructed that strategy specifically as it related to a concrete political goal—to liberate India from British rule. Beyond that, Gandhi spoke of the broader goals of a peaceful and spiritually awakened society. The method Gandhi advocates to achieve these goals personally is *ahimsa*, a virtue in Hindu, Buddhist, Jain, and Sikh traditions referring to the respect for all life and the avoidance of harm to other beings. The political method is *satyagraha*, a word coined by Gandhi to refer to nonviolent resistance. The spiritual fuel for *satyagraha* is *ahimsa*, while the material calculation that drives it is the observation that the British were unable to administer India without large swaths of Indian society continuing to participate in the colonial economy.

Satyagraha, which in direct translation to English means "adherence to truth" or "truth force," is inherently connected to the "truth" of righteous struggle for political freedom and personal transcendence. The adherence to a truth philosophy-strategy involves behaving as righteously as possible in all aspects of life, and organizing peaceful noncooperation that requires great sacrifice on the part of participants. By giving in to sacrifice and nonviolently refusing to abide by British administration, Indians could both materially throw off their colonizers and spiritually build dignity and fortitude for independence. Ultimately, the method and the end are inseparable.

Likewise for Martin Luther King, Jr., whose primary political goal when he developed and popularized his nonviolent strategy in the U.S. was to end racial segregation, with a broader, deeper goal of achieving an egalitarian society. Dr. King's nonviolent approach stems from a combination of his interpretation of Christianity, his study of Gandhi, and his strategic calculation based on a power analysis of the political and racial realities of the U.S. Like Gandhi, King's faith, his immediate political goals, his broader ideological orientation, and his nonviolent strategy are all interrelated.

While they differ in terms of their method, practitioner-theorists of revolutionary armed struggle are similar to Gandhi and King in that their methods are constructed to achieve linked political and ideological goals situated in specific historical circumstances. For the most famous theorists of modern guerrilla warfare—Mao Zedong, Võ Nguyên Giáp, and Che Guevara—the primary political goals were, respectively, to liberate China from Japanese occupation, Vietnamese independence and self-rule, and to overthrow the Batista dictatorship in Cuba.[16] For all three, the broader ideological goal was international communism (though each demonstrated a different conception and commitment to the meaning of communism). For each of them, the selection of guerrilla warfare as a strategy was based first and foremost on strategic calculations arising from Marxian analyses of the material contradictions of the regimes they opposed, as well as the observation that occupying forces are generally unable to directly govern the geographic entirety of a country. Furthermore, for all three, guerrilla warfare as a method was inherently linked to the struggle by the oppressed against the forces of imperialism.

The strategy of guerrilla warfare involves organizing in remote areas of a country where the regime's forces have little reach. In the initial stage of struggle, revolutionaries recruit everyday people to the cause, build community trust, and agitate for collective struggle in pursuit of a better future. In this phase, the guerrillas are not equipped to face the state's forces in open combat, and instead focus on organizing and building capacity. These remote areas grow into a second stage of struggle as "liberated zones" that are governed by rebels essentially as a parallel state, then they are able to engage in ambushes and limited battles that resupply the guerrilla forces and build their confidence while depleting the material and morale of the opposing army. Still, one of the main goals of this stage is to demonstrate that guerrilla governance is better than the state's rule. Only when the liberated zones grow to rival the legitimacy of the state do guerrillas transition to the third phase and engage in more conventional warfare. Mao, Giáp, and Guevara are clear that without the support of the people, specifically poor, marginalized, and exploited populations, the movement cannot graduate from the first phase and there can be no guerrilla struggle. This is why Giáp, probably the greatest guerrilla strategist in modern history, is explicit that the most important quality of guerrilla war is having a *just cause*. While the liberatory nature of guerrilla struggle is certainly open to debate, and the historical legacies of guerrilla wars are mixed, from the perspectives of its theorists, having a just cause and being "of the people" are essential components for successful guerrilla struggle.

Table 1. Strategic goals and methods for theorists of revolution

Theorist	Immediate Goal	Abstract Goal	Method
Mao Zedong	End Japanese Occupation	Communism	Guerrilla struggle
Võ Nguyên Giáp	Vietnamese independence	Communism	Guerrilla struggle
Che Guevara	Overthrow Batista regime	Communism	Guerrilla struggle
Mohandas Gandhi	Indian independence	Peace	Nonviolent struggle
Martin Luther King, Jr.	End U.S. segregation	Egalitarianism	Nonviolent struggle
Gene Sharp	Nonviolent action	Nonviolent action	Nonviolent action

In contrast to all five of the practitioner-theorists listed in Table 1, Sharp's goal is solely the promotion of means, not ends. Or, put another way, promotion of the means *is* the end. Of course, many social theorists study methods of struggle without an explicitly ideological component. What is noteworthy about Sharp is that he makes a partisan argument as though it were ideological, but specifically arguing for the use of a method, unattached to a cause. In other works, Sharp nods to the importance of decentralizing power for lasting political change, but these are asides compared with the emphasis he puts on methods of nonviolent resistance. He is ambivalent about the ethical application of nonviolent action against a legitimate government, but without discussing what constitutes legitimacy. And, even more strikingly, he is upfront that the consequences of overthrowing regimes using the tools he promotes are beyond the scope of his work. It is in this regard that Sharp's theory is most visibly at odds with the political Left. The distinction between strategic and principled nonviolent action is an important theoretical contribution, but it also has the dual consequences of depoliticizing the field of civil resistance that grew from his work and narrowly limiting its view of political struggle. These have deep implications for the theory's conception of power, since a theory of power that claims to be apolitical is either lacking or hiding something.

Think, for example, of the 2011 Egyptian uprising that initiated the overthrow of Hosni Mubarak. Many nonviolence advocates hailed this as a shining success of their theory; some pundits even (outrageously) claimed the revolt had been fomented by Gene Sharp himself.[17] While the uprising was by no means holistically nonviolent, those momentous three weeks in Egypt were a deeply inspiring example of popular power that rippled across the entire world. Two years later, another wave of massive protests in Egypt ousted Mohamed Morsi, the first democratically elected president in Egyptian history, and ushered back a military government similar to that which the 2011 protests had deposed. From a completely detached standpoint, these two movements appear nearly identical—both involved mass protests and occupations of public space that ended with the military removing the head of state. But the 2011 movement went up against an entrenched dictatorship, while the 2013 movement was supported by the remnants of that dictatorship, which continued to control large swaths of the economy and security forces. Or consider pro-Chavez and anti-government protests in Venezuela between 2002 and today, the "red shirts" and "yellow shirts" in Thailand between 2005 and 2020, the Gezi park occupation and anti-coup protests in Turkey between 2013 and 2016, and so many other examples of politically opposing civil resistance movements in the same country. If all we care about is civil resistance tactics, then all of these movements are essentially comparable as protests against a government. However, if we take into account social dynamics and political context, each pair of examples represents opposing movements with different or even opposite support structures. Promoting a method of resistance without a set of political principles to guide it ends up at best confusing matters and at worst reinforcing established authority.

Social power, in theory

Sharp bases his strategy on a very limited bibliography. Apart from Gandhi, his sources in *The Politics of Nonviolent Action* are largely drawn from Western classical political philosophy, and with a conspicuous lack of attention to social or revolutionary theory. This foundation leads Sharp to underestimate or outright ignore real-world dynamics and challenges associated with the types of leverage he proposes, with further consequences for his theory's applicability.

As other theorists of nonviolent action have noted, Sharp's approach to power "is individualistic and voluntaristic in orientation."[18] To the question of why nonviolent action had not been successfully used more frequently in history, Sharp answers that it is because people by and large do not understand power. Since the dynamics he proposes are meant to be universal, applying to all governments and peoples in all places and times, and since his theory states that all power is ultimately with the mass of people, then the existence of oppression is only due to the oppressed failing to act. In Sharp's words, "the degree of liberty or tyranny in any government is, it follows, in large degree a reflection of the relative determination of the subjects to be free and their willingness and ability to resist efforts to enslave them." He goes on to quote (white) South African philosopher Errol E. Harris as saying that "a nation gets the government which it deserves," and Tolstoy in arguing that the British had not enslaved the Indians but rather, based on their (at that time) failure to liberate their country, the "Indians who have enslaved themselves."[19]

Sharp's approach is consistent with his sources in classic Western political theory, a school of thought that has tended to bypass context and contemplate society against the backdrop of a theoretical universe in which all things are equal. Even leaving aside the deeply problematic implications of blaming oppressed peoples for their oppression while crediting the populations of imperialist societies for what domestic political liberties they have, this abstract framing, free from complex social dynamics and context, is predisposed to overlook factors that are important for strategic calculations. For example, Sharp does not factor in the complexities of capitalism, racism, patriarchy, or state bureaucracy, nor how different types of stratification in society mean that different people can benefit from and be oppressed by social systems in different ways.

Sharp builds on the theories of philosophers like Hobbes, Rousseau, and Comte for his understandings of the state and power. Bertrand de Jouvenel's *On Power*, John Austin's *Lectures on the Jurisprudence, or the Philosophy of Positive Law*, and Martin J. Hillenbrand's *Power and Morals* make repeated appearances as well. On the other hand, contemporary social theorists from Sharp's era and prior are all but absent from his bibliography, and he makes no reference to the revolutionary movements of the 1960s. Though he makes arguments on the subjects of violence, power, authority, social control, resistance, and the question of why people obey or rebel, Sharp does not consult, for example, Arendt, Du Bois, Fanon, Foucault, Gramsci, or Marcuse, nor does he put his work in conversation with movements that were making theory through action in Sharp's country such as the Black Panther Party, Student Nonviolent Coordinating Committee, or Students for a Democratic Society.[20] Accordingly, Sharp drastically underestimates the complex dynamics that pervade the space between theoretical nonviolent rebellion and social reality.

Sharp briefly discusses historical examples, but their purpose in the text is not to explore and draw out dynamics but simply to substantiate his own claims. The examples he uses further expose his inconsistencies, since several of them involve significant violence, which he sometimes acknowledges and sometimes ignores. For example, Sharp discusses what he calls the "predominantly nonviolent" Russian revolutions of 1905 and 1917, claiming that the turn to armed revolt in 1905 led to the revolution's defeat, while better adherence to nonviolent discipline in 1917 led to success.[21] Only the most cursory and insincere exploration of either of those historical events could justify claiming them as nonviolent, and the crude explanation of the 1905 revolution's defeat based on a shift from nonviolent resistance to armed resistance is wildly simplistic.

That he views the 1905 and 1917 Russian revolutions as fully distinct events in the first place reveals a conceptual limitation that continues to haunt civil resistance studies until today. Sharp mentions the political and social changes that emerged from the 1905 movement (i.e., the creation of a legislature and the rise of the *soviets*), but he nevertheless views the 1917 revolution as a completely separate revolt. The two can then be compared and judged as either successful or unsuccessful in their short-term goals. Such a two-dimensional approach entirely misses the importance of the 1905 revolution in changing Russian society and educating revolutionaries such that the 1917 revolution could have succeeded the way it did. But the purpose of this historical example in Sharp's work is not to illuminate the dynamics of the Russian Revolution, nor to learn from the experiences of its organizers; it is simply to convince readers that nonviolent action works better. In other cases, such as in describing prison resistance in the Soviet Union, Sharp simply states: "In some of these there was a great deal of violence," and then moves on without explaining what that means or discussing how that violence might have interacted with the nonviolent dynamics he is using the example to illustrate.[22] And the fact that Sharp is able to pivot from discussing the 1917 revolution as a successful nonviolent revolt to discussing prison resistance against the government that evolved from the 1917 revolution should draw our attention to the inability of Sharp's theory of power to comprehend or account for anything that happens between moments of acute uprising.

In a later publication, Sharp devotes a chapter to Hannah Arendt's report on the trial of Adolf Eichmann, the source of her famous adage, "the banality of evil."[23] However, like the historical examples mentioned above, Sharp only uses Arendt for a single point she makes, in this case, that cooperation from within Jewish community leadership facilitated the Nazis' extermination policies by convincing people to put their heads down and go along until it was too late. Sharp uses this observation to make the case that nonviolent noncooperation could stall future genocides, but he cherry-picks this single point out of an otherwise complex and historically informed argument.[24] Arendt was attempting to bring to light a number of less comfortable aspects of the Holocaust from the perspective not only of a political thinker, but of a Jewish person who escaped Germany herself. In *Eichmann in Jerusalem*, Arendt was critically evaluating the ways in which the Holocaust narrative was being manipulated in the new State of Israel through the theatricality of the Eichmann trial. Sharp extracts a single point (which happens to be the most controversial) from Arendt's argument and repurposes it to validate his theory of nonviolent action, never putting it back in conversation either with Arendt's nuanced treatment of power in that same work, nor with her other writing on totalitarianism, violence, and revolution.

Sharp's lack of attention to Barbara Deming's theory of nonviolent action is particularly instructive. In her 1968 work, *On Revolution and Equilibrium*, Deming makes a similar move to Sharp, that is, distinguishing principled nonviolence from practical nonviolence so as to better craft movement strategy. Deming makes her argument as an activist herself, in reference to the politics of revolution not just in India but in Cuba and Vietnam as well, and in direct response to Fanon's and Sartre's arguments for the use of political violence. Deming was committed to revolutionary militancy, and while she advocated for nonviolence as a means, she considered herself an ally of revolutionaries who applied other means. For example, Deming spoke supportively of the Vietnamese struggle for independence and of the Vietnamese Communists' achievements after expelling French occupation forces, and even met personally with Hồ Chí Minh during a visit to North Vietnam in 1967.[25]

Though she was a prominent contemporary activist writing on the same subject matter in the same country, Sharp does not cite or engage with Deming. Reading her work next to his, it is clear that Deming is committed to the politics and outcomes of social struggle, while Sharp is committed only to the tools of nonviolent conflict. The difference is more than a side note. Deming's work is about real-world nonviolent conflict that exists in lived experience and conditions characterized by complex social, political, and economic oppression, specifically in the service of a more nonviolent and egalitarian future. Sharp's work is about methods of political struggle in the abstract, in service of short-term goals in the abstract. I can't help but wonder what the field of nonviolence studies would look like today had it followed Deming rather than Sharp, but it is less of a mystery why Sharp's work was so much more marketable.

There are numerous consequences of Sharp's underestimation of social dynamics. A particularly important one for his theory of the power of collective consent and refusal has to do with social, political, and economic stratification. Focusing on the power of people withdrawing cooperation implies there was cooperation in the first place. Sharp appears unaware of the possibility that constant, ongoing resistance by those at the margins of society and at the bottom of systemic hierarchies are part of the status quo, and that many people at all levels of society might conform or resist in different ways on a daily basis.[26] Furthermore, people's position in society impacts the potential leverage available to them. For a member of a political regime or someone with a coordinating role in the formal economy, the dynamics of withdrawing cooperation might be relatively straightforward. But for those residing on the margins of society or engaged in the informal economy, or for those who are systematically degraded, excluded, imprisoned, or murdered by governments, withdrawal of consent has less, or at the very least different, inherent leverage. This is precisely why in some industries sabotage has been a necessary element of labor strikes. And it is why rioting is sometimes required to make people's resistance visible and effective, a dynamic that movement scholar Frances Fox Piven frames as "withdrawal of cooperation in the routines of civil life."[27]

The Nonviolence of Imperialism

Perhaps the most significant consequence of Sharp's abstract foundation is the (at best) naïve understanding that individual knowledge of power dynamics is the primary requirement to mobilize real-world power. Ironically, Sharp's own career stands as a prime counter-example to his theory in this regard. Nonviolent resistance is often viewed by adherents as opposition to imperialism; Sharp himself wrote extensively about political resistance against tyranny, and social movements on the Left have picked up Sharp's work and run with it. However, for the bulk of his career Sharp himself sought to work with Western governments and collaborated with institutions that are far from nonviolent. Here, I will dip only slightly into a whole can of biographical worms for the sake of clarifying the purpose and feasibility of Sharp's theories.

Throughout his academic career, which began at Oxford and ended at Harvard, Sharp's work was funded by, among others, the U.S. Department of Defense and the RAND Corporation. In 1985, Sharp published a book titled *Making Europe Unconquerable,* about methods of defending Western Europe against communism and weakening Eastern Bloc countries using civil resistance methods. The book's foreword was written by George F. Kennan, who had been U.S. Secretary of State, ambassador to the Soviet Union and Yugoslavia, and a main architect of the U.S.'s Cold War policies. As law and economics professor Marcie Smith puts it, "the book is basically a manual for how the United States could develop and resource 'pro-democracy' protest movements in the Eastern Bloc and defend them from Soviet retaliation."[28] Sharp's efforts to convince U.S. and European governments to train their personnel in the methods of nonviolent action never panned out (as Sharp himself might have predicted if he had infused his theories with a deeper understanding of real-world power), but many within the government, like Kennan, saw great value in his contributions for the purposes of U.S. foreign policy.

In fact, Sharp's connections to the U.S. government began decades earlier. In 1965, he left Oxford to finish his dissertation at Harvard's Center for International Affairs in order to work with Thomas Schelling (the economist who coined the term "collateral damage") while he was serving as an advisor to Project Camelot.[29] Project Camelot was a "peace research" initiative run by the Army Psychological Warfare Office looking into "nonviolent solutions to international projects"—the most exposed of a number of military-academic collaborations designed to better understand how to influence social movements and counter-insurgencies in foreign countries.[30] Schelling would write the introduction to *The Politics of Nonviolent Action*.

Sharp's research at the Center for International Affairs—the other CIA—where he held an appointment from 1965 to 1995, was funded by the U.S. Department of Defense in a Cold War context in which the Pentagon was intent on studying the nuts and bolts of social movements in order to incite and support uprisings against the Soviet Union and its allies while undermining the same types of uprisings domestically. Nominally nonviolent movements can function as excellent geopolitical weapons, since their success can weaken or overthrow a rival state, while state repression against the movement can be used to undermine that government's legitimacy on the world stage. At the same time, lessons on effective repression can be learned and applied against movements at home. In reading *The Politics of Nonviolent Action* as a government manual for how to instigate rebellion in an enemy state, as opposed to an activist manual for how to change society for the better, the writing style makes a bit more sense. Notably, this is all conspicuously absent in Sharp's popular and activist-facing biographies, which rarely so much as mention the significant parts of his career he spent working with governments and military advisors.[31] On the contrary, over the years, many advocates of nonviolent action have responded harshly to any and all accusations levied against Sharp and his organization, the Albert Einstein Institution (AEI).

The debate over Sharp gets weird. For example, after claims cropped up on the Left in the early 2000s that AEI was training dissidents in Venezuela and Iran, international relations scholar Steven Zunes wrote a series of articles and penned a sweeping letter of support for Sharp that was signed by numerous leftist luminaries, most prominently Noam Chomsky and Howard Zinn.[32] The letter "categorically" denies that the AEI (also referred to in the letter as the "Albert Einstein Institute") "has ever provided financial or logistical support to any opposition groups in any country; nor has Dr. Sharp or the AEI ever taken sides in political conflicts or engaged in strategic planning with any group." The letter goes on: "The Albert Einstein Institution operates with a very minimal budget out of Dr. Sharp's home with a staff consisting of two people ... and is quite incapable of carrying out the foreign intrigues of which it has been falsely accused." However, a quick look at AEI's annual report for 2000–2004 shows the Institution proudly highlighting their work training "groups in more than 20 countries."[33] In the section on Venezuela, the report states:

> Venezuelans opposed to Chávez met with Gene Sharp and other AEI staff to talk about the deteriorating political situation in their country. They also discussed options for opposition groups to further their cause effectively without violence. These visits led to an in-country consultation in April 2003. The nine-day consultation was held by consultants Robert Helvey and Chris Miller in Caracas for members of the Venezuelan democratic opposition. The objective of the consultation was to provide them with the capacity to develop a nonviolent strategy to restore democracy to Venezuela. Participants included members of political parties and unions, nongovernmental organization leaders, and unaffiliated activists.[34]

It would be one thing to defend Sharp's personal values and intentions—or even to defend the training of Venezuelan dissidents in the early 2000s—but the open letter appears to vociferously deny something that is not only verifiably true, but which Sharp's organization actually boasts about. The refusal to even entertain honest engagement with the less comfortable aspects of Sharp's career conceals an ongoing working relationship between many civil resistance scholars and military, government, and private capital interests. Many of the most prominent names in nonviolence studies are directly connected to institutions that are, to put it mildly, questionable as to their alignment with nonviolence.

One of the most astute interpreters of Sharp's work is Robert Helvey, the consultant mentioned in the AEI report above, who was an Army Colonel with the Joint Military Attaché School and met Sharp while he was a senior fellow at the Center for International Affairs. Helvey would become the president of AEI, and his AEI-published 2004 book, *On Strategic Nonviolent Conflict*, articulated, among other things, the "pillars of support" framework for understanding nonviolent strategy, a useful tool that would later be popularized among activists by the Momentum training program. Maria Stephan is a program director at the U.S. Institute of Peace, but was previously a senior fellow at the Atlantic Council, a think tank founded during the Cold War to strengthen U.S.-European cooperation and free trade. She was the lead foreign affairs officer with the U.S. State Department's Bureau of Conflict and Stabilization Operations when she co-authored *Why Civil Resistance Works* with Erica Chenoweth, who is now at the Harvard Kennedy School.

Peter Ackerman, co-founder of AEI and author of the 1994 book, *Strategic Nonviolent Conflict,* and the widely popular 2000 book, *A Force More Powerful* (which has been turned into a television series and a video game), was also a director at the British International Institute for Strategic Studies and the head of the international capital markets department at Drexel Burnham Lambert, a powerful multinational investment firm. At the time he co-founded AEI with Sharp, Ackerman was leading a notorious Wall Street junk bond scam that made him $165 million in 1988 alone but contributed to bankrupting the company by 1990; he avoided criminal charges by paying off colleagues in civil claims.[35] Ackerman also founded the Center for Applied Non-Violent Action and Strategies and is the founding chair of the International Center on Nonviolent Conflict (ICNC).

It is difficult to square the most prominent theorist of nonviolent strategy collaborating with vulture capitalists and addressing his work to military audiences, then becoming venerated by social justice activists. It is not as difficult to read this information in a conspiratorial light—giving a much darker implication to William B. Watson's frequently repeated book jacket quote that "Sharp is the Machiavelli of nonviolence." And while Sharp did at times write about the importance of decentralizing power more broadly, these are some of the least referenced areas of his work by his disciples. Sharp himself was likely a true believer—if anything, more naïve than nefarious. Earlier in his life he had been a committed pacifist, and he appeared to maintain a dogged belief in his version of nonviolence.

When political scientist Geo Maher published an article critical of AEI's role in Venezuela, Sharp himself reportedly sent Maher, then a graduate student, an email castigating and threatening him.[36] Shockingly, the main concern Sharp voiced in his email was not that Maher had accused AEI of training a right-wing coup government, but that he had connected their work to a campaign that used violent tactics! As his theory would suggest, the use of strategic nonviolence appears to be Sharp's main concern. For him, perhaps, if he could convince government and military forces to use nonviolent action, his work would have the most bang for buck. The eagerness of so many anti-imperialist thinkers to defend Sharp against accusations of U.S. government collaboration at least speaks to his trusted networks in radical intellectual *milieus*, and many continue to see Sharp's radical influences as more important than his neoliberal ones.[37]

Regardless of his intentions, Sharp's theory of strategic nonviolence is demonstrably applicable for U.S. foreign policy purposes, and that is something movements and analysts must remain aware of. His refusal to deal with politics, context, or vision for a liberated society make his theories of action well suited for state use against foreign governments. After all, if the goal is to incite a movement to collapse an enemy state, a movement's liberatory politics would only get in the way when the U.S. would later step in to install a friendly regime; much better for the activists to have less developed politics of their own, just the methods required to weaken their country's political system.

Conclusion

If Sharp was unaware of the ways that agents of U.S. foreign policy used his work, then his comprehension of the realities of social-political struggle was, in the end, astonishingly weak. If he was a conscious and willing collaborator with imperial strategies of the U.S. government, then he was something much worse than naïve. But that is a matter for his friends and biographers. Our concern is how Sharp's theories continue to effect understandings of movement strategy. We cannot deny that Sharp crafted an accessible and useful theory of political action that has turned out to be highly influential in activist communities.

In considering the substantial limitations of Sharp's theory of power, which resistance scholar Brian Martin sums up as, "too simple to capture the full dynamics of society, if it is not misconceived altogether," Martin wisely asks: "what is the point of having a theory of power in the first place?" He goes on: "If the aim is to advance the careers of intellectuals who stand by the side observing society but preferring to avoid interaction with it, then a complex, erudite theory serves admirably. On the other hand, if the aim is to provide some insights which can be used by activists, then a simple, straightforward, easy-to-apply theory is far superior, so long as it grasps certain basic insights."[38] Indeed. The question here pivots on the final qualification—*so long as it grasps certain basic insights*—as well as activists knowing when the theory is applicable, when it's not, and when the easy-to-apply approach gets in the way of radical change that necessarily takes place in a complex world.

Sharp's theory of power and the architecture of strategic nonviolence have been repackaged by contemporary movement-training programs and used to generate impactful campaigns.[39] The user-friendly strategic nonviolence approach is expedient in onboarding people to social movement activism and can be highly creative in applications of nonviolent tactics. But that approachability has a flip side—it can mislead eager participants into thinking the movement can be scripted in a classroom or retreat center. While the "what works better" framing is compelling for those interested in building power from below (myself included), it has also encouraged a mechanistic and apolitical view of movement tactics, leading some to approach movements as one would a cookbook, as though we can generate predictably successful short-term outcomes if only our inputs could be correctly measured.

"Textbook instructions for 'how to make a revolution' in a step-by-step progression," Hannah Arendt once said, "are all based on the mistaken notion that revolutions are 'made.'"[40] Organizations and campaigns are made, but revolutionary struggle encompasses a much wider range of interconnected actions, dynamics, and conditions. Emphasizing the ability of everyday people to launch and drive uprisings can be empowering and is important, but overemphasis on efficacy alone can lead to shortsighted analysis, in-fighting over messaging and branding, inability to understand or commit to long-term political struggle, and, most destructively, a sense that revolutions can be created, controlled, and directed by professional organizers.[41]

The Sharpian strategic nonviolence approach can also lead to a valorization and idealization of protest as such—meaning seeing protests as an indicator of success in themselves—especially when it references theory and research that claim to show a mechanical relationship between getting people in the streets and political change. The most egregious example of this can be seen in the application of Chenoweth's claim that no movement that mobilized 3.5 percent of a country's population has failed to overthrow the government.[42] This idea has been re-published and repeated *ad nauseum*, to the point that some nonviolent action trainings have encouraged activists to literally do the math around their target populations to discover the number of people needed to mobilize real change. During moments of uprising around the world in recent years, the *BBC* called it "the 3.5 percent rule" and *NPR* referred to it as "the magic number behind protests."[43] Even if that was what the underlying research actually said (and it's not—I'll get to that in the following chapter), prioritizing how many people are being mobilized leaves out entirely a theory of *how* those people will create desired change.

To be fair, Chenoweth has more recently cautioned against overzealous application of this number, for example in a 2020 Harvard Kennedy School monograph, where on the first page they state: "The 3.5% figure is a descriptive statistic based on a sample of historical movements. It is not necessarily a prescriptive one, and no one can see the future. Trying to achieve the threshold without building a broader public constituency does not guarantee success in the future." Correct as these remarks are, they come years after the 3.5 percent number made its splash, and to a large extent the damage has been done. When we present what seem like easy answers, we should not be surprised when they get repeated in the easiest ways.

Participation in protests does not itself lead to political change. Movement researchers have found that the majority of protests post-1960s and leading up to the 2000s were placid, routine, non-disruptive to the status quo, and initiated by the advantaged.[44] Many defenders of nonviolent discipline insist that nonviolent action is not inherently placid but rather can be both highly creative and deeply disruptive and is often initiated by oppressed communities. That is all true. But Sharp's theory, and applications like "the 3.5 percent rule," make it difficult to distinguish between them. And the fact remains that most nonviolent protest actions these days *are* highly routine and non-disruptive. Even when they are disruptive, the emphasis on escalating protest as a goal in itself limits our horizon of how people create social and political change.

Sharp's vision of nonviolent action is presented as expansive, his volumes detailing hundreds of different types of action, and proponents frequently point to the endless possibilities for new creative versions and adaptations. Again, it is true, there are countless ways to resist that do not directly threaten people or property. But there are more possibilities for resistance that do. Here we come back to the consequences of limiting our scope of potential actions to nonviolent discipline.

As Noam Chomsky has reminded us, "the smart way to keep people passive and obedient is to strictly limit the spectrum of acceptable opinion but to allow very lively debate within that spectrum."[45] According to Sharp, nonviolent action is the opposite of passive and obedient. But in the final analysis it serves the same purpose Chomsky describes at a meta-level of social control. If people cannot be contained, then limiting the form and scope of acceptable practices of dissent is the ideal way to reinforce a system that bends but does not break, giving people the sense that there is resistance going on and that social change is achievable for relatively little risk, when in fact the presuppositions of the system are being fortified by the limits put on the range of resistance. This is especially important for societies that purport to be democracies full of political and civil rights. From the perspective of foreign policy strategists, when deployed against adversaries those same limits on movement actions can be supplemented with international pressure, sanctions, and other forms of intervention, or the transgression of those limits can simply be ignored. That does not mean that politically radical and strategically minded nonviolent action cannot be disruptive and generative—certainly it can—but policing the boundary of nonviolent discipline limits our thinking about resistance and leaves us with a deeply diminished toolkit, filled with many of the wrong tools that happen to closely resemble the right ones.

Overall, Sharp's insights can be useful, but strategies derived from his theory of change are likely to share its shortcomings. Audre Lorde famously wrote: "the master's tools will never allow us to dismantle the master's house. They may allow us to temporarily beat him at his own game, but they will never enable us to bring about genuine change." This quote is often taken out of context, frequently to bolster the argument for strict nonviolence. Lorde was speaking of white supremacy, patriarchy, and homophobia embedded in ways that intellectuals organize the tools of analysis that we use to understand society. In the same essay, Lorde asks and then answers: "What does it mean when the tools of a racist patriarchy are used to examine the fruits of that same patriarchy? It means that only the most narrow parameters of change are possible and allowable." Following this logic, we might say that tools for change based on simplistic theory and developed in collaboration with U.S. government strategists can be used for liberatory purposes, but in applying those tools alone, only the most narrow parameters of change are possible.

3.

Why Civil Resistance Works with the Wrong Data

"In our dreams we can have our eggs cooked exactly how we want them, but we can't eat them."
—ANNA FREUD

The twenty-first century has seen massive, unarmed civilian rebellions in dozens of countries around the world, as well as countless more protests that have changed national conversations and influenced political developments. This wave of movements has often been characterized as *nonviolent*—Gene Sharp's theory come to life. Scholars in civil resistance studies have explained the surge in global uprisings using the logic of nonviolent action, making it appear as though the modern rebellion is nonviolent, with violent tactics being aberrations increasingly relegated to the past. While the majority of uprisings around the world in recent decades have taken the form of civilian resistance as opposed to armed resistance, most have also involved rioting and other acts of unarmed violence. Movement theorists who hail from a nonviolence framework have been highly resistant to incorporating property destruction and other low-level violence into the stories of movements in any way other than to blame losses and setbacks on these kinds of actions. The argument that nonviolent tactics are universally more effective than violent tactics has become accepted as conventional wisdom, due in large part to the research Chenoweth and Stephan present in *Why Civil Resistance Works*. Most activists and movement scholars think that the empirical evidence in that book says that

61

nonviolence is more effective for social movements than violence. It doesn't.

There are many conceptual slippages between researchers
and practitioners—academics and activists often use words differently—and the operational meanings of violence and nonviolence are a prime example. While activists today often debate
the use of violence in terms of unarmed actions like rioting, sabotage, and vandalism, much of the academic literature ostensibly addressing the same debate operationalizes violence as
warfare. As we will see, the most prominent studies that claim
to address the violence/nonviolence debate omit protester violence altogether, and therefore tell us very little about the types
of actions that are most relevant to movements today. Very
few studies investigate the impact of the types of violence that
are most common in twenty-first century social struggle from
below—unarmed collective actions like property destruction,
sabotage, arson, and physical altercations with police or political
opponents—not in contrast to but *within* the context of the types
of movements that scholars call nonviolent. This may be beginning to change in recent years, but there is much ground to cover,
and many misconceptions to undo. As it stands, opinions, often
strong opinions, related to one of the most significant debates
for social movements are largely based on assumption and con-
jecture, though typically framed as fact.

In this chapter, I dig into the research that rocketed civil
resistance studies to the influential field it is today: Erica
Chenoweth's Nonviolent and Violent Conflicts and Outcomes
dataset (NAVCO). When we examine the dataset up close, we
see it is poorly constructed to answer the questions most relevant
to movements today; it tells us very little about which strategies
or tactics are most effective for social transformation, and in fact,
the dataset itself is of questionable veracity.[1] Despite its renown,
NAVCO data hides behind a curtain of incomprehensibility. For
better or worse, datasets and statistical research methods carry
a great deal of weight in our society, and their apparent com-
plexity can discourage readers from exploring beyond the presented findings. When we are told that a university study proves

something with statistics, many people are prone to accept it—especially if it tells us something we want to believe. In this case, examining the codebook, appendix, and dataset itself line by line reveals a host of inconsistencies and problems, with serious consequences for our understandings of movement strategy.

**

It is no exaggeration to say that the most significant work in nonviolence studies since Gene Sharp is Erica Chenoweth and Maria Stephan's 2011 book, *Why Civil Resistance Works: The Strategic Logic of Nonviolence Conflict*. Whether or not you have heard of the dataset behind the book, if you are involved with social justice or follow protest movements, you have probably encountered NAVCO. Every time you see an article about how nonviolence is more effective, or about how mass participation in protests leads to change, chances are the author backs it up with Chenoweth's NAVCO data. The dataset and analyses drawn from it have become major bulwarks in holding the line against the suggestion that anything other than strict nonviolent action might play a part in the struggle for a more equitable world. Whenever riots come up, someone will point to an article based on NAVCO and reply: *but violence doesn't work—civil resistance works*.

Why Civil Resistance Works is based on research derived from the NAVCO 1.1 dataset, which catalogues 323 maximalist intrastate conflicts between 1900 and 2006, breaking them down into two categories: 217 "violent" (i.e., armed) campaigns and 106 "nonviolent" (i.e., unarmed) campaigns. By "maximalist" they mean campaigns that explicitly and immediately want to overthrow the government either by toppling a regime, ousting a foreign occupation, or seceding from a state. There is data on geography, economy, political system, and so forth, and holding these all constant, each campaign is assessed for its success or failure. Analyzing the data, Chenoweth and Stephan find that nonviolent campaigns are better at mobilizing large numbers of people and are thus almost twice as likely as violent campaigns to overthrow a government. This finding has been widely promoted as validating the superior efficacy of nonviolent tactics in resistance struggle.

However, NAVCO does not compare violent tactics to nonviolent tactics, it compares armed struggle to civilian struggle. Most importantly, *there is no measure in the data for riots or any type of unarmed violence at all.*

NAVCO was originally introduced in 2008 and then upgraded to NAVCO 1.1 for publication in *Why Civil Resistance Works*. At this writing, the dataset has been updated twice more, most recently in 2020. The latest iteration, NAVCO 1.3, extends the data through 2019 and counts 622 total campaigns, of which 320 are coded as nonviolent. When we add data on riots into NAVCO 1.3, we find that violent protests are commonplace in the types of struggles that are categorized as nonviolent.

Behind the Statistics Curtain

Before we add riots to the data, let's examine NAVCO's data construction. The dataset contains information on maximalist political campaigns from around the world that took place between 1900 and 2019 (in its initial version, between 1900 and 2006). The unit of analysis is the campaign, and each campaign is designated one data point based on its "peak" year, assigned based on the year of highest campaign participation, or where that cannot be determined, based on the year prior to campaign outcome.[2] A major finding in *Why Civil Resistance Works*, and one of the major points NAVCO data is commonly cited for, is the importance of mass mobilizations in achieving movement victories. However, the data is specifically designed so that the findings work around instances where data on mobilization numbers are absent, as data on crowd size from uprisings that took place generations ago can be unreliable or non-existent. And, while the dataset catalogues the beginning and ending dates of campaigns, which sometimes span many years, it ultimately measures a single year for success, though where that year falls in a specific campaign's trajectory is different depending on the case. NAVCO relies heavily on shaky numbers for movement participation and bases its findings, as said above, on a single "peak" year that the authors designate either based on their assessment of maximal participation or based on the year prior to campaign outcome.

Let us examine a specific campaign's data by way of example: the uprising that ousted Slobodan Milosevic in Serbia in 2000, a movement that has been influential among strategic nonviolence circles, specifically the *Otpor!* (Resistance!) student movement. In NAVCO, the campaign is named "anti-Milosevic" and its target is the Milosevic regime. Beginning and end years are 1996 and 2000. There are binary variables for "success," "limited success," and "failure," and each campaign gets a "1" for one of those and a "0" for the other two. The data catalogues limited success but the final analysis only looks at success vs. failure. In this case, under the variable for "success" the campaign gets a "1"; for "limited" and for "failure," it gets a "0." There are binary variables for "violent" and "nonviolent," for which this campaign gets a "1" for "nonviolent," and a "0" for "violent." Next come the type of maximalist struggle a campaign is assessed as having based on its target. This campaign gets a "1" for "regime change," and a "0" each for "independence from a foreign occupier," "secession," and "other." In the original NAVCO 1.1 dataset, each campaign was also assessed based on additional variables for region, polity score, the presence of a "radical flank" (contemporaneous armed struggle), the presence of regime crackdown, defections, and for an estimate of peak participation numbers. The researchers run logistic regressions on this data to get their central finding that nonviolent campaigns had higher success rates, as well as other findings regarding the superiority of nonviolent campaigns in causing repression to backfire, regime defections, and so forth.

As previously stated, in order to be included in NAVCO, a campaign is supposed to have "maximalist" political goals, meaning the overthrow of a regime, the ouster of a foreign occupation, or secession from a state. Based on this criterion, NAVCO excludes reformist political movements, cultural movements, or movements without overtly stated goals—although as we will see, the actual cases in the data are inconsistent in this regard.[3] To be considered maximalist, a campaign must make its goals of over-throwing the government explicit. But, of course, not all movements from below have explicitly revolutionary politics. Off the bat, NAVCO data tells us nothing about movements that do not directly seek to overthrow the government. That means this research tells us nothing about movements to defund the police or to achieve national healthcare, divestment campaigns, immigration reform campaigns, campaigns to free political prisoners, labor struggles, outing and holding accountable abusers and sexual predators, international solidarity movements, cultural empowerment movements, mutual aid networks, electoral campaigns, campaigns that target private corporations, and so forth.

In reality, many movements are not either reformist or revolutionary, but rather are ambiguous as to the nature of their claims *vis-à-vis* the state. As such, many scholarly approaches to revolution also include in their definitions the restructuring of political institutions, rapid cultural shifts, and other transformations in social processes and popular consciousness. And, of course, many social movements explicitly advance non-revolutionary claims while incubating revolutionary aspirations. Such elements are not considered in NAVCO. The dataset relates to a particular subset of social movements: those making explicit claims to state control. However, findings derived from this study, most famously that nonviolent tactics are more effective than violent tactics and that no movement in which 3.5 percent of a national population actively participated failed to overthrow the government, have been widely interpreted and publicized by activists as being applicable to social movements of all kinds. From nonviolence training programs to popular publications, these data have been touted as a key to helping us understand the dynamics of protest movements. If this were the only problem with the data, it would be significant, but there is an argument to be made for some reasonable crossover in the findings to non-maximalist movements—though even then, that argument should be made openly, not assumed or buried. However, this is far from the dataset's only problem.

Most importantly for our purposes, the NAVCO dataset

does not compare violent struggle to nonviolent struggle, at least not in the way activists typically discuss these terms on the ground. Rather, it compares civil war to civilian resistance. The "violent" category in NAVCO is derived from existing data on intrastate conflict, primarily the Correlates of War dataset, which catalogues wars between two armed parties suffering at least one thousand battle-related casualties.[4] In other words, "violent" in NAVCO means literal warfare. However, when it comes to the "nonviolent" category, NAVCO contains no variables for the presence of riots or any type of violence that falls short of war. In this data, riots simply vanish, as do other forms of non-nonviolent but also non-armed actions such as vandalism, sabotage, and fistfighting with political opponents. Unfortunately, this has not stopped the authors and others from using findings related to armed struggle to argue that riots are detrimental to movements.

Chenoweth used NAVCO data to argue that black bloc tactics employed during the #DisruptJ20 protests at Donald Trump's 2017 inauguration would hinder resistance to the Trump regime. This argument was picked up by many others, for example social theorist Amitai Etzioni, who used Chenoweth and Stephan's research in precisely the same way to argue that the black bloc and other non-nonviolent antifascist actions were destructive to the movement.[5] The example of DisruptJ20 is especially insightful since some nonviolence proponents claim not to consider property damage violence. But apart from the much-heralded Richard Spencer punch, the black bloc that day attacked property, not people. It was the "burned limousine and vandalized storefronts" that drew Chenoweth's criticism on the basis of their non-nonviolence.[6] Not only does NAVCO tell us nothing whatsoever about burning limousines, vandalizing storefronts, or punching Nazis, but these sorts of physically confrontational actions are common within the types of movements categorized as "nonviolent" in NAVCO data.

Chenoweth and Stephan justify omitting riots from the data primarily because of their unit of analysis: "Campaigns have discernable leadership and often have names, distinguishing them from random riots or spontaneous mass acts."[7] However, many movements today do not have discernable leadership (or at least it depends on who is doing the discerning), and movements are frequently named from the outside or after the fact. Furthermore, riots are not random; their outbreak is typically in direct response to police violence, public outrage at political leadership, or acute deprivation. Chenoweth and Stephan are content to dismiss violent actions within civil resistance movements because: "Often those who employ violence in mass movements are members of fringe groups who are acting independently, or in defiance of, the central leadership; or they are *agents provocateurs* used by the adversary to provoke the unarmed resistance to adopt violence."[8] However, the idea that researchers from the outside should decide who the legitimate leaders of a movement are, who is "fringe," and who is really an agent of the state is fraught, to say the least, but regardless, none of these factors justify erasing salient collective actions from analyses of resistance campaigns. While some argue that riots should be analytically distinguished from social movements, the categories are not mutually exclusive, and the forms of struggle at least interact as practices of resistance.[9] Especially when it comes to the contemporary violence-vs-nonviolence debate, riots and property destruction in protests are highly relevant forms of political action.

To sum up, even if the data in NAVCO was unassailable, it still would tell us little of value about most movements today, and would tell us nothing at all about strict nonviolence. It would simply indicate that modern unarmed movements have been more likely than armed movements to overthrow a government. It would not tell us anything about the effects of nonviolent discipline versus unarmed violence like rioting, just as it would not tell us anything about movements that do not seek the overthrow of the government or anything about the social or cultural transformations movements affect.

On top of these limitations, NAVCO data is of questionable integrity and contains a number of what appear to be significant coding errors. The dataset claims to only count "maximalist" campaigns, but in fact counts more than a few "successful" campaigns that should not qualify on this basis, while at the same time undercounting failed nonviolent movements.[10] Most troubling of all, NAVCO includes some "successful" nonviolent revolutions that have no supporting evidence.

The dataset codes successful instances of maximalist nonviolent campaigns—again, meaning a nonviolent uprising that overthrows a regime—in Argentina in 1987, Guyana in 1992, Ghana in 2000, Croatia in 2000, and Madagascar in 2002. The NAVCO Appendix includes a single source for each of these, in four cases an academic journal article and in one case a newspaper obituary for the former president of Guyana. None of these references discusses a maximalist nonviolent campaign. Two of them *do not mention protests at all*. A third specifically notes the "lack of large anti-government protests," another mentions demonstrations in passing, and the other discusses protests alongside riots and bloody armed conflict. While it is possible Chenoweth and Stephan consulted additional sources that they simply fail to record in the appendix, considering the prominence of this dataset and the sweeping claims about strategic efficacy it is used to advance, it is worth examining the sources that are listed. I will briefly discuss each of these examples in turn.[11]

"Argentinean protests against attempted coup, 1987"[12]

In this entry, the NAVCO Appendix describes an attempted *coup d'état* by military officers, after which the government, "aided by popular protests against another military dictatorship, compromised with the revolting officers, preventing major bloodshed from occurring." Even on its face, preventing major bloodshed should not necessarily qualify as a maximalist political goal by the NAVCO dataset's own standards, which again are campaigns to overthrow a regime, oust a foreign occupation, or secede from a state. The single source the appendix cites is a 1996 article in *Latin American Perspectives*, which discusses and compares extra-legal military action in Argentina and Venezuela. That article clearly states that the officers in Argentina "did not... attempt to take over the government" but rather were demanding "an end to the government's perceived campaign against the armed forces, and most specifically, an end to the trials and removal of the army chief of staff."[13] The article makes a single, passing reference to a civilian demonstration in support of the democratic government, but says nothing about a civil resistance–fueled compromise that prevented bloodshed, and in fact states that the officers were ultimately successful in achieving their desired concessions. None of this indicates that there was a successful maximalist nonviolent campaign.

"Guyanese revolt against Burnham/Hoyte autocratic regime, 1990–1992"[14]

In this entry, the NAVCO Appendix describes "a series of protests in the early 1990s" against the government of Desmond Hoyte, the outcome of which was that the "Guyanese revolt overthrew the autocratic regime." The lone source is Hoyte's 2002 obituary in *The New York Times,* which does not mention any protests but only describes Hoyte as "bowing to pressure" to introduce press freedoms and electoral reforms before he was defeated in 1992 elections.[15]

"Ghanaian protest against Rawlings government, 2000"[16]

In this case, the appendix points to the 2000 presidential election in Ghana, telling us that, "aided by a wave of protest against Rawlings, the opposition candidate officially won the presidency." Aiding a legal, scheduled electoral process should not qualify as maximalist political struggle—or there should be many more cases in NAVCO—but either way, the reference provided does not describe a wave of protests. The single source is an article in *The Journal of Modern African Studies* that describes the 2000 elections in terms of voter registration, turnout, oversight, and political process. It makes no mention of protests or demonstrations. The article does say that the 2000 elections were mostly smooth, with the "tragic exception being post-election violence in Bawku in the Upper East Region."[17]

"Croatian protests against semi-presidential system,
1999–2000"[18]

Here, "pro-democracy protests" are described as helping to elect a left-leaning government—again, not maximalist criteria—but the single source listed is an article about international criminal tribunals. The government transition is described in the source article simply as a defeat of the nationalist party in parliamentary elections by a center-left coalition. The only demonstrations mentioned in the article are by rightwing nationalists protesting against arrest warrants that had been issued for military generals accused of war crimes. Despite describing the government's fear of mass unrest, the article specifically notes the "lack of large anti-government protests" following the decision to arrest former officers and to cooperate with the International Criminal Tribunal for the Former Yugoslavia.[19]

"Madagascan pro-democracy movement against
Radsiraka [sic] regime, 2002–2003"[20]

This entry relates to an opposition candidate, Marc Ravalomanana, defeating incumbent Didier Ratsiraka in an election "aided by wide-scale protests." The source is a 2003 article in *African Affairs*, which describes two political opponents commanding the loyalty of different demographics as well as different military and paramilitary factions, both vying for control of the country, where "the threat of ethnic war was brandished by both sides."[21] The article does mention demonstrations and a general strike along with a "half-hearted attempt at repression by the security forces." It also mentions how a mob "protesting against shortages, sacked the houses of prominent Ratsiraka supporters."[22] Still, civilian demonstrations are barely a side note in the article, which more prominently discusses the importance of armed roadblocks and several "bloody clashes" between the two factions that threatened to plunge the country into civil war.[23] The article ultimately ascribes Ravalomanana's victory to his political maneuvering, pragmatic disposition, the support of the business class, and the actions of the army.

***

The problems with the cases above differ from one another. In Guyana, for example, there was a great deal of political turmoil leading up to the 1992 election, including opposition coalition talks and breakdowns, protests, riots, and more, many of these events geopolitically and racially charged. None of this is mentioned in the newspaper obituary cited in the dataset appendix, which gives the appearance of a research reference but merely obscures the complex situation that is being coded as a successful maximalist nonviolent campaign. In the cases of Argentina and Croatia, the reference for each appears to directly contradict the idea that maximalist nonviolent movements drove those political events. In Madagascar, the reference describes a tense election fraught with possibilities for ethnic violence, which was ultimately decided by political maneuvering and military loyalty. In the case of Ghana, the reference article simply discusses an electoral process and makes no mention of civil resistance. Incidentally, a recent longitudinal review of protests in Ghana, which discusses mobilizations from late-nineteenth century to the 2010s, includes nothing about anti-Rawlings protests in 2000.[24]

Highlighting the above examples is not to say that there were not nonviolent revolutions in these countries during those years—I was in none of those places at those times and history has certainly been good at erasing the role of movements in political and social change—it is simply to say that the sources listed in NAVCO do not reference any maximalist nonviolent campaigns. And these are only the most egregious of a host of discrepancies and question marks with NAVCO cases, categorization, and sources. Nevertheless, this dataset remains the most distinguished civil resistance research to date and its conclusions are widely celebrated. Chenoweth and Stephan's book won numerous prestigious accolades and is continues to serve as the bedrock for the empirical claim that nonviolence is more effective than violence in activist communities, scholarly discussions, and the broader public.[25]

Due to the questionable nature of the data, I am wary of

repurposing NAVCO to seek reliable findings as to what kinds of actions generate movement success, but I do think it is worth using the dataset to prove a point about the myth of the nonviolent revolution. I therefore took the "nonviolent" cases from NAVCO 1.3 as a starting point and added data on riots in order to show just how common protester violence is in civilian uprisings.

Putting the Violent in "Nonviolent" Struggle

While it is difficult to quantitatively measure low-level violent acts within protests, some data on major riots are captured in one of the most prominent global datasets on contentious political action. Arthur S. Banks's Cross-National Time Series Archive (CNTS) dataset contains a variable for riots, and spans the years between 1815 and 2020, covering the entirety of NAVCO 1.3. In CNTS, a riot is defined as: "Any violent demonstration or clash of more than 100 citizens involving the use of physical force," and primarily derives its data from analysis of articles published in *The New York Times*.[26] I add this data on riots to the "nonviolent" campaigns in NAVCO 1.3 to assess the presence or absence of riots. The simple question this method is designed to answer is: did at least one major riot occur in each nonviolent campaign?

Out of the 285 comparable "nonviolent" cases in NAVCO 1.3, a full 233 were associated with at least one riot (see Table 2).[27] In other words, even accepting the questionable cases in NAVCO, such as the five described above, *riots occurred alongside 82 percent of maximalist civil resistance movements*. Furthermore, riots occurred in 80 percent of successful cases. This is a slightly lower ratio than cases that were coded in NAVCO as unsuccessful, of which 84 percent were associated with at least one riot, but still four out of five successful nonviolent campaigns in NAVCO were associated with at least one riot. The civil resistance that NAVCO juxtaposes to armed struggle is in fact not nonviolent in a strict sense, but more often than not involves rioting, if not as an integral part of campaigns then as a catalyst or coexisting alongside nonviolent demonstrations.

Table 2. Riots in NAVCO 1.3

Civil resistance campaigns (NAVCO 1.1)	Riot	No riot	Total
Successful	106 (79.7%) (45.5%)	27 (20.3%) (51.9%)	133 (100%) (46.7%)
Unsuccessful	127 (83.6%) (54.5%)	25 (16.4%) (48.1%)	152 (100%) (53.3%)
Total	233 (81.8%) (100%)	52 (18.2%) (100%)	285 (100%) (100%)

Of the fifty-two comparable cases in NAVCO without a riot in CNTS data, 52 percent were coded as successful, compared with cases that included at least one riot, of which 48 percent were coded as successful. On its face, this might appear to add weight to the assertion that strictly nonviolent movements have better success rates, however, five of those successful cases with no data on riots are the cases mentioned above that do not appear to have involved maximalist civilian campaigns. If these were to be omitted, the percentage of successful cases without a riot would fall to 47 percent, below that of campaigns that involved riots. And these are not the only questionable cases. In fact, for nine of the twenty-seven successful campaigns with zero associated riots in the data, CNTS also records zero nonviolent demonstrations. Furthermore, the dataset I am using for riots and protest events is a blunt instrument. More focused research of unarmed violence within civil resistance has found these campaigns to be more effective than those without unarmed violence.[28]

Even using CNTS data on its face, only 18 percent of "nonviolent" cases in NAVCO 1.3 had no riots recorded in the data leading up to or during the campaign. Qualitative sources point to evidence of riots or riotous actions in many more instances than the data represents. The CNTS dataset is missing information for several key years of social struggle: for example in anti-colonial uprisings against European occupation, many of which involved both riotous and nonviolent demonstrations. And for the countries that do not have missing years of data, there are likely missed instances of riots. The dataset draws its riot data from an English-language news source, a limited data collection method that likely involves under-reporting errors and selection bias.[29] *The New York Times* can and does fail to report on riots that take place. For example, the successful "Tulip Revolution" in Kyrgyzstan in 2005 is one of the successful nonviolent cases in NAVCO that is not associated with riots in CNTS data, but other news sources reported widespread rioting.[30] Even some nonviolence scholars admit this uprising involved a great deal of violence on the part of demonstrators; an ICNC monograph on nonviolent discipline in three of the "Color Revolutions" describes in Kyrgyzstan street battles between protesters and police that involved multiple deaths, the destruction of at least one police station, and the smashing and looting of government buildings.[31]

Importantly, while there are clearly under-reporting errors in CNTS, it is very unlikely that there are *over-reporting* errors. Media can easily miss or fail to report on riots that occur, but *The New York Times* is unlikely to report major riots that did not occur. So while the actual number of riotous events is likely to be significantly higher than is recorded in the data, it will almost certainly not be lower. Furthermore, the data only includes major riots (e.g., those involving more than one hundred participants and being destructive enough to merit the attention in international media as riots), while smaller riotous actions within otherwise nonviolent protests, equipment sabotage, and targeted vandalism remain unaccounted for. If we had data on those types of extremely low-level "violence"—actions that are absolutely treated as violence when they take place in protests today—it is highly likely that the number of purely nonviolent uprisings would fall to near zero.

There are, of course, campaigns that commit themselves to nonviolent action and maintain nonviolent discipline that contribute to overthrowing governments. But these are still impacted by contemporaneous riots taking place against the same government. A campaign cannot be reasonably or accurately analyzed in isolation from coexisting forms of resistance in the same country against the same authorities. It is for this very reason that NAVCO 1.1 contains a variable for the (armed) violent flank effect—the effect a contemporaneous armed challenge has on an unarmed mass campaign. Scholars considering the violent flank effect (sometimes called the radical flank effect) in civil resistance have maintained the focus on violence-as-armed-struggle, which deepens the erasure of unarmed violence by making it seem as though violent actions within nonviolent movements have been accounted for when they have not.[32]

There is broad acknowledgment among civil resistance scholars that violent campaigns coexist with nonviolent ones. Prominent nonviolence proponents have long admitted that there is "virtually no case" of a purely nonviolent struggle.[33] Civil resistance scholar Jonathan Pinckney uses a diagram (see Figure 1) to visually demonstrate the overlap between civil resistance campaigns and armed struggle.[34] However, as Figure 1 shows, this acknowledgment is still filtered through a model that equates violence to armed struggle. The line between "civil resistance" and "violent resistance" is drawn between "mixed struggles" of armed and unarmed struggle and "civil resistance with an armed wing," meaning movements that are driven by civilian mobilizations in a context where there is also an armed struggle being waged in the same country. However, literature on nonviolent struggle as it stands only applies its analysis to actions that conform to strict nonviolence, so while civil resistance campaigns might include the spectrum in Figure 1, Figure 2 represents the types of actions that are considered legitimate for civil resistance campaigns: strict adherence to nonviolent discipline. When unarmed violence is considered, this "purely" nonviolent struggle historically accounts for—at very most—18 percent of civil resistance movements, and likely much closer to zero. In other words, real-world civil resistance struggle typically involves some mix of violent with nonviolent actions—not nonviolent civil resistance alongside armed violent flanks, but unarmed collective violence as part of civil uprisings (see Figure 3).

Figure 1. Violent resistance versus civil resistance in theory

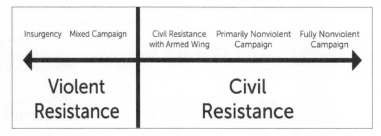

Figure 2. Violent resistance versus civil resistance-as-nonviolence

Figure 3. Martial resistance versus civil resistance

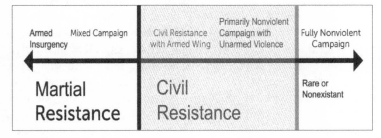

Chenoweth and Stephan theoretically acknowledge as much, and qualify their categorical comparison as being between

"primarily" nonviolent and "primarily" violent campaigns.[35] However, they go on to use "nonviolent" synonymously with "primarily nonviolent," which negates the potential salience of the violent actions that oblige the qualification. Furthermore, in the literature, the acknowledgment of the non-purity of nonviolence tends to be processed through a violence/nonviolence model that blurs the lines between different types of "violent" actions, and tends to focus on armed struggle. By continuing to focus on warfare or terrorism as instances of violence in the research, civil resistance scholars like Chenoweth and Stephan have evaded honest engagement with unarmed violent actions that are not only commonplace in civil resistance movements but are precisely the types of actions being debated by activists and organizers today. The problem is not just that violent actions are ignored, it is that, like Sharp before them, they quietly roll the real-world effects of violent actions into their argument for the strategic logic of nonviolence, thus presenting a false picture of resistance.

When unarmed violence is added into the equation, interpretations of NAVCO data change dramatically. For example, one of Chenoweth and Stephan's major findings is that nonviolent campaigns lead to democratic outcomes more reliably than violent campaigns. The effects of civil resistance movements on political liberalization appear to be especially emphasized by nonviolence advocates in the security and foreign policy realms. However, subsequent research that examines the effects of contentious protests shows that riots have democratizing effects.

Sociologists Mohammad Ali Kadivar and Neil Ketchley use event-level data to examine the impact of unarmed collective actions that inflicted physical damage in 103 nondemocracies over the course of more than a decade, as well as qualitative analysis of eighty democratic transitions, and found that riots were positively associated with political democratization.[36] It is precisely this type of effect that is concealed by incorporating riots' effects into civil resistance, calling it primarily nonviolent, and evaluating it as wholly nonviolent in relation to the violence of warfare. It should also pose questions about the persistence of the strategic nonviolent narrative: if it is clear that riots are common in unarmed movements, and if the data shows that they have positive effects on the outcomes that theorists claim to care about, why do they continue to be left out—in fact not only be left out, but frequently made into counterexamples—of the civil resistance story?

There is something else I noticed when I added data on riots into NAVCO: In the cases that had riots, the vast majority of those riots occurred at the beginning of a campaign. In 74 percent of all civil resistance campaigns, riots are recorded in the year leading up to a campaign or the first year of a campaign. Of the campaigns associated with riots, 90 percent see a riot at the beginning of the campaign—92 percent of the time for successful campaigns. There are certainly instances where less-violent movements culminated in a riot that collapsed the government, for example when Serbian protesters used a bulldozer to smash through police lines and burned government buildings during climactic protests of the anti-Milosevic movement in 2000.[37] In most cases, however, riots seem to explode at the onset of civil resistance uprisings. In other words, riots appear to catalyze civil resistance movements.

This is especially important because it contradicts the demobilizing effect nonviolence theories say violent actions have on civil resistance movements. According to Chenoweth and Stephan, the central mechanism of movement success is its ability to mobilize large numbers of people on a consistent basis. This is, of course, an assertion most movement people can agree on—our opponents' ultimate weapons are capital and police violence; ours are masses of people. According to nonviolence theorists, any violence on the part of protesters supposedly undermines a campaign's ability to get masses of people in the streets, leading to fewer and smaller acts of protest, and thereby hurting movements' chances for success. The following chapter explores this proposition by examining occurrences of riots and nonviolent demonstrations within the same country over time.

4.

Molotov Cocktails and Mass Marches

*"Rock throwing ... is a first step across an invisible line between
obedience and resistance."*

—STAN GOFF, FORMER U.S. ARMY SPECIAL OPERATIONS,
AFTER FACING RESISTANCE WHILE OCCUPYING HAITI

The primary factor that Chenoweth and Stephan point to in order
to explain their findings is that movements that mobilize more
people more consistently tend to win, and they argue that nonviolence is associated with higher levels of mobilization, making
it more effective. But, as we have seen, their methods do not test
the relationship between strict nonviolence and increased mobilization, nor the relationship between violence and demobili-
zation. Sharp's framing argument is that nonviolent action is "a
prerequisite to advantageous power changes" and that, "as a consequence, nonviolent discipline can only be compromised at the
severe risk of contributing to defeat."[1] Sharp and other nonviolence scholars point to a variety of mechanisms that are supposed
to make violent tactics harmful to movements, for example
that violence invites repression, negates the backfiring effect of
repression, alienates public support, presents a barrier to participation, and makes it less likely for regime officials to defect. As I
discussed in chapter two, all of these arguments relate to a single,
central claim that violent tactics demobilize support for and limit
participation in nonviolent actions.

In this chapter, I test the claim that unarmed violent
action demobilizes nonviolent protests using data on riots and

nonviolent demonstrations from ten countries representing different geographic regions, cultures, governance, economies, and histories of resistance. Examining the data on riots and nonviolent demonstrations in these countries over seventy-five years, in all cases we find that riots are broadly associated with increased nonviolent mobilizations. I then discuss what we can learn by putting this finding in conversation with the tools that nonviolence scholars have developed to analyze movements, and flesh all this out using the case study of the 2011 uprising in Egypt.

Data and Methods

In order to test the relationship between riots and nonviolent mobilizations, I use annual data from CNTS, the same dataset I used in the previous chapter to add riots to NAVCO. This widely used dataset contains variables for both riots and for nonviolent demonstrations, with data collection based primarily on coverage in *The New York Times*. The riot variable is defined as: "Any violent demonstration or clash of more than 100 citizens involving the use of physical force."[2] The nonviolent demonstrations variable is defined as: "Any peaceful public gathering of at least 100 people for the primary purpose of displaying or voicing their opposition to government policies or authority," and the data exclude "demonstrations of a distinctly anti-foreign nature."[3] I present data analysis on ten countries: the United States, South Africa, Philippines, Mexico, Iran, Britain, France, Ethiopia, China, and Brazil. For each of the ten countries, I use annual CNTS data between 1946 and 2020, with a total of seventy-five observations each.

The CNTS dataset has data going back well over a century, but for all countries there is a gap in data around World War II, so the longest timespan without gaps in data is 1946–2020. I have chosen countries that have data on riots and nonviolent demonstrations for every year in this time period, whereas many countries have more recent gaps in data, for example post-colonial countries that won their independence more recently than

WWII or those such as the former Soviet Union that fractured since then. Countries with missing data are difficult to compare especially considering that gaps are often related to political crises. I further select a subset of these countries based on their geographical distribution and other qualitative factors that lead me to believe the data will tell us something useful. Using an annual measure over seventy-five years gives a wide-angle view of the overall relationship between riots and nonviolent mobilizations in these countries, showing how movements have escalated and demobilized over time.

For each county's data, I use three models. Model 1 is an ordinary least squares (OLS) regression to test the relationship between riots and nonviolent demonstrations within each year. This is especially significant considering the annual scale of the data, since uprisings can rise and fall in the span of a year. The dependent variable is nonviolent demonstrations and the main explanatory variable is riots. In other words, if there are more riots in a given year, we want to know if this is associated with more or less nonviolent demonstrations in that year. In the second model, I include lagged variables for riots and nonviolent demonstrations to test the impact of actions from the previous year on nonviolent mobilization in the current year. Regression analysis is a basic statistical technique used to test the degree to which one variable in an equation is impacted by another while holding other factors constant. It is essentially the main tool that Chenoweth and Stephan use in *Why Civil Resistance Works*, except they use a version that is designed for binary variables. Finally, in model 3, I test the same effect as model 2 using a first order autoregressive time-series model, which might offer slightly better accuracy. In all cases I include a measure for Gross Domestic Product (GDP) per capita as a control variable.[4]

Unlike Chenoweth and Stephan, I omit the outcome variable. I do this for several reasons. First, political outcomes are complex and unwieldy things, and thus fraught to squeeze into a single data point. An extra-legal change in formal government with no accompanying shift in systemic power, institutions, or culture should not necessarily designate a successful revolution.

And in some instances, today's revolution is tomorrow's counter-revolution. That should not necessarily change our analysis of the actions that led to an initial overthrow, but it might complicate the story of resistance if certain factors left a movement vulnerable to rollback. As a South African activist I spoke to, quoted in chapter six, put it: "Can you imagine if they had said, 'Okay, no apartheid from '94 to '95, then it will resume again'? That is not victory." Yet, in NAVCO, it would be coded that way. I wanted to avoid this confusion.

Second, using an outcome variable means strictly defining movement goals. Basing a study only on maximalist campaigns excludes most movements from consideration, even many that we might consider revolutionary. Most protest mobilizations are not explicitly maximalist, and often we see a mix of reformist and revolutionary claims either organizationally or in the aspirations of participants. For a study to apply to movement communities across issues, goals, and frames, it should measure level of overall mobilization, which is generally accepted as positive and necessary for movement power. Finally, as some of the cases I detailed in NAVCO demonstrate, it is at times unclear the degree to which a movement was the *cause* of a government collapse as opposed to a component in that collapse. We can avoid having to parse and quantify these factors by simply looking at levels of mobilization.

Results

In all three models, the riots variable is positively correlated with the nonviolent demonstration variable within the same year at the highest level of statistical significance. Results are reported in Table 3. The adjusted R-squared measure—the measure of how much variation in the nonviolent demonstrations variable is explained by riots and GDP variables—varies by country, but in many cases this simple regression displays a great deal of explanatory power. Model 2, which adds lagged variables for riots and nonviolent demonstrations, tends to increase the explanatory power. In all three models, riots and nonviolent demonstrations in the same year are positively correlated and statistically significant in every country.

Table 3. Riots and nonviolent demonstrations, 1946–2020

	BRA	CHN	ETH	FRA	GBR	IRN	MEX	PHL	RSA	USA
Model 1										
Riot	1.04***	0.28***	1.03***	0.96***	1.24***	0.77***	0.85***	1.26***	0.65***	1.05***
	(0.19)	(0.09)	(0.11)	(0.08)	(0.22)	(0.12)	(0.13)	(0.22)	(0.05)	(0.17)
GDP	0.45***	1.57***	0.19	0.09***	0.17***	0.29**	0.50***	1.12***	0.24	0.45***
	(0.11)	(0.22)	(0.70)	(0.03)	(0.05)	(0.12)	(0.09)	(0.31)	(0.16)	(0.08)
Constant	-0.93	0.79	-0.01	-0.91	-1.59	0.10	-0.93	-0.03	-0.12	-2.78
	(0.50)	(0.55)	(0.14)	(0.57)	(1.17)	(0.51)	(0.45)	(0.42)	(0.57)	(2.33)
N	75	75	75	75	75	75	75	75	75	74
Adj R2	0.48	0.66	0.69	0.71	0.43	0.37	0.54	0.37	0.68	0.47
Model 2										
Riot	0.75***	0.32***	1.13***	0.80***	0.84***	0.75***	0.74***	0.71***	0.60***	0.62***
	(0.20)	(0.10)	(0.11)	(0.11)	(0.15)	(0.13)	(0.15)	(0.19)	(0.07)	(0.18)
Nvd single lag	0.08	0.18	-0.30**	0.14	0.79***	0.03	0.31**	0.64***	0.07	0.48***
	(0.11)	(0.12)	(0.12)	(0.14)	(0.14)	(0.12)	(0.12)	(0.09)	(0.12)	(0.1)
Riot single lag	0.51**	-0.01	0.26*	0.14	-0.13	0.03	-0.26	-0.17	0.05	0.07
	(0.23)	(0.10)	(0.16)	(0.15)	(0.18)	(0.17)	(0.17)	(0.21)	(0.11)	(0.2)
GDP	0.39***	1.18***	0.09	0.08***	0.00	0.27**	0.47*	0.25	0.26***	
	(0.11)	(0.33)	(0.77)	(0.03)	(0.00)	(0.13)	(0.10)	(0.25)	(0.17)	(0.00)
Constant	-1.16	0.63	-0.10	-1.03	-1.20	0.08	-0.55	-0.09	-0.33	-2.3
	(0.50)	(0.57)	(0.14)	(0.59)	(0.81)	(0.54)	(0.47)	(0.33)	(0.61)	(2.07)
N	74	74	74	74	74	74	74	74	74	73
Adj R2	0.53	0.66	0.72	0.72	0.75	0.36	0.57	0.64	0.68	0.62
Model 3										
Riot	0.77***	0.32***	1.10***	0.83***	0.77***	0.75***	0.76***	0.65***	0.60***	0.65***
	(0.18)	(0.09)	(0.12)	(0.09)	(0.09)	(0.12)	(0.18)	(0.15)	(0.06)	(0.16)
Riot single lag	0.58***	0.03	-0.03	0.23***	0.25*	0.06	-0.12	0.12	0.09	0.31
	(0.16)	(0.08)	(0.10)	(0.08)	(0.14)	(0.08)	(0.21)	(0.26)	(0.09)	(0.22)
GDP	0.42***	1.46***	0.06	0.09***	0.21	0.28*	0.54***	1.28**	0.27	0.47***
	(0.12)	(0.19)	(0.67)	(0.03)	(0.20)	(0.16)	(0.16)	(0.55)	(0.19)	(0.11)
AR 1	0.19	0.16*	-0.29**	0.00	0.78***	0.02	0.34***	0.68***	0.06	0.48***
	(0.16)	(0.09)	(0.12)	(0.15)	(0.07)	(0.13)	(0.12)	(0.06)	(0.09)	(0.09)
Constant	-1.23	0.78	-0.07	-1.13	-0.60	0.09	-0.75	0.09	-0.33	-2.61
	(0.85)	(1.07)	(0.22)	0.83	(7.91)	(1.08)	(1.14)	(1.80)	(1.07)	(5.77)
N	74	74	74	74	74	74	74	74	74	73

Nvd = nonviolent demonstration
GDP expressed in thousands
*** Correlation is significant at the 0.01 level (2-tailed)

The lagged variables display varying results. In nine of the ten countries, the lagged nonviolent demonstration coefficient is positive, and in four of those cases it is statistically significant

(Britain, Mexico, Philippines, and the United States). That means that, in these cases, increased nonviolent demonstrations in one year are positively correlated with increased nonviolent demonstrations in the following year. In one case (Ethiopia), the coefficient is negative and statistically significant, meaning increases in nonviolent demonstrations in the previous year are associated with decreased nonviolent demonstrations in the current year. For lagged riots, six are positive and four are negative, with two of the positive coefficients (Brazil and Ethiopia)—but none of the negative lagged-riot coefficients—being statistically significant.

Model 3 tells a similar story as model 2, but now eight of the lagged riot coefficients are positive and three of those are statistically significant (Brazil, France, and Britain); two are negative and are not significant. The autoregressive term for nonviolent demonstrations in the previous year is positive for eight countries and significant in five of these (China, Britain, Mexico, Philippines, and the U.S.), negative for one, which is also significant (Ethiopia), and approximately zero for one (France). Once again, accounting for previous nonviolent demonstrations, previous riots, and GDP, riots and nonviolent demonstrations are positively correlated in every one of the ten countries at the highest statistical significance.

The clearest takeaway is that riots are associated with increased nonviolent demonstrations within the same year in every country. When interpreting these results, it is important to bear in mind the annual timeframe of the data. Much can happen within a year—some uprisings rise and fall within a matter of weeks, sometimes months, while others wax and wane for years. In each of these countries, within a given year, riots are associated with increased levels of nonviolent protest. Adding events from the previous year to the equation does not alter the correlation between more rioting and more nonviolent mobilizations.

Nonviolent demonstrations from the previous year tend to have a positive impact on nonviolent demonstrations in the current year, consistent with how civil resistance theories would expect movements to build power—more actions beget more actions. However, in one case, prior mobilization is correlated with fewer protests in a given year. Riots in the prior year are sometimes associated with increased nonviolent mobilizations and sometimes with decreased, although the positive effects are more sizeable and are more statistically significant. What do we make of this? Given the varying associations and generally small effects of protest events from a previous year on those in the current year, it is likely that much of the action in many moments of uprising takes place within the span of a year.

The relationship between these two variables is especially evident when viewed as a graph. Figures 4–13 show nonviolent demonstrations in the lighter grey, and riots in the darker grey line. The x-axis is years and the y-axis is number of events. As is abundantly clear, nonviolent demonstrations and riots tend to move together. Spikes in the two variables often occur in different proportions, but in nearly all cases they rise and fall contemporaneously. In other words, when we see sharp increases to one, we usually see an increase in the other. There are few instances in any country of a significant spike to one variable in isolation from a rise in the other. Most importantly for our purposes, there are very few examples of nonviolent uprisings without accompanying riots. On the contrary, the largest rises in nonviolent demonstrations in every country are also associated with rioting in those same years. Increases in mobilization of each type of collective action tend to occur together, indicating that riots and nonviolent demonstrations in uprisings are related to each other and/or to similar causes, exogenous influences, and collective action frames.

Put simply, moments of civilian uprising comprise both riots and nonviolent demonstrations. Shocks to riot and to nonviolent demonstration variables are very closely associated in most years. In some instances, the peak of a spike in the nonviolent demonstration variable follows the peak of a spike in the riot variable, while in other instances a peak in riots follows a peak of nonviolent demonstrations, but the largest shocks to both variables occur in the same annual time frame. Again, it is abundantly clear that moments of civilian uprising involve both riots and nonviolent demonstrations.

Figures 4–13. Riots and nonviolent demonstrations, 1946–2020

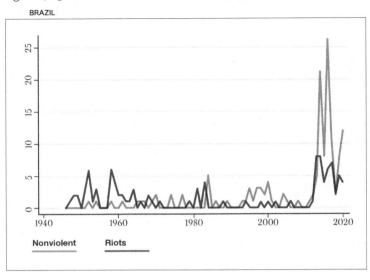

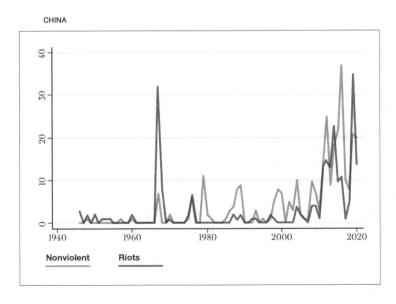

ETHIOPIA

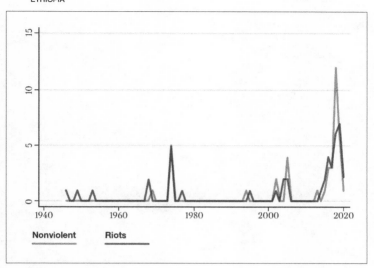

FRANCE

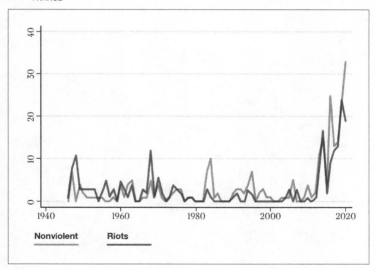

GREAT BRITAIN

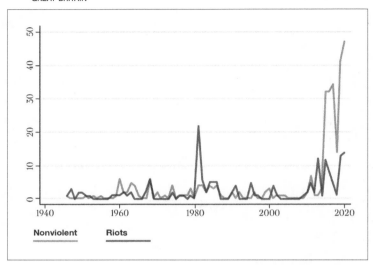

IRAN

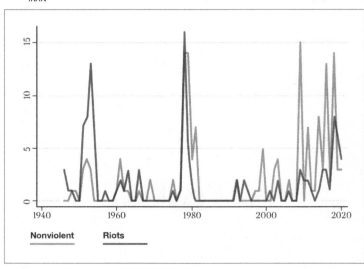

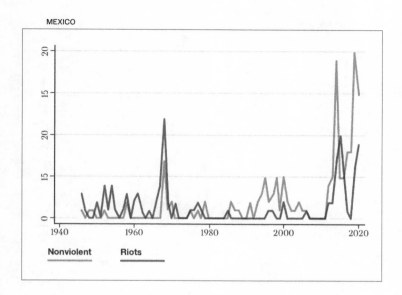

MEXICO

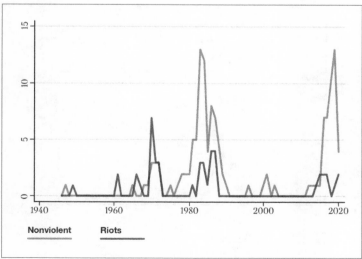

PHILIPPINES

SOUTH AFRICA

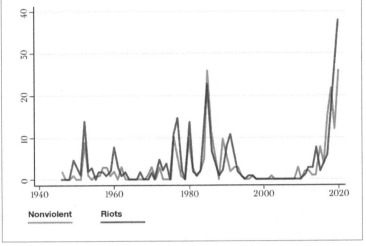

Nonviolent   Riots

UNITED STATES

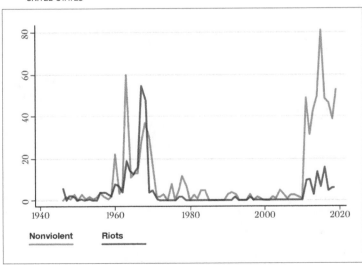

Nonviolent   Riots

While the data presented here strongly indicates a positive association between rioting and nonviolent demonstrations, my goal is not to argue the inverse of strategic nonviolence. These data do not suggest that rioting necessarily leads to increased mobilizations, nor that there is a mechanical relationship between violent protest and movement growth. But the positive association between the variables for riots and nonviolent demonstrations in these data is unmistakable. Nevertheless, it seems that some civil resistance scholars are committed to finding evidence to support the claim that violent actions hurt movements no matter what, and such people will find some traction with the data I present. For example, while riots and nonviolent demonstrations are positively associated in every country within the same year, there are countries in which riots from a previous year are associated with fewer demonstrations in the current year.

A study by researchers Luke Abbs and Kristian Gleditsch used nonviolent campaigns from NAVCO as a starting point and add CNTS data on riots to evaluate how rioting effects levels of nonviolent protest.[5] They initially find that riots are positively associated with nonviolent campaign onset, and that nonviolent protests increase following a riot. However, they end up arguing the reverse. Adding a measure for lagged nonviolent protest, Abbs and Gleditsch find that the effect of previous riots turns negative, meaning that we are less likely to see a nonviolent campaign launch where there were riots in a previous year. (Though, as shown, NAVCO might not be the most reliable source for nonviolent campaigns.) They then switch the dataset and category of analysis to examine correlation between riots and campaign termination in countries in Africa and Central America between 1990 and 2013, finding that riots are associated with the end of a campaign. Based on this finding they conclude that riots scare people away from participating in protests and demobilize movements.

What is striking about this argument is the authors understand that the end of a campaign on its own does not tell us much; campaigns can end because they failed to mobilize people, but they can also end when they've been successful in extracting concessions from the state or because of other changed conditions. Abbs and Gleditsch admit that "rioting is more common in successful campaigns (thirty-five percent of campaign months) than in unsuccessful campaigns (twenty-five percent of campaign months)."[6] Yet they still insist that riots are detrimental to movements.

Even if it was true that nonviolent protest begets more nonviolent protest, while rioting decreases civil mobilizations, the data here present us with a paradox: the relationship between riots and nonviolent demonstrations works in both directions. When we make riots the dependent variable in the regression, nonviolent protest is positively correlated with more riots in the same year at the highest level of statistical significance in all countries.[7] The coefficients are generally lower in this direction, but are all positive and significant. So if it is not the case that riots lead to increased protests, then it *is* the case that increased protests lead to more riots, which are then supposed to lead to decreased protests. At very least, there is a dynamic relationship between these types of resistance.

The GDP per capita variable is included in the models as a control, but interestingly, the coefficient is positive in all models for all countries and statistically significant in many, but it turns negative and significant in most cases when riots are the dependent variable. This means that increases in GDP per capita are associated with more nonviolent demonstrations but fewer riots. Based on the structure of the data visible in the graphs, this effect likely has to do with the comparative scale of one variable versus the other. Regardless, years with increased riots also see increases in nonviolent protest, and *vice versa*, indicating that violent and nonviolent protest are mutually constitutive of moments of uprising.

Overall, it is clear that the data do not support the claim that riots demobilize civil uprisings, nor that nonviolent demonstrations are more successful in growing their numbers when there are no riots. Let us look again at Figures 4–13: there are few examples in any of these countries of significant spikes in nonviolent demonstrations absent any rioting, and the largest escalations in nonviolent protests in every case are accompanied by riots. The dynamics of both rioting and nonviolent protests appear to be mutually constituent of civil uprisings.

Strict nonviolence is not a prerequisite to advantageous power changes for movements, as Sharp would have it, but instead what activists have called a "diversity of tactics" appears generative for uprisings.[8] In fact, approaching these types of mobilization—riots and nonviolent protest—as distinct variables is itself part of the problem, especially because there is likely a great deal of grey area in between. Again, to be clear, my findings here are not meant to prove that riots work *better* than nonviolent protest, but to show that rioting is common during civil uprisings, and that in many contexts major riots are associated with overall increased mobilization.

I do not intend to recreate here the problems of inaccessibility and opacity that I complain about in other quantitative studies. The findings I present have distinct limitations.[9] These are ten countries out of many. The data are annual and national in scope, and so capture only a wide view of movement uprisings in these countries. The supposition that spikes in protests within the same country tend to relate to the same cause or collective action frame are not part of the statistical models but rather rely on theory and observation. The data points are each sizeable demonstrations or riots, but between them no distinction is made for scale—a protest with one thousand people and one with one hundred thousand are both represented by a single point in this data. The data do not record protest or riot intensity, nor do they distinguish between more and less disruptive nonviolent actions.

The models also admittedly involve few variables. This is partially because I do not think they require more for the points I am making, and that in this case a simpler model tells the most important parts of this story. Because riots and nonviolent protests are both collective modes of expressing discontent, it is highly unlikely that a relationship between these variables in these disparate countries will be spurious, even with few exogenous factors. Still, adding more variables could conceivably tell a different story. Perhaps most problematically, the data records events as either riots or nonviolent demonstrations, which erases the nuances of protests in which some participants engage in property destruction, or those that begin as peaceful protests but escalate to more forceful actions in response to police repression or some other catalyst.

A brief note on data collection. The most recent iteration of the CNTS dataset extends data on protests and riots through 2020. For the USA analysis, however, I omitted the final year in the data. This is because of the magnitude of data corresponding to the racial justice uprising in the summer of 2020. Often called the George Floyd Uprising, named for the man who was murdered in broad daylight by former police officer Derek Chauvin in Minneapolis on May 25, 2020, this uprising in many ways picked up where previous Movement for Black Lives mobilizations had left off, in this case directly sparked by George Floyd's death and other highly publicized murders of unarmed Black people in the U.S. including Breonna Taylor, shot to death by police in her home in the middle of the night, and Ahmaud Aubrey, murdered by white vigilantes as he went for a run near his home. The uprising that followed was fierce and massive. CNTS data counts so many protests events in the year 2020 that they essentially wash out the rest of that country's data.

Figures 14–15. Riots and nonviolent demonstrations in the U.S., 1946–2019 and 2020

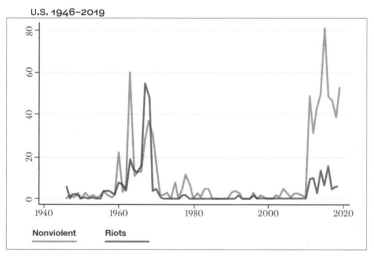

U.S. 1946–2019

U.S. 1946–2020

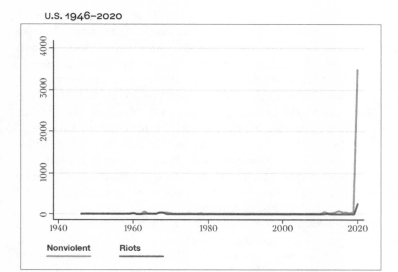

The George Floyd Uprising is widely considered the largest civil uprising in U.S. history, and this graph certainly highlights its size; the spike in protests in 2020 flatlines the rest of the graph. Note that the spike in riots, while smaller by degrees than the nonviolent protests in 2020, is still significantly larger than the largest spikes in either variable in the rest of the timeline. If the 2020 year is included in the analysis, the positive association between riots and nonviolent demonstrations increases by a factor of twelve. However, for the sake of accuracy I chose to omit this year in the models above. Despite the enormity of the George Floyd Uprising, the change in scale in the data likely has more to do with changes in news reporting and data collection than with protest events themselves. The uprising brought acute media attention that took pains to count every action in a way they previously had not. I have no doubt that the George Floyd Uprising was the largest in U.S. history, but I am skeptical it was *fifty-seven times* larger than the height of uprisings of the 1960s, as the CNTS numbers indicate.

This case should draw our attention to the construction of the data in all countries I examine—the data are only as good as the news reports CNTS draws from. Indeed, as protest movements in the 2010s became a global news story, we tend to see spikes in both nonviolent demonstrations and riots in most countries during this decade (though not of a difference in scale like the U.S.). This might well be due to real increases in protests and riots, but it might also be related to increased attention to these events. Once again, we should be cautious not to overestimate the accuracy of these analyses in terms of their specifics. This study solidly demonstrates that riots do not demobilize nonviolent demonstrations, and that riots are correlated with increased nonviolent demonstrations; it should absolutely not be taken to say that riots will predictably result in a certain number more nonviolent demonstrations.

The results presented in this chapter do not suggest that rioting is always a good idea, nor that rioting automatically leads to higher levels of mobilization. These statistical methods are basic and the data blunt. And in general, quantitative data analysis will only get us so far in understanding the vastly complex and dynamic events that fuel the contentious politics of social change from below. But these analyses are more than sufficient to demonstrate that violent protest and nonviolent protest tend to occur together, either intertwined or alongside one another during moments of uprising. That rioting often brings enhanced repression or changes the political landscape in a way that alters possibilities for movements should not be controversial. But nonviolence theorists have gone to lengths to argue that rioting and other types of unarmed violence have negative impacts on otherwise nonviolent movements. The data and analysis presented in this chapter contradict this assertion. Riots do not necessarily demobilize nonviolent demonstrations, but overall are associated with increased protests, especially during moments of uprising.

Rioting in Civil Resistance

Just because a dichotomy is false doesn't mean we can't learn things from it. Despite its problems, the study of nonviolent action has given us many useful concepts and tools for understanding the dynamics of movement power. Nonviolence researchers since Sharp have identified strategic factors that unarmed movements generate and contend with that have significant material impacts on movement success or failure. Main areas of emphasis have included the importance of mass participation, resilience in the face of repression through discipline and tactical diversity, the backfiring effect of repression, the ability to create leverage against regimes through disruptive collective action and strategic withdrawal of support, and social polarization as a result of direct action. While nonviolence is assumed to be crucial to all of these dynamics, it is in fact required for none of them. The perception that nonviolence is the fulcrum that moves the disruptive leverage that movements can exert on governments rests on the misconception that riots are alien to civilian uprisings. This misconception is coded directly into civil resistance research like NAVCO and reproduced in broad claims about the superior efficacy of nonviolent methods.

The field of strategic nonviolence has constructed a discourse around nonviolence that hides real-world violent actions by broadly referring to armed conflict as "violent" and unarmed conflict as "nonviolent." When researchers like Chenoweth and Stephan admit that violent resistance sometimes works, they use examples of armed struggle; when they return to the superior efficacy of nonviolent struggle, violent moments in those episodes disappear. As Foucault reminds us in his 1978 work *The History of Sexuality*, it is not just a matter of whether or not a topic is discussed, it is *how, when, and where* that topic is discussed and not discussed that shapes its discourse. It is not just that nonviolence scholars don't talk enough about unarmed violence, it is that the ways and places riots are mentioned or neglected function to erase them from the story of resistance.

Take Chenoweth and Stephan's data on "primarily nonviolent" campaigns for example. Chenoweth and Stephan claim to study primarily nonviolent campaigns, but they go on to describe those same campaigns as nonviolent. The qualification "primarily" is there in the first place so it can be omitted in the last. If "nonviolent" was used alone, the obvious deviations from strict nonviolence in those campaigns might stand out, but if the word "primarily" is inserted in the proper place to acknowledge the impurity of the nonviolence, then we can go back to analyzing those "nonviolent" campaigns without qualification. In other words, when riots are mentioned by civil resistance scholars, it is in such a way as to negate their consideration and allow the strategic nonviolence argument to proceed unchanged.

In the context of unarmed social movements, riots are not only common, but they can be accurately and effectively analyzed in the same strategic framework as nonviolent repertoires. In other words, it is not simply a matter of riots being "in between" nonviolent action and warfare on a two-dimensional spectrum of collective political violence. Violent protest actions are essential components in the collage of collective actions that compose and color civil resistance struggle. Riots, as civilian collective actions, fit into the civil resistance framework in every way except for their physical destructiveness. Contrary to the belief that violent actions undermine the logic of civil resistance, central concepts in civil resistance theory can be clarified and enhanced by making unarmed violence a legible part of movement repertoires.

Here I will focus on five civil resistance concepts, three that are articulated by nonviolence scholar Kurt Schock—*mobilization*, *resilience*, and *leverage*—and two additional concepts that could be assessed as part of these three categories but that involve their own dynamics—*the backfiring effect* and political *polarization*.[10]

Mobilization: One of Chenoweth and Stephan's foremost findings is the importance of mass participation for campaign wins. Though they acknowledge that the quality and diversity of participation is important, according to NAVCO research, numbers are the primary indicator of success.[11] Importantly, participation in a campaign is not the same as public opinion about a campaign. Chenoweth and Stephan claim to measure "active and observable engagement of individuals in collective action," not public opinion polls.[12] This is an important distinction, which I will come back to in a moment when we talk about polarization.

First, Chenoweth and Stephan's arguments for why violence

reduces active participation, such as the need for strenuous physical training, the hardships of commitment to violent struggle, and moral barriers to using violence, relate mainly to armed insurgencies, not protester violence.[13] Second, participation is not a monolithic feature of movements. There are multiple forms of participation and various, fluctuating structural and systemic constraints and opportunities that impact participation at different levels of engagement. In other words, people take part in social movements in different ways. If we are only focused on how many people are in the streets, we would miss a lot of the ways people participate in and support movements—just as we would miss many of the ways people participate in and support guerrilla campaigns if all we were to look at was the number of people holding guns. Riots might frighten some people away from participation in nonviolent actions, but there are also good reasons to believe they might also politicize people and rouse them to action.

The Iranian Revolution, which in many ways was an early forerunner to twenty-first-century-style civil resistance revolutions, involved at least twenty-three riots between 1977 and 1979 according to CNTS data. Importantly, this violence was not a separate violent insurgency or radical flank, but rather took the form of unarmed street violence *as* civil resistance. According to political scientist Karen Rasler's event-level analysis of the Iranian Revolution, 44 percent of protest actions in 1977 and 1978 were violent.[14] Nevertheless, the Iranian Revolution mobilized an unprecedented 10 percent or more of the country's population.[15] Neil Ketchley's work on the 2011 revolution in Egypt, discussed in more detail below, shows that participation in nonviolent mobilizations across Egypt increased following the outbreak of riots. While violence might indeed reduce movement participation in some circumstances, there is a great deal of evidence for instances where riots have positive impacts on movement participation.

Statistically speaking, riots do not demobilize movements, even in the U.S., where riots are roundly rejected in mainstream media as illegitimate forms of protest. And on an event level, we don't want for examples. The flames, concussion grenades, and property destruction that greeted Donald Trump's 2017 inauguration did not appear to reduce participation the following day in the Women's March, which was among the largest nonviolent marches in U.S. history—nor did it appear to curtail resistance to the Trump regime for the years that followed. Likewise, waves of the Movement for Black Lives began with riots in Ferguson and Minneapolis, respectively, and were followed by escalation and spread of mostly nonviolent actions.

Resilience: Resilience refers to activists' ability to weather repression, recover, and adapt. While some sociologists have supposed that a movement's resilience is connected to its ability to mobilize resources and exploit political opportunities, civil resistance scholars have tied resilience to a movement's ability to innovate, modify, and vary actions in a way that outflanks authorities, undermines a government's control, and drains the regime's legitimacy. Put another way, movements are more resilient when they employ a *diversity of tactics*.

There are certainly reasons to believe that unarmed violence challenges a campaign's resilience. Violent actions often carry heavier legal penalties, and engaging in them can expose activists to enhanced repression; protracted, expensive, and draining legal cases; and worse. There are activists I know well, and some I spoke to as part of this research, who have been deeply burdened by the effects of extended trials, jailtime, and extra-judicial retaliation by police as a result of alleged participation in riots. Without at all discounting these very real costs—which are not exclusive to, but very likely to be exacerbated by, violent protest actions—there may also be significant emotional benefits to riots, both for participants and onlookers, which strategically enhance a movement's overall resilience.

Emotion has often been starkly juxtaposed with rationality in scholarly discussion of social movements (and in the social sciences in general), but even "rational action involves underlying commitments that are best rendered through an emotional lens and vice versa."[16] In other words, resilience of individuals and groups has a lot to do with how people feel about themselves and their struggle. Riots and images of them can play a crucial sustaining role. The subjective impact of participation in or alongside physically confrontational protests is easily overlooked in studies that focus on short-term political outcomes, but might be especially salient for longer-term movement trajectories. The following two chapters are dedicated to exploring these possibilities through the experiences of rioters themselves. What previous research exists on the political-emotional experience of riots speaks to this point as well. For example, sociologist Javier Auyero quotes an activist in Argentina recounting how participation in a riot had transformed her from a "beaten down" woman who had taken "thirty-six years of crap" into a "commando woman" who was ready to take action.[17]

Leverage: To many social movement and civil resistance scholars, leverage means people's collective ability to impose sanctions on a target. These sanctions can come in the form of attacks on the flow of everyday life or the refusal to participate in crucial areas of government or the economy. Put simply, the leverage of a movement hinges on their disruptive capacity—their ability to interrupt business as usual. In and of itself, the assertion that riots are disruptive is likely an uncontroversial one, which is part of the point—it is clear to all that riots are disruptive. Beyond the material disruption to civic routines, riots are disruptive to people's mindsets about those routines far beyond the location where they break out.

Of course, nonviolent tactics can be disruptive too; well-planned and cleverly executed refusal or nonviolent blockades can be highly effective in interrupting the flow of power. However, many of the standard tactics that are considered nonviolent by non-profits, government, and mass media—in other words the most affirmed forms of protest—are very often not disruptive. For example, research has found the majority of protests in the late-twentieth century U.S. were placid, predictable, non-disruptive, and initiated by the advantaged.[18] These "performances of *potential* disruption—permitted marches, pre-arranged business union strikes, public delivery of petitions, and the like—ultimately derive their leverage from the threat of actual, material disruption."[19] In other words, what leverage there is in non-disruptive protest is there because of the implicit threat that they carry by being associated with types of protest that are disruptive. Not all disruptive protests are violent, but violent protests are usually disruptive.

The interplay between violent collective actions and more conventional nonviolent approaches has a lot to do with the mounting difficulty movements have disrupting oppressive systems. In order to be effective, social movements must be "sufficiently pungent to disrupt the workings of the system" and remain so in order to resist the draining of disruptive capacities through cooptation.[20] Instead, however, non-profits and advocacy groups, especially in Western democracies, often deploy non-disruptive repertoires that have the appearance of contention, but which by design fail to exert meaningful leverage over authorities. The gap between the standardized performance of disruption and what it would really mean to be in conflict with the state and capital interests creates what sociologists Seraphim Seferiades and Hank Johnston call a *disruptive deficit*.[21] The disruptive deficit of conventional protest in tandem with the neoliberal capacity to manage the communication of social grievances and coopt dissent produces a vacuum likely to be filled by political violence. In the face of decrees by professional activists and social movement organizations that all participants must adhere to strictly nonviolent forms of protest, especially when it is clear to the aggrieved that these forms are ineffectual, some turn to violent forms, which, while less respectable and perhaps less strategically oriented, are at least manifestly disruptive. As Seferiades and Johnston put it, "in seeking conciliation through exclusively conventional protest, institutionalized claimants end up inadvertently fomenting the kind of political violence they most dread and despise."[22] Even in instances where rioters themselves might not see their actions through an explicitly political framework, riots alter the political terrain on which organized movements struggle. Riots, in the words of Frances Fox Piven, "give muscle to the demands of a movement."[23] In this way, riots can generate both energy and leverage in civil resistance uprisings.

The logic of the *backfiring effect* is central to many of the arguments asserting that violent tactics hinder movement success, including arguments relating to mobilization, resilience, and leverage.[24] Claims around the backfiring effect have to do with the juxtaposition of violent repression to nonviolent protest, which is thought to highlight the illegitimacy of a repressive regime versus the legitimate claims of nonviolent protesters, and thereby shift public opinion in favor of protesters. Violence on the part of protesters, the argument goes, increases the perceived legitimacy of repression and decreases public support for resistance. Though it is one of the most commonly repeated arguments for nonviolent discipline, this narrative relies on a number of fallacies. Among these are: the presumption that movement success requires each action to lead to increased public sympathy, the reliance on media to represent protest actions accurately, and the idea that perception of protest is unaffected by systemic biases.[25]

In a highly publicized study, political scientist Omar Wasow has argued that riots in 1968 were responsible for the presidential election of Richard Nixon by pushing white moderates to vote for a "law and order" agenda. This research received a great deal of promotion in nonviolence circles, and in fact was cited by Chenoweth years before it was published.[26] In 2020, famous activist and nonviolence scholar George Lakey used Wasow's results to argue that rioting in Portland, OR, could end up leading to Trump's reelection or seizure of power.[27] However, once again, despite the hay that has been made of this research, it does not say exactly what the headlines make it out to be.

Wasow's study finds that, in majority white residential areas, the 1968 riots resulted in a small (around two percent) average loss of Democratic vote shares when compared with a "counterfactual scenario that Martin Luther King, Jr. had not been assassinated on April 4, 1968, and therefore 137 violent protests had not occurred in the immediate wake of his death."[28] Let's unpack that. First, there is a big difference between protest designed to influence an electoral cycle and rebellion against systemic oppression. Second, with all due respect to predictive statistical modeling, when it comes to major historical events, I'm skeptical that we can assemble enough data to accurately predict what would have happened if what happened didn't happen. It's difficult enough to accurately analyze what actually did happen. In Wasow's counterfactual scenario, not only were there not riots but there would also have been Dr. King—a factor that seems like it would have additional and unmeasurable impacts on political outcomes that would go far beyond the 1968 election. In any case, two percent of white swing votes is actually a surprisingly small difference considering the scale of the 1968 rebellions; it may be consequential for the U.S. two-party political system that operates on tiny margins in particular places among the most indecisive people, but from a sociological lens it's miniscule. It is not at all surprising that a Black rebellion could lead some white people to cling to authorities. Indeed, effective polarization, as we will discuss below, requires such a sacrifice in the short term.

Before moving on, however, it is noteworthy that other studies have found the opposite effects of protest on both voting patterns and media coverage. A study of the post-1992 Los Angeles riot found a liberal shift in policy support at the polls, and research on the 2016 election concluded that Black Lives Matter protests, including both nonviolent and violent actions, led to higher turnout among Black voters without having a significant impact on white voting behavior.[29] In any event, movements' impacts on elections displays only their most institutionalized effects.

The backfiring phenomenon likely has more to do with factors apart from absolute adherence to nonviolence on the part of the protesters. Pre-existing disposition toward security forces, the appearance of disproportionate or illegitimate repression, and agreement or disagreement with the underlying grievance being protested all factor into the ways repression will be read by onlookers. It is uncontroversial that protester violence can be expected to increase the likelihood and severity of repression, but while some have argued that repression demobilizes activists, other research demonstrates that repression can have an overall positive impact on mobilizations. A violent response from police can diffuse activists, harden their resolve, create disillusionment about the established order among onlookers, and set off "micro-mobilization" processes that expand opposition to a regime.[30] Under certain conditions, riots can thus generate a similar back-firing effect as civil resistance theorists have claimed results only from nonviolent actions.

Chenoweth and Stephan note that one of the pivotal moments of the Iranian Revolution was sparked by a protester throwing a brick through a window, an action that triggered intensified repression, which in turn led to increased mobiliza-tion.[31] They suggest the involvement of an *agent provocateur*, but nevertheless describe the action in terms of its positive impact on movement growth. Likewise, riots in Ferguson and Baltimore in 2014 and 2015 did not appear to demobilize nonviolent Black Lives Matter actions, but rather added to the resurgent moral cri-sis of institutional racism in the U.S., as well as to growing dis-comfort with militarized police forces. Regarding the 2020 wave of the Movement for Black Lives, a Monmouth University poll found that 54 percent of U.S. Americans believed the burning of the 3rd Police Precinct in Minneapolis was a justified response to the murder of George Floyd.[32] One guesses the same poll would have yielded different results had the question been hypothetical.

Like Chenoweth and Stephan's suggestion about an *agent provocateur* in Iran, police and liberal groups were quick to blame property destruction in Minneapolis and elsewhere in the summer of 2020 on outside agitators. And, like the Iranian Revolution, though it might be important for a host of other reasons, when it comes to an overall analysis of an uprising, in a sense, it does not matter who threw the first rock or set the first fire. *Agents provocateurs*, like anyone else, can make miscalcula-tions, and their actions can end up escalating protests and mak-ing them more powerful.

The *agent provocateur* is a common character in the arguments of civil resistance theorists, who often use them as evidence of the strategic superiority of nonviolence.[33] As such, it is worth taking a moment to address this. It is of course true that *agents provocateurs*, as well as their close cousins, informants, are widely used by state forces to weaken and destroy movements, and activists would do well to educate themselves on identifying and dealing with such threats in a responsible way. But it does not follow from the existence of *agents provocateurs* that nonviolent tactics are always more strategic. Since just about all uprisings involve some who engage in non-nonviolent actions, and all serious movements are likely to have undercover state agents working to destabilize them, there are no counterexamples. And the suggestion that anyone who is engaging in violent action could be an agent of the state is a dangerous notion that easily leads to paranoia—hardly a productive quality for movement building. Furthermore, while undercover agents sometimes encourage protesters to start rioting, the police are always demanding out loud that protests remain nonviolent—in neither case does movement strategy benefit from unquestioningly doing the opposite.

When nonviolent actionists accuse violent protesters of undermining the backfiring effect, they are saying that protester violence reduces the likelihood that the average onlooker will sympathize with the protest, that it drives popular opinion away from the movement. In fact, both protester violence and repression can have impacts in both positive and negative directions. In other words, violent actions are polarizing.

Polarization—the "widening of political and social space between claimants in a contentious episode"—might be interpreted as a reduction in mainstream public support for a time, but it is also closely linked to the consolidation of opposition forces around an issue and the possibilities for widespread rebellion.[34] This dynamic is key to the logic of direct action in civil resistance, powerfully explained in Dr. King's famous 1963 "Letter from a Birmingham Jail." Put simply, direct action forces people to take sides. Riots are exciting and frightening, they shock people and bring deep-seated political opinions to their emotional surface. In some circumstances, this might have an overall demobilizing effect on movements. In others, it can lead to the type of polarization that clarifies social-political cleavages, galvanizes supporters, and increases people power.

Writing of the French Revolution, sociologist John Markoff describes how peasant insurrections posed no military threat to the vast French war machine but rather represented a threat to the "moral unity of army and nation," making them a distinctly effective engine of social change.[35] The physical challenge to authority involves different subjective and material dynamics for a riotous crowd than it does for a less violent one, but nevertheless it typically does not present a straightforward military threat to the armed forces.[36] Few rioters are likely to think they can defeat the army in combat, but a government that calls on its military to put down a rebellion risks a swift corrosion of legitimacy.

The riskiest form of polarization has to do with the armed forces. In many countries, police and the military are not the same; they have different political-social functions and often hail from different sectors of society. The job of police is to control their fellow citizens and protect some from others. In practice, this means protecting political, social, and capital hierarchies, or in other words, keeping people in their place. On the other hand, at least in theory, a state's military forces exist to protect the citizens of that state from outside threats. Soldiers are trained to use violence to defend their country. When they are ordered to use that violence within their country, they are often highly effective in quelling immediate unrest, but turning their guns on fellow citizens can also lead to rapid deterioration of morale. When a political leader is forced to call in the army to put down a rebellion, they gamble not only with their legitimacy but their entire regime. The moment soldiers refuse orders to shoot their fellow citizens is the moment the president flees the country.

Police are used to behaving violently with citizens of their own country (and certainly with people who live there but are not citizens) and they are trained for crowd control. Yet police often catalyze rioting with their own actions, either through direct violence against community members or via heavy-handed repression of a protest. Once it begins, rioting can be intimidating for police, but the authorities face a similar dilemma with most violent crowds as they do with peaceful protests in how much force they are willing and able to apply in an attempt to end the disruption—or risk spreading it. The decisions police make, in terms of how they will engage rioters, occur at all levels of the chain of command, including both rational and emotional considerations such as personal or political commitments, a fear of mobilizations escalating, fear of being physically hurt, desire or hesitance to physically hurt others, duty to follow orders, and so forth. These considerations by authorities are common to both disruptive nonviolent and violent civilian actions, although emotions and consequences are more extreme during violent protests.

Movements are fluid, evolving and adapting tactical repertoires over time as participants and authorities engage, learn, and change from their experiences in relationship with each other. In this area too, imagining an impermeable separation between violent and nonviolent actions limits understandings of resistance to oppression. Many activists in the U.S. who were mobilized by the riots in the 1960s later joined and led nonviolent social movements.[37] And rioters can be experienced activists who previously had only participated in nonviolent actions. The ways in which people can change through their participation in different types of contentious political actions to a large extent drives the trajectories of movements, spans periods of abeyance when movements appear to wane, and informs repertoire diffusion and innovation in moments of uprising.

Finally, a brief word on *regime defections*. Chenoweth and Stephan claim nonviolent campaigns are more likely to result in loyalty shifts among regime elites, which in turn increases the likelihood of movement success.[38] However, regime defections are a double-edged sword. Sociologist and nonviolence researcher Sharon Erickson Nepstad argues that regime defections, especially from the military forces, can help oust a president, but subsequently present dangers to an unarmed movement's ability to consolidate their victory.[39] If elements of an oppressive regime defect intact, they are likely to use their resources and networks to reassert authority in the aftermath of a government's collapse. This dynamic will come into play in the 2011 Egyptian case outlined below. Regardless, the issue of defections is more directly relevant to the difference between martial conflict and civil conflict than it is to the difference between riotous and peaceful protests within a civilian uprising.

***

Based on the study of social protest in the U.S., famed sociologist William Gamson argued that the use of violence frequently coincided with success, concluding: "Violence should be viewed as an instrumental act, aimed at furthering the purposes of the group that uses it when they have some reason to think it will help their cause."[40] The reality is more complicated, as interviews with rioters in the following chapters reveal. Just because nonviolence is not categorically more effective does not therefore mean that the reverse is true. There are many reasons to believe that violent tactics can hurt movements; these reasons are well circulated by nonviolence scholars. From a movement perspective, riots and unarmed violence, like any set of tactics, are likely to have potential benefits and costs depending on context and on a variety of factors. But in order to effectively analyze the impact that different types of actions have on movements and individuals, violent actions must be fully incorporated into the analytical framework. Below I briefly discuss an exemplary case study to illustrate.

The 2011 Egyptian revolution is an iconic uprising and a *critical case* of civil resistance for which there exists excellent existing quantitative, qualitative, and experiential research.[41] The trajectory of the Egyptian uprising saw riots open the way for nonviolent protest to increase and grow, in this case on a very short timeline. Interactions between riots and nonviolent demonstrations in the 2011 Egyptian revolution highlight both the observable ways that riots can aid movement growth and how an analytic approach that ignores riots is liable to misunderstand what is really happening during uprisings.

Riots and Mass Protest in the January 25 Revolution

The Egyptian revolution, one of the so-called "Arab Spring" revolts of 2011, was widely cited within civil resistance and nonviolence studies fields as an exemplary case of nonviolent civil resistance.[42] The moment was undeniably characterized by civil resistance in the sense that collective actions were civilian based and highly decentralized, and it sought to overthrow an authoritarian government through popular mobilizations. The movement created and utilized popular slogans, drew massive grassroots support, occupied public space, sparked nationwide solidarity protests and labor strikes, made use of creative and adaptive tactics, and was successful in ousting the country's head of state. And the movement included widespread rioting.

Following the stunning overthrow of the Tunisian government by a spontaneous civil revolt, Egyptian activists who had previously been planning protests against police violence for January 25, found the streets full of political newcomers, inspired by a new sense of possibility.[43] Protesters emerged from all walks of life, focusing their frustration and anger on the Mubarak regime and taking up the popular slogan of the Tunisian uprising: "The people want to overthrow the regime!"[44] In only seventeen days, the people forced the removal of Hosni Mubarak, who had held power for almost three decades. In addition to its swift success, civil resistance scholars extolled the Egyptian movement for creating a nonviolent "global sensation" and "accomplish[ing] what years of violent rebellion could not."[45] Then-U.S. president Barack Obama also emphasized the nonviolent nature of the Egyptian protests in his speech following Mubarak's overthrow.

In fact, nearly one hundred police stations were sacked and burned in the opening days of the revolution.[46] Throughout the three-week uprising there were numerous confrontations with police and government-backed gangs involving massive street fights and the heavy exchange of projectiles. In the words of political scientist Mona El-Ghobashy, it was "four continuous days of street fighting, January 25–28, that pitted people against police all over the country," which transformed an episode of protest into a "revolutionary situation."[47] The January 25 Revolution involved spectacular acts of nonviolent resistance and contained widespread nonviolent sentiment, but to the extent that the seventeen days between January 25 and Mubarak's ouster can be viewed as a bounded episode, it was far from nonviolent.

More than simply being present alongside peaceful demonstrations, rioting and other violent actions interacted dynamically with less-violent and nonviolent mobilizations.[48] While the riots were largely separate from the large demonstrations that made international news, the attacks on police stations were meant as retaliation for lethal force used against nonviolent protesters, and for police brutality in general, and were designed to open space for nonviolent protests to continue.[49] Political scientist Neil Ketchley's research on the contentious politics of the January 25 revolution brings out the ways that violent rioting and nonviolent protests appeared "both synergetic and complementary" in their combined ability to create a revolutionary situation.[50]

In the first days of the revolution, nonviolent protesters, many of them seasoned activists, had initial successes evading authorities and amassing in streets and public squares. However, as police regrouped, protesters were beaten back and temporarily demobilized by sheer force of repressive violence. There was also another group of "early risers" in the revolution, who have received much less media or scholarly attention. These were local crowds, often from poorer urban districts, who attacked local police stations with increasing frequency and ferocity in the opening days of the revolt.[51] It was this group that forced the police to retreat from attacking protesters in city centers in order to defend their stations, creating unpatrolled streets for nonviolent protesters to retake, and providing time for them to grow their occupations of public space, most notably Tahrir Square. Overall participation in the revolution *increased* following riots, with the largest mobilization taking place two weeks later, on February 11, the day Mubarak would end up being deposed.[52]

Riots targeting police stations created immediate, material sanctions against agents of the regime for their use of force against nonviolent protesters and compelled authorities to make decisions under duress about where, when, and how to deploy their forces. The backfiring effect did not function exactly as nonviolent actionists predict, since initial repression of nonviolent protests was largely effective. Instead, repression was followed by violent protests, which then suffered the highest casualties as a result of increased police repression, but which also cleared the way for nonviolent activists to regroup and grow. The backfiring effect in this case was multifaceted, relating *both* to increased repression that generated a riotous response from some and then the subsequent decreased security presence that provided a nonviolent mobilizing opportunity for others. Massive nonviolent demonstrations ultimately caused the crisis of legitimacy that led to Mubarak's ouster, but it was anti-police riots that created space for the larger mobilizations to gather momentum and reach the tipping point.

What makes the 2011 Egyptian case possible to characterize as "nonviolent" for those who labeled it as such is: 1) its *civil character*—that it took the form of civilian mobilizations as opposed to the martial mobilizations of armed struggle; and 2) the *relative* difference in acute violence applied by protesters and authorities—not its participants' refusal to engage in any violent actions. As activist and political scientist Rabab El-Mahdi put it: "There is no doubt that the anti-regime demonstrations were nonviolent compared to the state-security use of ammunition. However, by the 28th of January all NDP (National Democratic Party) headquarters and most police stations were set on fire."[53] In other words, the Egyptian uprising could only be considered nonviolent in comparison to the repressive force used by the state. However, in order to justify the label of "nonviolent"—perhaps, as El-Mahdi suggests, in order to make the revolution seem more approachable for Western middle-class audiences—violent actions were left out of the story or pushed to the margins. To claim that movements no longer deploy civil violence, but "instead, from Tunis to Tahrir Square, from Zuccotti Park to Ferguson, from Burkina Faso to Hong Kong, movements worldwide have drawn on the lessons of Gandhi, King and [nonviolent] everyday activists" is to misrepresent civil resistance by highlighting only a narrow scope of real-world movement lineages and repertoires.[54]

There is a final element of the 2011 Egyptian example that bears discussion. Mass protests did not ultimately overthrow the Mubarak regime—the army did. Protests and riots escalated to the point that military leadership made the command decision to remove Mubarak from power, but this is not the same as directly forcing a leader to step down. Just as we must not sanitize movement tactics, those who study civil resistance must be careful not to overstate victories. There was an outpouring of enthusiasm in the months that followed the January 25 revolution, and for good reason. That uprising led to waves of momentum for popular movements and occupations of public space around the globe. Despite the transformational moment, however, it was the army that oversaw the transition to Egypt's first open election, and when their candidate lost, they created conditions for another crisis of legitimacy that would enable them to depose the elected president and reinstall an authoritarian ruler from their ranks. Many Egyptian protesters opposed leaving Tahrir Square after the army's coup for fear of precisely this outcome. Here again, a ones-and-zeros measure of campaign success is vulnerable to missing important post-campaign developments that should inform future movements.

The field of civil resistance studies has been largely oriented toward activist application, which makes it all the more crucial that limitations in its analyses are brought to light. Making the full scope of real-world resistance tactics legible in the analytic frameworks, which make meaning of civilian resistance, enables us to more effectively explore the dynamics that animate these movements, as well as the factors that lead them to achieve their goals or influence subsequent setbacks.

Conclusion

The distinction between movement strategies organized around unarmed civil resistance and those organized around armed martial resistance is important and useful. As long as states have been making war, there have been studies of martial strategy, and when it comes to armed resistance, there are canonical treatments of guerrilla warfare. When it comes to civil resistance, however, the strategic canon is tainted with the refusal to admit that civil resistance is not inherently and completely nonviolent. We do ourselves no favors by pretending movements have historically been something they are not.

At times, violent actions might indeed hurt a civil resistance movement's chances for success, or perhaps complicate what success means. In other cases, the use of violence is beneficial to movement goals. In still further cases, the immediate outcome of an action might be ambiguous, or its direct strategic elements less important moving forward than the impact that action has on participants and onlookers. Riotous actions involve trade-offs for any movement as a whole, as do any set of tactics. A broad analysis of data on contentious political events reveals that, overall, riots are associated with increased street protests. In some instances, as in the 2011 Egyptian uprising, riots can play a materially tactical role in these mobilizations. In instances where the direct tactical outcomes are less clear, riots can have important symbolic, emotional, and experiential effects that inspire, educate, and sustain movement participants. When we make riots and other forms of forceful or physically confrontational direct action legible in the civil resistance framework, many of the dynamics nonviolence researchers have identified become more realistic and thus more useful. In order to explore the power of street rebellion, riots and rioters must be fully incorporated into the story of resistance.

Incorporating riots into civil resistance frameworks is not just a matter of adding tactics to the legible repertoire, we must also change the way we look at resistance. The strategic nonviolence framework directs us to look at whether or not violence works. The debate often proceeds as though we are discussing moves on a chessboard—does the riot help us or hurt us in achieving our goals? Approaching strategic and tactical questions in this way is sometimes appropriate and necessary, but exclusively discussing acts of resistance in these terms is also misleading. First, riots are sometimes a collective reaction to injustice, and as such they are likely to continue to happen as long as police forces continue to hurt vulnerable people with impunity, and more broadly, as long as conditions of grotesque inequality and destruction-for-profit continue to dominate the world's power relations. In this sense, asking whether or not riots *should* happen is pointless. It is more productive to try to understand rioters than to try to logic them out of existence. Second, looking at movements through a vulgar strategic lens can often mean missing the emotions that are necessarily wrapped up in acts of resistance. Terms like "strategic thinking" or "strategic logic" can contribute to a common but false distinction between rationally driven instrumental action and irrational, emotionally driven action. Resistance, like just about everything, is an emotional process, and so emotions must be part of strategy.

Up until now, this work has largely focused on what nonviolence theory gets wrong and why that is a problem for movements. Riots have for too long been left out of the conversation about resistance and movement strategy. In order to help bring them back in, I will now turn to the words of rioters themselves.

5.

The U.S. Black Bloc: Anarchy and the Effervescent Riot

"It is not a matter of being compelled to break eggs before an omelet can be made; but of the eggs doing their own breaking in order to be able to aspire to omelethood."
—IDRIES SHAH, PARAPHRASING RUMI

As we have seen, riots are intertwined with uprisings from below, however, very few studies have asked rioters about their experiences. Theories of "crowd hysteria" have largely been debunked, but nevertheless the idea persists in popular consciousness through notions of mob or herd mentality. This view can make it easy to forget that rioters are people too—possibly even people you know. Considering the rising levels of contentious protests around the world, more and more people are experiencing these moments. After a riot or protest that teases the boundaries of a riot, the people who were part of it go on participating in society, and often in movements. Understanding the subjective dynamics of rioting and how those experiences impact participants is therefore essential to understanding the social effects of contentious protest.

This chapter presents the experience of rioting in the words of anarchists in the United States who have taken part in black bloc actions. The black bloc originated as an anti-surveillance protest tactic in which participants cover their faces with bandanas or masks and dress in black, making it difficult for authorities to distinguish between individuals in a group. In addition to some measure of security through anonymity, the practice of dressing alike and "masking up" allows for "the creation of an illu-sory stable identity" that can be adopted by participants pursuing an empowering collective visual within larger protest actions.[1] The practice has grown to an aesthetic and political statement about militant street resistance, is widely associated with anar-chists, and involves groups of people who often engage in confrontations with police or political opponents during demon-strations. Since black bloc describes an informal, often ad hoc group of people in a protest wearing black (or sometimes another color or costume in common), there is a great deal of variation in how these groups and individuals behave. Many black blocs do not destroy property or engage in violent action, and in the ones that do, there are often individuals who do not. However, the collective willingness to confront authorities, threaten property, or physically protect other protesters is a primary characteristic of these formations.

When it comes to perception of anarchists in the U.S., black bloc formations are given disproportionate public attention. Black blocs leapt to national prominence in the wake of the 1999 "Battle of Seattle" riots against the World Trade Organization, an event that is widely considered pivotal in the "anarchist turn" toward more horizontal left politics, and since then anarchism has been all the more closely associated with black bandanas and thrown projectiles.[2] The black bloc again received a surge of attention after violent protests at Donald Trump's 2017 inaugura-tion, becoming intertwined with militant antifascists or "antifa."[3] By 2020, then-president Trump would target "violent anarchists" and "ugly anarchists" as domestic terrorists and the prime perpe-trators of all things evil.[4] The Trump administration went so far as to label three major U.S. cities— New York City, Seattle, and Portland—"anarchist jurisdictions" because of recurring confron-tational protest actions in those areas.

It is not only the Right who target the black bloc; liberals too wring their hands over what to do with "black-clad insurrection-ary anarchists."[5] In 2012, progressive commentator Chris Hedges famously referred to black bloc anarchists as "the cancer of the Occupy movement," labeling them "criminals," "hooligans," and calling them "a gift from heaven to the security and surveillance state."[6] Hedges's take is notably similar to that of Charles Marino, a private security expert and former advisor to the Department of Homeland Security, who wanted to put "Antifa and Black Lives Matter on notice" for their "destructive, violent" and "criminal" acts.[7] And while softer in language, the same sentiment is apparent in journalist John Horgan's imploring anti-Trump protesters to renounce violence, saying that too many "have been seduced by the macho glamour of violence and by the rough justice of combating state oppression with brutality of their own," and in activist and trainer George Lakey's suggestion that riots in Portland, OR, were a gift to Trump's "law and order" agenda.[8] The commonalities here are that the black bloc is violent and thus represents a threat to order, whether that order is attached to law or protest strategy.

The media contributes heavily to this association, as anarchists are commonly featured in Hollywood cinema as antagonists fomenting senseless chaos and destruction.[9] This association between anarchists, villains, and chaos makes experiential analysis all the more important, especially regarding the actions that appear closest to the stereotype—groups of masked rioters lighting fires, breaking windows, and fighting police. Indeed, many black bloc participants probably differ from the majority of rioters in not only being willing to riot, but often holding an ideology that highlights the riot as one of the principal forms of resistance. At the same time, while rioters can be a difficult subset of protesters to reach, the willingness to get physical, destroy property, and confront the police makes black bloc participants a prime source of experiential knowledge about rioting. Accordingly, while there has been very little interview-based research on rioters, a disproportionate amount of what does exist involves the black bloc. The most prominent work is Francis Dupuis-Déri's 2014 book, *Who's Afraid of the Black Blocs?*, while David Graeber's *Direct Action* and AK Thompson's *Black Bloc, White Riot* offer insight from experiential standpoints. Still, there remains a lot to learn about the riotous experience from those who participate.[10]

Anarchists in the U.S. have made headlines in recent years for rioting in racial justice protests, for mutual aid models during the COVID-19 pandemic, and for their general demonization by rightwing politicians. Depending on who you ask, the political philosophy goes back to nineteenth-century Europe, fourth-century China, or Indigenous practices around the world. The root of the word "anarchy" (*an-archy*, from the ancient Greek *anarkhia*) literally translates to "without ruler" or "without government," making anarchism the pursuit of a society without coerced authority. Anarchists distinguish themselves from other types of socialists and communists by opposing not only capital exploitation, but also the use of the state to transform society. For anarchists, the state is not a tool that can be wielded for liberatory purposes even in the hands of the oppressed, but rather it is a mode of organizing society that is inherently oppressive. Anarchists pursue a free and egalitarian society through values and practices like voluntary cooperation, community accountability, mutual aid, and direct action.

Despite anarchists' association with terrorism and assassinations of corporate and political leaders in the late-nineteenth and early-twentieth centuries, the underlying political philosophy of rioters today is profoundly optimistic. Anarchism invokes "a spirit—one that cries out against all that's wrong with present-day society, and boldly proclaims all that could be right under alternate forms of social organization."[11] Though active in political struggles around the world during the twentieth century, it was following the collapse of state socialism in the Soviet Union and China's turn to capitalism when anarchism re-emerged as a defining current in the radical Left.

The nineteenth-century specter of the cloaked anarchist with hand-held bomb has been thoroughly replaced in the twenty-first century with the image of a masked anarchist with brick in hand. However, the black bloc formation that fuels this association is relatively new to the U.S. One activist I spoke with, Arjay, now in his fifties, described having heard about the black bloc from the Autonomen, a German anti-authoritarian group, and subsequently working to incorporate it into the U.S. protest repertoire:[12]

In '89 it was the anarchist gathering in San Francisco, and the Autonomen were there to do a workshop, and I remember people asking them if they were going to be at the DOA [day of action] tomorrow. The idea was to open up a squat in Berkeley, but somehow the cops found out about it and they were there. We had this huge march, it was hundreds of people, masked up, ready to open up the squat and then the cops stopped us. And the Autonomen were there, despite saying, "no we can't violate our visa by being in the streets doing illegal action," but they were right there. And we liberated libations from a Coke truck at one point... which were then used as projectiles to throw at the cops. We couldn't open the squat so people just started throwing Coke cans at the cops in front of the building. And people had wrist rockets—you know, we came prepared—and we went up and down the main street in Berkeley and took out tons of windows, and it was pretty awesome in some ways and problematic in other ways. Yeah. But the black bloc wasn't a concept that was in the movement lexicon [in the U.S.] ... After that we started thinking about how we could bring it here.

From then, it did not take long for the black bloc to work its way into activists' repertoire. The first black bloc actions in the U.S. hit the streets in 1990, and by the World Trade Organization (WTO) protests in Seattle in 1999, there were numerous groups experienced in the tactic. By Occupy Wall Street in 2011, it was a staple of contentious protests, and by 2020 black bloc anarchists were being discussed by activists, politicians, and media across the country.

The Embodied Symbol of a Riot

In the late 1980s, Zi was an activist with the Youth Greens, then a radical wing of the Green Party before the organization's move into electoral politics. Zi was part of an affinity group that participated in what she and several others I spoke to referred to as the first black bloc in the U.S., on Earth Day 1990.[13] She had been led to that action by years of frustration and growing disgust with the inaction that characterized the political protests she had been part of. For example, she described peacefully counter-protesting an anti-abortion march, an issue for which she felt strongly, leaving her feeling disheartened: "It was super depressing! I just didn't feel like it was an effective style of resistance to what we were being confronted with.... I felt pretty defeated on the protest front."

In another instance Zi remembers, even the appearance of being angry was policed by "the nonviolence people" in conventional protests. "I would go to these protests ... and they were *so* boring. Like this one time, me and my friend, we baked a cake to feed the protesters, and the cake said, 'Fuck you George Bush,' and this lady who was part of the protest comes up to us and is like: 'That's violence.' *To our cake!* It was so depressing." She laughed, cradling her bowl-sized teacup in both hands as she recalled this incident—chuckling first in amusement of the cake she and her friend had made, and then incredulously at the person who had denounced it. We're sitting in the back corner of a café frequented by punks and their hipster flank. Now in her fifties, Zi exudes an aura of wisdom, punctuated by a playful smile.

As a teenager, Zi had rebelled into anti-authoritarian counterculture. She had friends who were anarchists, but their politics had felt reactive and not particularly interesting to her. At that time, she still had what she now describes as a liberal outlook, believing that the only change that was possible came through persuading one person at a time, though she became increasingly disheartened with that prospect. "And then I read Murray Bookchin's *Remaking Society*, where he talks about how neurotic everybody is and how it's a product of capitalism, and I was like— Oh! That's what it is! You know, maybe we all don't have to grow up and be as awful as our parents are." As it turned out, she had just moved to an area where social anarchists were organizing. "So I got involved," she says, "and that was nice because there were teachers and there was a structure that I could come into that had older people and wasn't just my peers throwing bowling balls through army recruitment windows. So that was more my style."

Black bloc tactics emerged in the U.S. just as the Soviet Union was collapsing and the U.S. was rising to global political hegemony. The U.S. military was intervening, bombing, and invading other countries with increasing shamelessness, and the neoliberal, non-profit approach to social movement organizations was solidifying control over resistance. Francis Fukuyama was famously declaring that we had arrived at the "end of history," that we had passed the final stage of ideological conflict, that change could thereafter be processed through the liberal state and economy. The typical protest during this time was calm and peaceful, and social movements were replicating the form of protest from previous generations, but with conciliatory or reformist content. Before long, the façade of contention amidst growing urgency resulted in a "loss of political meaning" for many protesters.[14]

Zi continued attending protests that did not feel powerful during the time she was being exposed to radical politics, which led her to seek out those who were interested in "actually doing something." Zi was inspired by the black bloc tactic in Germany, which was being popularized among anarchists as a method to physically defend squatted residences against the police. Zi's group decided to organize a black bloc action at a major city's Earth Day march in 1990. The plan was to break off from the large, permitted march and cause chaos, highlighting the seriousness of climate change and the need to treat it like the crisis it is. She described arriving that morning: "It was kind of scary ... when we got there, the black bloc was meeting up a little before the big march was convening. And they had lit a dumpster on fire and pushed it into the street ... and it was like, oh shit there's a fire in the middle of the street! And in that moment, it felt like the tables had turned, you know?"

Speaking at a faster pace: "I mean, this isn't a 'Fuck you George Bush' cake anymore—this is fire in the street!" Zi laughs excitedly, then pauses to slurp from her tea cup before adding,

"I remember being scared but also enlivened." Then the action began. "It felt cohesive. Which I guess I had never really felt before. You know, when I had gone to protests before, it was usually with one friend of mine. And it was just us standing around feeling alienated, you know? This was like—we're all in a group, and the adrenaline is going.... It felt like we were one cohesive unit, all moving together, but all doing our own things."

In addition to "cohesive" and "enlivened," Zi and many black bloc-ers I spoke with frequently used words like "exciting" and "thrilling" to describe their moments in action. Several articulated the feeling as "euphoria." For all interviewees, the feeling did not last beyond the action itself, but for many the sensation would lead to lasting shifts in political consciousness.

Zi related a coincidence that juxtaposed for her the difference between her previous, alienated experience with conventional protest and the adrenaline-fueled sensation of the bloc. While her bloc was moving from one target to another, they passed by the main Earth Day march, and she happened to spot an old friend from her hometown. The two had been close until a falling out when Zi had begun radicalizing: "And she was standing there, watching the protest go by on the other sidewalk. And she was crying. Just watching the protest and crying at how awful the world was or something. And I was just like, *fuck that*—just crying in response to this crisis we're in. Because ... a couple years ago I would have been there too. I would have been on the sidelines right next to her, feeling overwhelmed and hopeless and crying. But instead I was in a cohesive unit, energized and running down the street trying to change things in a different way."

Zi became visibly animated and smiled widely when describing the heightened sensation of participating in the riot, speaking as though she were in the streets in that moment, revealing how powerful those embodied moments are for her even today. The feelings retained their positive effect over time, though Zi acknowledges that in the immediate material sense the actions she was describing made next to no difference: negligible property destruction, likely covered by insurance or the taxpayer, and not directly impacting the climate change crisis. Yet the feeling of rioting gave her a physical impression of rebellion and freedom that would have a lasting impact on her life.

She describes the transformation that she experienced following her participation in an "unarrest," the act of physically wresting an arrested comrade out of police custody: "I felt really empowered by being part of a group like that. And that was something I wanted people to know was possible. And the unarrest, you know? That we didn't have to just go along with the power over us. That we could physically remove ourselves from that kind of power and violence and control, feeling really just a fundamental shift in my capitulation to authority. I was in kind of an abusive relationship at that time, and it was the end of my tolerance for that. It just seemed like a lot more was possible."

Through the act of fighting a friend out of police custody, Zi, in the moment, organically connected the coercive authority of the state with abusive interpersonal dynamics. The internalized empowerment of resisting the police led to a personal revolution that affected her clarity, disposition, and drive to liberation in all areas of her life. To view that particular black bloc action in purely instrumental terms of whether or not it advanced a short-term strategic goal would be misleading. Zi reported the sensation of the riot instilling in her a deep sense of empowerment that not only had a lasting impact on her political engagement, but transformed her personality.

***

Violence, according to Hannah Arendt, "is distinguished by its instrumental character."[15] We tend to think of violence as Arendt does, as a tool to accomplish something tangible. Early studies of social movements understood it the same way: "Violence should be viewed as an instrumental act, aimed at furthering the purposes of the group that uses it when they have some reason to think it will help their cause."[16] Ironically, the strategic nonviolence school now approaches all movement actions instrumentally, and argues against the use of violent tactics precisely on the basis that they are not instrumentally effective. However, when we examine the riot's affective qualities, a central theme that emerges is how the violence of the riot is largely *symbolic*.

There are instrumental qualities to particular actions, of course; through looting, for example, people can acquire goods in addition to the semiotic effects. Unarresting a person is principally about keeping the arrestee out of police custody, but the accompanying sense of empowerment in doing so is no less significant.[17] For many, the experience of participating in a violent protest has subjective effects that supersede the direct material effects. Police authority and private property are sacred in liberal society, and the physical violation of one and especially both is a powerful experience for many in the black bloc, with images of those actions inspiring others as well via widely reproduced and circulated riot imagery.

In strategic discussions about riots, there are two main types of arguments: material sanctions and propaganda. It is true that riots' destruction is the quickest way that marginalized and oppressed people have of levying material costs on elites. Especially in the case of widespread rebellion, this can run into the millions of dollars and damage entire economies for years to come. Material calculations around such destruction factor into thinking about riots and the social problems that cause them. This is evident for example when, leading up to the verdict in a trial of a police officer who murdered an unarmed Black person, many local storefronts and even those in other cities preemptively board up their windows. However, as many rioters themselves understand, the destruction of most riotous actions is barely a rounding error for major corporations.

Propaganda arguments go in two main directions. First, riots can highlight a social problem, forcing it into public conversations and the immediate agenda of elites. As political scientist Daniel Gillion succinctly puts it: "Nonviolent protest brings awareness to an issue; riots bring urgency to an issue."[18] Second, some anarchists have connected the riot to the strategy of "propaganda by the deed," or the idea that the way to spread rebellion is to show people how it's done. Here the propaganda being spread is the doing of the riot—not increasing the pressure on policy makers to shift their priorities, but inspiring other aggrieved people to mobilize in deconstructing the current system.

Like the black bloc itself, propaganda by the deed is frequently associated with insurrectionary strains of anarchism, which have long stressed the importance of visible acts of rebellion against authority as a strategy to destabilize governments and raise consciousness among the people. According to CrimethInc's podcast, *The Ex-Worker*, "an insurrection is an act of revolting against a civil authority or government, so an insurrectionary anarchist would be an anarchist who is in favor of revolts against civil authority or government, or more specifically, one who believes that smaller revolts against authority will lead to larger revolutions."[19] This tendency within anarchist circles draws from a number of traditions including nihilism and situationism, and has at times created significant tension and controversy within anarchist circles. Indeed, many of the anarchists I spoke to identified with this tendency, but many did not, and some who participated in black blocs had none too kind words for "insurrectionaries." Nevertheless, the tendency's influence on black bloc practices and rioting in particular makes it important to grapple with here, especially concerning "the focus on immediate and existential revolt."[20]

There are obvious limitations to the ability of a riot, as discussed here, to directly transform society. In most cases, we are talking about relatively short events, and in some instances just moments within protest events. However, in the words of black bloc participants, we see how the riot, even if momentary, also has the direct ability to transform individuals and collectives. Riots symbolize the embodied persistence of political struggle, infuse participants with a visceral sense of which side they are on, and can alter participants' understanding of their relationship to authority.

Georges Sorel famously advocated the use of violent tactics from the Left.[21] The French social theorist's argument was widely derided by the Left of his day (the turn of the twentieth century), but generations later his ideas were taken up by insurrectionary anarchists and others who have attempted to conceptualize an insurrectionary riot as the direct conduit to broad social transformation.[22] To Sorel, the growth of a liberal middle class was preserving the capitalist system by blunting its fundamental antagonisms and giving people hope in the system—what in the U.S. came to be called "The American Dream." In Sorel's words, violent action by the proletariat could "so operate on the middle class as to awaken them to a sense of their own class sentiment" and allow the class war to proceed.[23] For example, stores boarding up their windows in anticipation of a riot is akin to signaling which side of the struggle this company is on. In his discussion of the black bloc, AK Thompson has highlighted the relevancy of Sorel's theory today, but says that it needs to be revised in order to turn middle-class "dissident energies" against the system.[24] In the words of black bloc rioters, we see evidence of this revision in action—both a version of Sorel's theory and its inversion.

For Sorel, violence had to be done *to* members of the middle class in order to raise *their* consciousness in terms of their interest in fighting to *preserve* the system. In black bloc participants, the violence of the riot has a similar consciousness-raising effect, but as a result of violence being done *by* the rioter (many of whom in this case, though by no means all, are white and come from middle-class backgrounds), raising their *own* consciousness in terms of their interest in fighting back *against* the system. The key is the empowering sensation of physically opposing authority, which on the one hand counters the pervasive sense of alienation in society in general and in conventional protest specifically; and on the other hand clarifies antagonisms with authority. But the impacts of physical resistance also appear more complicated. Zi is white and comes from a working-class background, but for her the experience unarresting a comrade from police custody was also automatically connected to abusive dynamics in an interpersonal relationship, revealing that the experience of rioting can have an intersectional impact, empowering a person to resistance wherever they face oppression or coercion.

This is not to say that riots are only for rioters. Strategic approaches to rioting, however, are prone to overlook the experiential power of rioting, which itself is intertwined with the communicative power of that form of resistance.

✳✳✳

For Em, being in physically confrontational protests clarified the social role of police: "It only takes one or two experiences being beaten up by cops in the streets to really, really understand in a physical, almost animal way that these people are not here to help you." Some people—in the U.S., particularly Black people, Indigenous people, people of color, and poor people—grow up with this dynamic as a lived reality. Others get a small taste of it through deviant behaviors, in this case political protest, and that experience, combined with the feeling of fighting back, can be particularly transformative for people who were not socialized into the most violent realities of systemic oppression and exploitation.

Like Zi, Em also found her way to black bloc tactics as a result of unsatisfying experiences with conventional protest: "There are so many experiences of disempowerment, including in movement organizing. I didn't personally feel like I had power in any of the political protests I saw and was part of." She focuses on the experience of being violently attacked by police while protesting nonviolently. "It's not like we were smashing windows or setting fire to their cars, it was like I'm standing *here* and not *there*," she said, pointing at the floor under her and then two feet away. "So then it becomes like just the pure experience of authority."

Em is from a white, middle-class family of libertarians from a rural area of the country. She was politicized as a young adult, and got involved in local labor struggles and anti-war mobilizations. She is a proud anarchist, and literally wears it on her sleeves. As she became more engaged with radical politics, Em describes a mounting feeling that conventional protests were not only insufficient, but were backward, sapping her of the will to fight. Em's initial forays into activism quickly led to hopelessness: "Most of the stuff I had gotten was depressing on an intellectual level, like, the world is fucked and Big Brother is watching you, I get it. But what can you *do?*" Being physically attacked by police despite not representing a threatening presence during nonviolent actions— "the pure experience of authority"—had created both frustration and a feeling of sheer disempowerment.

In contrast to that feeling, Em was invigorated by entering the contentious space outside of strict nonviolent protest. In Em's words, "taking action with people who weren't defeatist was amazing." Importantly, this was not necessarily tied to taking any specifically violent actions, but rather to the type of contentious gathering that does not adhere to a narrow conception of nonviolent discipline, thereby opening the potential for physical transgression. In describing the feeling associated with these "unleashed" actions, she quotes another activist from the Battle of Seattle.[25] "There's this guy on a megaphone," she says, "and it's this really intense moment, there's tear gas raining down, and he said: 'I know you think that's fear in your chest right now, but it's not—you've just never felt freedom before.' I still have a hard time saying those words, it's so powerful." She is still speaking softly, but faster, and is physically animated, gesticulating with her hands as she describes herself identifying that feeling during a subsequent action she took part in. "It was absolutely terrifying, but it also had that feeling! You know, once you crack open that understanding of, 'am I allowed to do this and that?'—once a fissure opens in that, there is a whole other range of possibilities before you, and it's so beautiful. It's thrilling ... like, oh my God, the world is so much more interesting, and there is so much more to be done.... And I thought of that quote and I was learning to examine that particular adrenalized experience, you know? And do I know how to handle the sensation of freedom? And when have I ever had the opportunity to try?"

Learning about the political struggle required to fight for a better world is one thing; feeling it is another. For Em, the embodied understanding of the need and possibility for a new world is elevated beyond what would be possible simply through intellectual learning. The feeling of expansiveness and beauty that accompanied physically forceful collective actions, or actions in which she felt free of constraints on how she was supposed to practice resistance is itself important. Even defenders of riots typically describe them as destructive forces—perhaps destroying what needs to be destroyed, but destructive nonetheless. Riots might indeed be destructive, but participants also describe a generative sensation that both sustains their long-term political engagement and imbues in them a vision that, as the anti-globalization movement insisted, another world is possible. The first time Em felt her child kick in the womb, she tells me with a smile, she and her partner were blocking a street during Occupy.

**

For Ely, being an anarchist means being willing to break rules, and the rule of nonviolence is among the most repressive we have. We're sitting at a trendy bar in an otherwise run-down area; I had arrived early and picked a table as far as I could from the bar and the stereo speakers. Ely was easy to spot when she arrived, with her facial piercings, faded black movement tank top, and purposeful swagger. I couldn't help but remark on the fancy location she had selected, a momentary lapse in my interviewer persona probably due to my experiences growing up in a city that had aggressively gentrified when I was a kid. She shrugged and replied that the bar has good pizza—they put their leftovers in the dumpster every night at 11.

Ely had grown up seeing unreasonable authority everywhere—in family, school, and the street. Everywhere authority, and everywhere lying and abuse of power. "How could anyone *not* be an anarchist?" She radicalized in high school, but the anarchism she encountered was primarily in the punk scene, which she described as misogynist and alcoholic: "Fuck the system— let's drink ourselves into a stupor," she mocked. The "intelligent anarchism" scene, as she called it, taught her a lot, but was also discouraging—all analysis without the action. She went on to discuss how finding people who not only studied but practiced anarchism through direct action changed her, leading toward a life of radial politics: "Once you realize how fucked up the world is, it's either swallow the pill and buy in, or kill yourself, or just wallow in despair. Then you meet people who fight back, who practice an alternative, and it becomes the only way." Ely is not referring simply to rioting here, but to a collection of anarchist practices that go along with taking the streets for many black bloc participants. When I asked which was most important to her, she responded: "Anarchism is a process, so some people live communally, some people dumpster, some people organize in their workplaces, some people fight the cops and fuck shit up. I say: *All of the above*."[26]

Anarchism, to Ely, is all about becoming. Breaking through nonviolent discipline is a necessary part of that. There is nothing wrong with a nonviolent action, but there is something wrong with being told you *must* be nonviolent in your action. A commitment to nonviolence, for Ely, is not about *becoming* but about *remaining*. That commitment is necessarily reformist, relying on existing power structures of society to create the change we need if we only add a little polite pressure. The rules of society say you must be nonviolent in your protest, and so by accepting that in your strategy, psychologically you've already foreclosed your chances of becoming something other than a subject of the current order of things.

***

The feeling of embodied resistance can have transformative effects on a person's consciousness and identity. Zi's experience following the unarrest shows the power that the rioting experience can release, manifesting not only in subsequent movement participation, but in personal relationships and identity. Here it becomes clear that the influence of rioting impacts society even beyond the sphere of social movement activism—itself an abstraction within a social whole—via the production of altered subjects, characterized by lower obedience to authority, lower tolerance of abusive power dynamics, and an embodied knowledge that more is possible in the world.

Well over a century ago, scholars in Europe were debating the social causes and effects of crowds and riots in a conversation that would become formative for the modern field of sociology. In his study of Indigenous Australian rituals, Émile Durkheim observed a phenomenon he called *effervescence,* where people who live lives that are typically isolated come together in a raucous group, resulting in a distinct type of heightened experience that feels so intense and all-encompassing to the participant that it is perceived as supernatural.[27]

For Durkheim, effervescence is essentially a mechanical product generated by the assembly of living human bodies in one place for a unified purpose. Earlier in his career, Durkheim had harshly critiqued theories of crowd psychology, which held that crowds essentially hypnotize participants and impose a collective sentiment on otherwise rational individuals—like the Borg in *Star Trek*—as lacking in empirical rigor. Durkheim's effervescence was supposed to be more scientific, but it ultimately reflects many of the same flaws. For Durkheim, social boundaries and individual discernment break down in the wake of the effervescent experience. The notion that people become wholly susceptible to outside influence and that, in the crowd, "the passions released are of such an impetuosity that they can be restrained by nothing" reflect the least empirically grounded aspects of Le Bon's crowd hypnosis—and bear little resemblance to the experience of rioters I spoke to.[28]

Some of the more sophisticated attempts to understand riots in contemporary sociology continue to portray the rioting crowd as being prone to violent excesses through dynamics of the crowd itself. Sociologist Randall Collins examines various types of violence, including the riot, using photo, video, and other types of evidence in an attempt to update Durkheim's theories of the crowd and use them to help us understand the "micro-interactions" involved in violent encounters. One of the primary take-aways for Collins is the idea of "forward panic," essentially the culmination of tension/fear in an aggressive frenzy. Here Collins draws primarily from soldiers in war, genocidal massacres, and police officers beating unarmed suspects, where he sees the release of accumulated tension/fear by members of a superior force exploding in an unconstrained violent outburst. Forward panic is "violence that for the time being is unstoppable."[29] The theory is meant to apply to violence in its many manifestations, which, like nonviolence theorists, enables Collins to swap in examples of one type of violence in order to explain another and make associations across vastly differing situations and geographies. In one of the more outrageous examples, Collins describes war crimes by Imperialist Japanese forces in China during WWII as being "like rioters on a looting rampage," as though mass torture and murder of civilians by soldiers was sociologically comparable to rioters taking goods from stores.[30]

Tension and fear are aspects of the riot to be sure, but nothing remotely like wanton "violence that for the time being is unstoppable" comes out in interviews with the rioters I spoke with. The riots they describe involve varying scenarios, including those in which there was a massive and violent police presence, those in which the police were two steps behind, and some in which police were entirely unequipped to respond, but the main targets were corporate or public property, and destruction was relatively limited. In some cases, the target was the police themselves or non-police fascists, but even then, no opponents were seriously injured. That isn't to say that people in this sort of riot never hurt anyone. But if the riot itself sets participants on a collective trajectory toward tension and fear that culminates in a climax of wanton violence, as Collins describes, we would see a lot more carnage resulting from black blocs.

Most activists I spoke to did express a distinct and profound emotional high from riotous moments in the streets, including an electrifying sense of being, purpose, power, and cohesion in the group, which in some ways resembles what we could call effervescence. However, contrary to Durkheim's effervescence, for these activists the experience is not just to do with assembly of purposive bodies in motion, but rather is inherently connected to the contentious power dynamics of their particular type of assembly. The sensation they describe is, at its core, embodied political struggle, which at once grounds the heightened sensation in opposition to identified material oppressions and offers a feeling of freedom from them—what some interviewees describe as a glimpse into a liberated world. In other words, in the context of a society in which we are increasingly alienated from one another, and protests against the sources of that alienation are often empty and performative, the feeling of bodies coming together in physical opposition to oppressive authority generates an exceptional feeling—a *contentious effervescence*.[31]

This feeling appears as powerful as Durkheim theorized effervescence to be, but is also far more nuanced in its effect on the individual participant. That the black bloc generated the feeling that "we were one cohesive unit, all moving together, but all doing our own things" is itself evidence that Zi felt both a heightened collective experience and an experience in which she retained her sense of self and autonomy. The self might be altered in that moment (some participants, like Em, reported self-awareness of this alteration in real-time) but nevertheless remains a discrete self, connected to, yet distinct from the group. These first-hand accounts challenge the underlying supposition common to Durkheim's crowd effervescence, Le Bon's crowd hypnosis, and Collins's forward panic that the self is lost in the overwhelming trance of the crowd experience in a slide toward violent action, yet they build on the idea that riotous crowds involve a psychologically and emotionally powerful affect.

***

The sensations described by black bloc participants were ephemeral, not lasting beyond the action itself. However, interviewees frequently associated these feelings with lasting shifts in political consciousness, personality, and worldview. Em specifically connects what she called the "euphoria" of collective action to freedom itself. The sensation of embodied freedom emerges when the repressive sense of obligation to the rules of a society is "cracked open." Em goes on to describe how having felt the "sensation of freedom" deeply affected her perspective moving forward:

> I think there are aspects of my personality that have been formed by those breakthrough moments... There is an aspect to radicalism that says, "better things are possible" and that gives you the ability to predicate other things on that assumption, and that isn't always tangible to you if you

haven't had those concrete experiences.... Sometimes that ends up being institutionalized and sometimes it ends up being a high you chase, and in my case it's more just been like I am not afraid to demand that the world be different, because I've seen the potential for other things. And I take a lot of comfort from that. I don't anticipate that I'll be able to see the changes I envision in my life or my child's life, but just understanding that power structures as they are now are not fossilized and not permanent, I feel like all of these things can be broken and transformed, and I think that's a real gift.

Here, Em relates the deep and lasting impacts on her political outlook and resolve, deriving from those exceptional moments of collectively breaking foundational rules of authority. This account supports the theory that collective political action generates effervescence in crowds, but it also adds a crucial element to it, since these activists do not find the effervescent feeling in conventional protest, and in fact report its opposite. Not only did participants not relate empowering, humanizing, or magical feelings to conventional protests they had participated in, many came away with feelings of disappointment, dejection, and depression. Some interviewees did describe empowering emotions related to participation in movements (as opposed to particular actions), for example Occupy Wall Street.[32] However, at the action level, there appears to be a difference between the sensations of an avowedly nonviolent protest and those that at least contain the possibility of physical contention.

In this case, it is not collective action as such, but a particular kind of contentious political action that is the source of the effervescent moment and its lasting effects. That the collective action contains the potential for violence or property destruction, violating the sanctity of private property and police authority and thus representing a political fight, is integral to the sensation, as in: "This isn't a 'Fuck You George Bush' cake anymore—this is fire in the street." At the same time, the sensation is not solely dependent upon the potential for violent action either; it is an embodied connection between that contentious space and political struggle. A reflection from Em points in this direction: "I think some people go seeking that [high], and I don't think you always can. I don't think you can always will those circumstances; I think they're emergent in struggle. But you have to be willing to put yourself in the place to have that moment. And I think those moments are really magical."

The "magical" sensation described is both deeply connected to political orientation and to the willingness to cross a line of disobedience, symbolized in this case by willingness to engage in property destruction—though importantly, not necessary by actually doing it. Some interviewees did not personally engage in any violent actions during the black bloc actions they related, yet described the experiences in terms of collective identity. The effervescence, while liminal in its sensation, constitutes a "breakthrough," which in a sense represents the birth of a new political subject. This new subject has both enhanced sense of political possibility, and the visceral understanding that politics is a fight.

The riot, as discussed here, is in many ways a symbolic act. Or, more precisely, it is a collection of material actions that carry deep symbolic meaning. As Zi and many other respondents alluded to, smashing a corporate window during a protest is not really about destroying that window in the tactical sense, and, in fact, is barely about the cost of replacing it—it is about smashing a concept. This viewpoint substantially aligns with James Baldwin's assertion that "looting" a television during a riot is not really about acquiring the object, it is a judgment on the value of commodities in a community that has been systematically robbed, and it is saying "screw you."[33] By damaging property during a riot, the corporate window or the TV or the car is converted into a symbol of that which has been taken, that which has been imposed, that which stands between people and liberation. The symbolic meaning and the material object here do not stand juxtaposed but are mutually reinforcing; the symbolic meaning of the object has political weight through and because of the real action of rioters destroying it.

The symbolic element of rioting also does not imply rash or nonstrategic thinking. In fact, most respondents, including those quoted in this chapter, were strategically minded activists who voiced frustration with the Left's insufficient attention to strategy. As Em put it in describing a seemingly successful action in which her group initially backed down lines of riot police and occupied a bridge, "And that's a great metaphor for the Left, right? It's like, we take the bridge, and now what?" She went on, "we can have these militant marches or even, you know, take over the road or a bridge for a few hours, but we don't always have the structure or numbers to take the next step. How do you turn these actions into levers of real political power?" This measured appraisal belies the notion that riots are spontaneous and irrational outbursts of mob violence enacted by people who are devoid of strategic sensibility, and also points toward the need to situate the riot's symbolic importance in conjunction with a strategic outlook.

***

Not all respondents had the same experience or perspective on acts of violence in the black bloc. For one activist, Owe, participating in the black bloc over decades of activist experience was central to her political identity, but for most of that time she personally believed in nonviolent strategy. Though many of the black bloc actions she was a part of involved physically confrontational actions by others, Owe preferred to focus on medic work and protest art. Her belief in nonviolence made her an exception among respondents, but her experiences too speak to the emotional power of the black bloc formation itself: "I definitely remember that it was exciting. You know? It definitely made us feel a sense of unity. There were nerves because we could get arrested or beat up, but also me and the folks I was with, all of us had gotten arrested and beaten up before.... It did feel like we were with like-minded people who were all fighting for the same kind of vision of radical social change, not just a discourse around the Democrats and Republicans, but a sense that the whole system is rotten from the inside."

Amidst the café humming all around us, Owe is poised and focused, her voice relaxed but serious, especially when speaking of the fight for justice. Unlike many others quoted in this chapter, Owe had been inspired to radicalism by the Congress of Racial Equality and other civil rights groups, and was a believer in many of the tenets of strategic nonviolence. Many of her former comrades, however, and in one case a close friend and roommate, did engage in property destruction and the use of physical force during protests and antifascist actions.

> Well I think at the time, I did not smash a window and I was not interested in that, but I also felt like if somebody in my group is smashing the window of a multinational corporation to draw attention to it being a problematic place, then maybe it's misguided but I don't see it as the biggest sin. I'm like, why are people focusing on this minor property violence when, you know ... people are getting beaten by the police and that's not the public narrative, the public narrative is look at these few anarchists who were breaking windows in a store that was closed, and the company has money to pay for it.

Owe personally did not partake in violent actions, but she understood why others did, and was ready to take to the streets alongside and defend them. And, as it turned out, the rise of mainstream fascism amid Trump's 2016 bid for power had shifted her perspective in favor of protester violence, but she still has never personally engaged in violent actions during protests. Interestingly, while Owe did discuss feelings of unity and empowerment in the bloc, she was one of the few who did not speak of those moments with the excited affect that others did, nor did she describe effervescent-like feelings. The difference might not be that she had never personally engaged in violent actions during the effervescent moments—several others reported acutely heightened sensations in moments of collective physical transgression in which they personally were not engaging in violent actions—but rather that Owe did not *believe* in those actions, instead holding an articulated belief in nonviolence.

Another activist, Jay, nowadays works for a movement organization that professes nonviolence, but he cut his teeth as a teenager in antifascist groups that would seek out Nazis to fight. Whether at punk rock shows or public demonstrations, Jay was part of a group that was there to beat the fascists down, and sometimes to get beaten up, but one way or another to fight. Jay comes from a working-class Jewish family that resides in a mostly white, Christian suburban area that was starkly split between rich and poor neighborhoods—what he described as a breeding ground for fascists. Before he had political analysis, in fact before he knew just about anything else, he knew that the existence of Nazis was abhorrent, and so his political career began there. He quickly found himself among the type of people who oriented their politics around fistfighting white supremacists: "We literally thought that's how you change the world—punching one Nazi at a time." He laughs, and takes a drag from his smoke. "Or maybe not, you know, but it was something."

Jay is now a career activist in the non-profit sector, with many self-critiques about it. He looks back on his time in antifascist actions as strategically misguided, but he also speaks of the feeling of those fights as having empowered him to the possibilities of direct action. And there were elements of those experiences that were educational, especially concerning the role of police: "Police are always on the side of the fascists," he said. It is one thing to hold political views that associate the police with the far-right, but confronting Nazis and seeing the police come to their defense viscerally illustrated for Jay the politics of the police. Aside from their institutional origins in slave patrols, police departments in the U.S. have long been infiltrated by overt white supremacists.[34] A recent media leak in Portland, OR, exposing police for directly collaborating with far-right forces during public fights with antifascists was shocking to those who are insulated from these realities but came as no surprise to many antifascists, who routinely observe the police taking the side of fascists in street confrontations.[35] But it goes deeper than individual fascist sympathizers and collaborators. For Jay, seeing Black police officers in riot gear defending the most vicious neo-Nazi groups from antifascists—"having the job of protecting people who would kill them in a dark alley if they had a chance"—specifically highlighted for Jay the role of the police force as an institution.

Jay still believes it's important that people shut down fascists in public wherever they show themselves, and says he wouldn't give up those experiences for anything, but he also grew to believe that his skills were better used in other areas of organizing. The shortcomings of the "punch-a-Nazi" strategy, for Jay, were not that punching Nazis is wrong, but that to him it didn't foster the growth of alternative political and community institutions he feels are most important for building power against systemic oppression, which is where he decided to spend his energy. Even so, when describing the feeling in moments approaching, during, and just following a fight, he smiles.

***

To Geo, it isn't about the black bloc itself—at the end of the day, that's just an aesthetic—it's about what you're doing when you're bloc-ed up. Geo is a tough-talking trans-masculine anarchist from a big city. Their family is from a Spanish-speaking island in the Caribbean, as are most people from the neighborhood where they grew up. They see themselves as continuing a long and powerful tradition of Latin American anarchists, and resent the association of anarchism in the U.S. with whiteness. At the same time, they also acknowledged that anarchist and punk scenes *are* largely white, and described struggling with implicit racism among comrades. However, the most important thing to them is having a crew that is down to fight the cops and "fuck shit up." As long as people are willing to listen and learn, Geo is comrades with anyone who wants to get free, and to them, a big part of that is being willing to riot.

When they have taken the street with their affinity group, they described the feeling as "awesome," "magical," and "beautiful." Geo has many negative feelings for cops based on personal experience, but when describing moments of physical confrontation they talk more about positive sensations and their love for their comrades than about animosity toward their adversaries. "You never really *feel* your crew like when you're fighting the cops. You have your differences and your conflicts, you know, but when you're together out there … it's a different kind of feeling.… It's beautiful." Their eyes wander to the distance as they speak about those moments in the streets, seemingly transported back to that feeling. So many people I spoke with used the word "beautiful" to describe the feeling of rioting. The consistent repetition of this word, which might otherwise seem incongruous in relationship to a riot, recalls the famous print from the May 1968 uprising in Paris featuring a woman at a barricade throwing a brick, along with the slogan: *La beauté est dans la rue*—beauty is in the street. The experience of rioting reveals the interconnectedness of resistance not just between individuals, but across time and space.

Speaking of beauty, whereas older anarchists I talked to tended to present the black bloc as primarily tactical, Geo, among the younger activists I spoke to, described it as an aesthetic first and an anti-surveillance tactic second. Another activist I interviewed called it "the Cool," and a number of people associated it with CrimethInc.'s slick and fashionable publications. Geo acknowledged the tactical usefulness of the bloc, and they certainly took security culture seriously (we are speaking in the woods without our phones present, and well out of cell phone reception just in case). In fact, being in a bloc had once helped someone very close to them directly evade capture by the police. Still, they had initially described it in terms of "a look." Older activists like Arjay and Zi admitted that they used to think the black bloc was a lot more effective before seeing news coverage of their riots, when they realized they could easily tell who was who among their friends.[36] Just as surveillance technology has advanced, anti-surveillance black bloc tactics have likewise developed over time, with experience, and can still be highly effective. Even in the high-profile felony riot trials of Disrupt J20 defendants, prosecutors using video evidence were unable to identify many individuals in the group. That Geo sees the black bloc as a style at least as much as a tactic may have more to do with increasingly conventional protest actions undertaken in black bloc gear.

In fact, approaching the black bloc as an aesthetic reveals a whole new range of social-psychological impacts—feeling tough, unified, formidable, and cool.[37] Geo talked about the look half-cynically, but also clearly adopted and liked it themself. Zi talked about the look too, saying that when she first encountered images of the black bloc, they looked "serious," "badass," and "cool," and described how wearing the outfit and mask, bloc-ed up with others, gave her a feeling of "oneness," "unity," and sense of "connection" with a crew that was aligned in the commitment to fight authority and looked the part together. Many anarchists I spoke to shared similar views. But Geo's comments in particular remind us that simply wearing tactical gear does not imply anything about tactical action. Many black bloc gatherings have ended up being no different in practice than your typical Sunday afternoon protest.

In fact, late in our interview, Zi would describe one of the last black bloc actions she participated in as being just as depressing as the pre-bloc marches that had driven her to seek out the tactic in the first place. In this instance, the bloc was blocking traffic in an intersection, but was spread out, not moving, and was not really disrupting anything. The police didn't seem to care either. As she describes it, with a combination of contempt and amusement on her face, "It didn't seem like we had to be wearing black." As it turned out, the black costumes were badass and cool not just aesthetically, but because of what they represented, because they were connected to a particular type of resistance.

***

Like the black bloc itself, burning barricades or throwing rocks at the police in some circumstances have tactical applications, but in most cases, these acts symbolize a fight in a deeper way than they directly engage in the fight. This is not to say that riots do not constitute a real fight, but rather that the real power of the riot lies in its political meaning more than the specific actions involved. Rock-throwing cannot defeat even moderately armed police in an unbridled confrontation of force, and dumpster fires are not terribly difficult to put out or move. Even major riots that escalate to widespread property destruction can be put down with the full application of deadly force that the police (and certainly the military) have at their disposal. The riot is not directly fighting authorities as much as it is asking questions of authorities and everyone watching.

The police make their own strategic and emotional calculations about their use of force, not the least of which is fear of riots spreading or developing into complete social breakdown. The fact that police do not immediately open fire with live ammunition on rioters, but instead tend to use personal shields, batons, and "less lethal" weapons like rubber bullets and tear gas, and in some instances do nothing at all, tells us that they worry about the ramifications of escalating the violence. The physical violence on both sides of the riot is therefore typically marked by the quality of restraint. But rioting symbolically represents the opposite of restraint, especially in a political context where nonviolent tactics are standard.

It is worth quoting Owe at length, as she connects the symbol of protest violence with strategy against the overwhelming violence of the U.S. state:

> We're in such a violent society, I think there needs to be people drawing attention to that in some way. And who knows, maybe there is a zone where property destruction, if done on a massive level, could it be effective if it was actually scaled up? I don't know, I'm not personally going to go down that route, but it's always a question of scale with tactics. If you think about economic boycotts in previous eras, where people say "I'm not spending money on this business in our neighborhood," what's the twenty-first century version of that? Where it's not just like how you spend your money—that doesn't do much anymore; corporations are so large, and finance capital is totally insulated,

so economic boycotts are less likely to have a real effect. So what could create a similar kind of sanction? That's part of the process of figuring out what our strategy might be. And setting things on fire certainly sends a message. And let's be honest, it's as good an idea as the next.

Here Owe is grappling with a central problem for those struggling for justice: nothing yet has worked. There have been victories, massive ones in some places and times. But on the balance of it, the world remains deeply violent, divided, and unjust, governed by a profit-driven economic super-system that is fast destroying the ecosystem on which all life depends, with those most vulnerable paying the price first. No strategy has been proven to hold the key, no matter how confidently it has been presented, so in a sense we are all grasping for answers. The riot is manifestly disruptive to the status quo and it sends the message that there exists resistance. In a professionalized protest sphere that seems more and more disconnected from actual political contention, rioting enables participants to access a feeling of being in the fight.

With respect to the scope of political violence, the riotous actions discussed by black bloc participants are so minimal they can barely be considered violent—in a few cases fistfights with fascists and throwing objects at police, but for the most part vandalizing public or corporate property. Indeed, some argue that property destruction is not in fact violence. But to say that breaking a window or incinerating a police vehicle is *not* violent would also be misleading; there is a palpable and undeniable difference between a protest in which property is physically attacked and one in which physical destruction is off limits. An action where people are throwing things and lighting things on fire *feels* different than one that enforces nonviolent discipline. But, as we have seen, the lines of the debate between violent and nonviolent tactics tends to be drawn toward the nonviolent extreme. The "violence" being discussed here, which is qualitatively different from actions in which property destruction is forbidden, is primarily symbolic. Widespread rebellions that destroy millions of dollars' worth of property can certainly levy serious material sanctions on a country's economy, but these are comparatively rare as riots go, and early participants do not know at the time how far their actions will spread. More reliable are the existential sanctions on a regime's legitimacy.

The destruction of public property as dissent is a physical acknowledgment of the deep consequences of structural violence through embodiment of the counter-violence required to forcefully resist from below. The feeling of violating the sanctity of private property and of police authority delivers for many a transcendent sensation that both clarifies political conflict and reduces the psychological-emotional barrier between our political reality and a vision of a liberated world. These forms of low-level violent resistance symbolize the fight—and one's position, and perhaps identity in it—in a way that can be deeply felt in the body. Amidst an atomizing and bureaucratic neoliberal system that is consistently and relentlessly disempowering, feeling the embodied power of collective resistance can be transformative.

It is not simply neoliberalism in some abstract sense that is disempowering, but also non-profits, organizations, and movement-training experts that are shaped by neoliberal constraints—what Owe referred to as "gaslighting by the entitled." Rioting takes place in reference to conventional protests underwritten by a non-profit industrial complex that popularizes the notion that change is made through their sponsorship and their talking points alone.[38] Em described how this elite-captured organizing can have deep impacts on a person's identity: "There are so many experiences of disempowerment. Including in movement organizing. I didn't personally feel like I had power in any of the political protests I saw and was part of... I think there are important parts of identity that are formed through experiences of power, either being repressed by power or having the opportunity to wield power."

The black bloc and similar formations are modes of action designed to counter the disempowerment of the system with the embodiment of fighting back, contributing to the formation of more empowered identities.

***

In the previous chapter, we saw that riots can lead to greater numbers of protests, in some cases leading to widespread rebellion, and we saw how they can function strategically within and alongside nonviolent resistance. In this chapter, we see how rioting has subjective impacts on participants in the moment, and also how those actions can play a nourishing role for radicals' will to resist. Movements ebb and flow, always facing overwhelming odds, and strategic questions are perpetually in play in a deeply unjust world. While we are debating strategy, setting things on fire as an expression of sheer resistance is, as Owe put it, "as good an idea as the next." In this way, in addition to having catalytic potential, images of riots can play a sustaining role for movements between uprisings and in times of abeyance, reminding us that the will to resist is there. The riot might not in and of itself transform broader society, but then again, no single tactic does. The riot can transform individuals and collectives, and it can send a message. The riotous moment imbues participants with a sense of empowerment and the visceral knowledge that they can resist, that society can be changed for the better.

6.

South African Fallists:
Decolonization and the Humanizing Riot

Confronting my rage, witnessing the way it moved me to grow and change, I understood intimately that it had the potential not only to destroy but also to construct.

—BELL HOOKS

When we examine the riot in terms of how the experience alters subjects, we must consider what forces have shaped our relationships to authority in the first place. Here we must talk about colonialism and decolonial struggle. Speaking with South African activists, whose interviews are presented in this chapter, it quickly becomes clear that their student movement was inseparable from the struggle to decolonize the country.

At least since the Haitian Revolution of 1791, revolutionaries have grappled with decolonization.[1] Imperialism is not merely military occupation; it is the violent imposition of an *order*—government, organization, logic, knowledge, and culture. Therefore, movements that seek to throw off imperial domination sooner or later face the elements of colonialism that run deeper than political office, affecting the ways we understand ourselves as subjects. The political language of decolonization as we know it comes from the twentieth-century liberation struggles of Africa, Asia, and the Americas, and in particular from Frantz Fanon—who, not coincidentally, also figures prominently in the discourse around violent resistance. Decolonization is about overthrowing colonial occupations *and* undoing colonial ways of thinking and being. In other words, decolonization is the process of disordering the colonial order, and re-ordering the world into something just. And, as Fanon put it in the opening sentence to his most famous work, *The Wretched of the Earth*, "decolonization is always a violent event."[2]

Fanon was a revolutionary and clinical psychotherapist from Martinique who, after studying in France and practicing in Algeria, joined the Algerian resistance against French occupation. Fanon's written work is largely about what it means to recognize, expose, and disrupt colonial regimes of state and mind that have been both aggressively beaten and more subtly socialized into people over generations through colonial relationships and institutions. To Fanon, it would not be enough—in fact, it would not be possible—to overthrow colonialism without destroying the colonizer living inside the mind of the colonized, which manifests itself through insecurities and inferiority complexes. In order to achieve the liberation of the mind, body, and nation, Fanon pointed toward the power of violent revolt. To Fanon, revolutionary violence is not instrumental in the vulgar material sense, but is also about colonized people embodying their full humanity by fighting back and winning on their own terms.

The concept of decolonization has to do with upending colonial regimes that outlast colonial governments, which brings up questions like what it takes to practice languages of knowing, communicating, and relating that can jettison the imposed colonial mindset. To writer and philosopher Ngũgĩ wa Thiong'o, the essence of decolonial practice is about decentering Western epistemologies, which is to say, moving away from European colonial ways of thinking and knowing, which have been forced on most of the world as other bodies of knowledge were erased.[3] Here, the university is a centerpiece of struggle.

In March 2015, a student activist at the University of Cape Town (UCT) threw human excrement on a statue of Cecil Rhodes. The statue was removed a month later after escalating protests, but until then it sat looking down at that campus, once part of Rhodes's personal estate, for well over a century. Rhodes was a British diamond magnate and an architect of European colonization, particularly in southern Africa, where he presided over the

Cape Colony in what is now South Africa, and helped to found the country of "Rhodesia," which was named for him and is now Zimbabwe. Student organizers in what would become known as the RhodesMustFall (RMF) movement (after their Twitter hashtag), vandalized and covered the statue, occupied an administrative building, and held public actions until the UCT management agreed to take it down.[4]

Beyond his personal profits, Rhodes was a true believer in British imperialism, and was a pioneer in colonial occupation, administration, and ideology. In 2015, students decided they had had enough of his statue at UCT, and took direct action. Anticolonial protests quickly spread across the country and beyond, including to Oxford University, home of the renowned Rhodes Scholarship, which is funded by Rhodes's fortune.[5] The action against the statue was the spark, but the movement was about much deeper issues, not least the institutional legacy of colonial education. And the legacy of colonialism in the South African educational system is not subtle: "The movement within the politics department was trying to demand Black lecturers, demand a course of African politics in the politics department, which wasn't there," a University of the Witwatersrand professor told me with a bitter laugh, before affirming my gaping mouth: "It's shocking, completely shocking."

Later in 2015, movements bearing the hashtags Outsourcing-MustFall (OMF), which focused on low-wage university workers who are outsourced from private companies, and FeesMustFall (FMF), which focused on university tuition, picked up the baton of decolonial struggle in South African universities, with the participants of all these movements coming to be known as Fallists. This chapter focuses on Fallist activists who participated in university uprisings in 2015–2016. My interviews mainly focus on participants in FMF, which arose in 2015 in response to proposed hikes to university tuition, with many also directly associated with OMF and RMF. The FMF movement temporarily blocked a national fee increase after disruptive and sometimes physically confrontational protests and campus occupations at universities across the country. When the government announced fee increases the following year, a second, smaller and more politically radical wave of protest challenged the hikes again, this time unsuccessfully. FMF was most prominently associated with the 2015 uprising at the University of the Witwatersrand (Wits) in Johannesburg, though many schools and campuses were home to uprisings, and it directly followed and overlapped with OMF campaigns.[6] Both FMF and OMF followed and overlapped with the RMF campaign, and all three struggles were intimately connected, each representing deeper, intertwined political goals focused on class, race, and gender inequalities, and the decolonization of higher education in South Africa. RMF in particular went global, with decolonization campaigns targeting colonial symbols, institutions, and curricula at universities around the world.[7]

The different Fallist campaigns highlighted different aspects of the struggle but all were understood by participants as inherently connected.[8] In the words of a Fallist interviewee from UCT: "FeesMustFall is an extension of RhodesMustFall because it was a direct progression from symbolic decolonization to material decolonization of the universities. Insourcing is about decolonization too. Because those workers travel from townships to work for some private company like they are still second-class citizens or even slaves, like this is not their country! They can't afford to send their kids to school on their wages, so even FMF is directly connected to the workers as well."

Beyond being interconnected, all of these campaigns were steeped in intersectional politics, unavoidably challenging the fallacy of the "single-issue" movement.[9] Fallist movements cannot be understood as anti-colonial without also understanding them as queer-feminist and anti-capitalist. Intra-movement tensions and conflicts along intersectional lines arose from the outset and were present throughout, and activist accounts do not shy from discussing the messiness and power of a radical movement working through internal anti-Blackness, misogyny, transphobia, and class contradictions.[10] Full discussion of South Africa's decolonial student movements are important, and many exist, as you can see by following the citations herein.[11] This chapter must be understood in this context, but the analysis here will go in a different direction, examining the affective experiences of participation in riotous actions.

Fanon shows up prominently in this chapter, not the least because student activists frequently cited him and his influence. Fanon's theory, therefore, precedes and seeds the movement, and provides a potent analytic framework for understanding it. This multi-level dynamic between theory and practice flows through these interviews. The experiences of student activists, many of whom are graduate students of the social sciences, often involved direct reference to political and social theory, as well as reflexive engagement with those theories.

Humanizing Violence and the Decolonial Riot

Similar to many of the stories that brought activists in the U.S. to black blocs, the disruptive tactics of the Fallist movements mobilized participants who had been disillusioned by conventional protest. One Wits student writes about hearing of a protest at the university gates, and wondering, "was this another one of [the elected student government's] frivolous ploys to seek attention from the university management?" However, upon discovering that students were forcibly barricading the gate to protest tuition hikes, he says: "without second invitation I joined the blockade."[12] The forcefulness of the protest imbued it with reality and made it viscerally worthwhile.

Domestic and international media focused on protests at Wits, a prestigious and historically white university, where students occupied and shut down campus in 2015.[13] From a campaign-oriented lens, which is to say, if we tried to understand FMF as an isolated and contained episode, we might say it was a student struggle over university fees, and in fact that is frequently how it was portrayed in international media. However, many other universities rose up as well, and from activists' perspectives the struggle was not limited to fees but was intertwined, from its inception, with the struggle for workers' rights, and beyond that the struggle to decolonize higher education and national politics.

Kay, El, and Tee were three Wits undergraduates who had all participated in FMF actions. I'm speaking with them on a grassy part of campus, on a brisk, beautiful day, interrupted more than occasionally as one of them exchanges a shouted greeting or congenial insult with a passerby. I had set up an interview with Kay at a coffee shop nearby, but when we met, he suggested sneaking me on campus instead, where we could talk with his friends in order to understand more perspectives, and I eagerly agreed.

Kay: Okay, we got the zero percent [rate increase] but that's it, and only for one year. FeesMustFall is about fees of course but it is also about deeper changes.

Ben: Do you think the government is capable of making the deeper changes FeesMustFall needs?

El: Yeah, they can. They have been around for a long time in the struggle and in the state. They have a lot of know-how about the system and how it really works. But they don't want to do it.

Tee: They're comfortable.

Kay: They're so comfortable! It's true.

Tee: It's like if I'm dating this girl, and after a while I know she won't leave me, I can just go days without showering, because I don't care even if I'm filthy. That's what the ANC [African National Congress] is like. [Laughter]

El: They're so comfortable, man.

Ben: So how do you get the changes you need?

Tee: You have to make them *uncomfortable*. And to make them uncomfortable, you have to compromise yourself.

El: He's telling the truth.

Ben: What do you mean?

Tee: You have to compromise yourself. You have to do things you don't want to do. You have to throw stones, even risk your life. That's what you have to do if you want to make these people in power feel uncomfortable. Then things might change.

El: There were problems and no one was listening. After FeesMustFall, now they're listening.

Kay [to El and Tee]: But do you think FeesMustFall was successful?

Tee: I think so.

El: No!

Kay: No, man. Because FeesMustFall won the zero percent, but it was only for one year! Can you imagine if they had said, "Okay, no apartheid from '94 to '95, then it will resume again"? That is not victory.

Tee: Yes, but now they are listening. That is why FeesMustFall must continue.

To these students, the goal was the removal of fee increases and related student interests, and at the same time the struggle was also about the legacy and present condition of the ruling ANC. The "zero percent" Kay referenced was the initial campaign's apparent victory; in December 2015, after months of escalation and amidst demonstrations and riots in Pretoria, then-president Zuma announced that there would be a "zero percent" increase in student fees for the upcoming year. Like many Fallists, this friend group was divided on the underlying goals and impact of the movement. While these students did not specify the "deeper changes" that they sought, they alluded in multiple ways to the connections between the ANC revolution against apartheid and their political moment.

Like many participants, these students characterize their movement as both a continuation of the struggle against apartheid and also as a movement targeting the protagonists of that prior struggle. In comparing FMF negatively to the anti-apartheid movement in terms of Fallists' failure to secure more lasting results, Kay describes the ANC as having been necessary and successful in the struggle of their time only moments after naming that same party as the enemy of the change he wants to see.

∗∗∗

For Cee, a student at UCT who participated in the Fallist movements, Fallism was a direct extension of the long process of decolonizing South Africa. He says, "Our parents did their thing, now we have to do ours." Unlike the three Wits students I had spoken

with on campus, Cee's demeanor is all business. He makes eye
contact when he speaks, and when we sit down, he wants to get
right to it, talk FMF and politics. "The ultimate goal is to create
a new society," he explains. "These struggles like FMF are about
winning changes that can bring more poor people to the universities and it is about making the universities for Africans. And
about creating a new movement culture that can do these things...
of course I respect the anti-apartheid movement; apartheid had
to end, and they ended it. And for a while there was euphoria
around that and for good reason. And people tested how much
they could change society in the new system, and they found that
there were big limitations, mainly capitalism. But some people
thought their job had been done and they left the movement to
the state. Now it is our turn."

The Fallist movements in many ways represent a congealing
of discontent from the left over ANC political stagnation, mis-
management, and corruption. While the 1990s in the U.S. had
represented a time of political torpor for Left social movements,
in South Africa that decade marked a time of radical possibility.
After the fall of apartheid and the election of Nelson Mandela, the
ANC government enjoyed great popular support, and, for a few
years, a honeymoon period when movements largely demobilized
and petitioned their concerns to the state from within the system.[14]

The consolidation of liberal democracy in this decade also
came with a turn toward a neoliberal economic program, and
the exacerbation of mounting social justice grievances. The mid-
2000s saw renewed escalations of both peaceful demonstrations
and unrest across the country, and in a sense the Fallist movements codified and articulated growing national discontent with
the path of the ANC revolution.[15] The repression that the state
and the universities brought down on Fallists through police
and private security, the latter often referred to by students as
"bouncers" as well as less polite monikers, makes unmistakable
the cleavages between movements on the one hand, and university management and the ANC on the other. While many student
activists discussed the ANC and their previous revolution with
nuance, understanding, and often esteem, authorities displayed

no such love for the activists. In addition to standard riot suppression techniques by the police—such as tear gas, rubber bullets, and imprisonment—private security routinely threatened, physically attacked, and sexually assaulted activists with impunity.[16]

While there was some disagreement in the FMF movement between those who emphasized the tangible need to remove fees and those who emphasized the cultural-political struggle to decolonize the university system, most activists I spoke with agreed that both were integral aspects of the movement. The larger political tension appeared between those who believed the ANC government could ultimately be pushed to continue the decolonial revolution they had started decades ago, or whether Fallism represented a new revolutionary movement to remove the ANC altogether and replace it with something new.[17] The latter position was referred to by multiple interviewees using the part-literal, part-figurative term, *burn it down*, as in, "the *burn it down* contingent did such and such." This tension was exacerbated by the resources and clout that ANC-backed student government officers wielded, at times organizing the movement, and according to some, at other times working to demobilize the movement from within.

The language and praxis of decolonization were common threads in both positions described above, but far more pronounced in the "burn it down" contingent. Decolonization in this context points to the colonial legacy of apartheid and European colonialism more generally, manifested in everything from stark and persistent racial wealth disparities, to faculty composition at universities like Wits and UCT, to Euro-centric curricula and material. In addition to South African revolutionaries who had advocated more radical paths during the anti-apartheid struggle—such as Black Consciousness Movement leader Steve Biko—Fanon's work made frequent appearances in interviews both explicitly and implicitly. As mentioned previously, Fanon is famously associated with his prescription of political violence for colonized people as a method to reclaim dignity and agency. At times activists would simply use his name to stand in for the argument that revolutionary violence is an essential aspect of struggle.

For Fanon, violent revolt against the oppressor is a necessary means for oppressed peoples to reclaim the dignity and
self-respect that it takes to create and govern liberated post-
colonial countries (a position that incidentally bears similarities to Gandhi's arguments for nonviolent refusal in the face of
oppression). Fanon has often been pigeon-holed into his advocacy for violence in ways that obscure other elements of his theory that are needed to properly understand the violence element.
As Arendt once put it, it is as though only the first chapter of *The
Wretched of the Earth*, titled, "On Violence," has been widely read.[18]
Beyond chapter one, Fanon discusses problems with excesses
or misdirection of violence, including the ways it can distort the
politics of a movement and lead to counter-revolution. Fanon's
approach to violence, or more specifically, the type and scope
of violence he prescribes, is meant as a radically democratizing
force, aimed not only at liberating a people from colonialism,
but also preventing "a new postcolonial elite from imposing a
regime of symbolic violence which might incorporate and pacify
the people."[19] A quarter-century on from a regime that succeeded
in some areas but is failing tremendously in others, Fallist references to Fanon speak directly to this type of nuanced revolutionary violence, or if you prefer, counter-violence.

Fallists represent the ambiguity of political struggle within
and against a post-colonial regime. This ambiguity is clearly visible in the space Fallists occupy with respect to the university
system. They target the colonial education structure, and advocate metaphorically and also in some cases literally for burning
it down, and yet they are students, their academic training as evident in their interviews as it is in the writing and analysis Fallists
have produced.[20] During the Wits campus occupation, students
held nightly study meetings—"Wits Protest Sociology," some
called it—where they would unpack and reflect on the activities
of the day. As one activist explained, "because at the end of the
day we are still students, and the academic project must continue."[21] An activist collective that produced an edited volume on
Fallist struggle describes the tension: "There is something about
a decolonial moment that requires incoherence. Or just perhaps

is incoherent. Conversely there is something about an intellectual tendency or perhaps just an academic one that seeks to impose order: coherence."[22]

Fallism grew from that space between the incoherence of decolonial revolution and the coherence of academic intellectualism trying to articulate revolution. And, unlike their predecessors in the anti-apartheid movements, Fallists were in an awkward position concerning their targets in the state as well—those who were in fact those same predecessors. The ANC does not represent sheer, unadulterated colonialism, racism, and oppression like the apartheid National Party government had, but rather something far more complicated. Lest today's revolutionaries be tempted back into thinking the revolution can be furthered from within the system as it stands, protester violence—fires, barricades, property damage, and scuffles with police and security—held the political struggle in a revolutionary space.

***

Many Fallists described riots in terms of the adrenalized experience in the moment. Emee, an activist at UCT who was associated with both the 2015 and 2016 waves of the movement, was involved in several fights with police and security, and became perceptibly animated when discussing those moments beyond strict nonviolent protest. In her words: "Fighting the police and security was a rush." Most of our discussion took the form of quiet talking, but sitting at an outdoor table at a trendy café in a bohemian area of Cape Town, she began raising her voice when discussing riotous moments as though forgetting we are in public: "You must understand, we were so *angry*! So when I was at the barricades and it was so big, it felt like history in the making." She is speaking even more rapidly: "Even when I was shot with a rubber bullet, I should have been afraid. It was like getting hit with a bat, I couldn't breathe, but it also gave me even more of an adrenaline rush."

Ess, a graduate student activist at University of Johannesburg (UJ), describes a protest in which she did not personally engage in violent actions, but where the presence of protester violence inspired a similar reflection as those who had. In this case, police had violently dispersed a student road blockade near campus, prompting some students to throw rocks at the police: "It gave me energy... It was necessary! We needed that. Because they're treating us like animals, like people without rights, like non-beings. And I think that when we throw stones, it's a way of reclaiming our humanity again. You know, to say we also have some form of agency in the fight... It gave me courage to see that."

For Ess, low-level violence against authority gave her energy and courage, and generated the empowering feeling of having "agency in the fight." Here, the act of throwing rocks counters feelings of dehumanization and affectively enhances the empowering experience of the crowd for a person who did not directly participate in the rock-throwing, indicating that the subjective power of the tactic extends beyond the individual actor to a group experience and collective identity. Ess uses "we" to refer to the stone-throwers even though she was not a stone-thrower on this occasion. Her identification with the action while not directly participating provides further evidence against canonical theories of crowd behavior, which hold that the rioting crowd typically imbues participants with a contagious and unrestrainable urge to violence. In fact, studies show that many participants in riots do not directly engage in violent actions, but here we see a positive affective experience from participation in the collective riot from an individual who does not herself engage in the described behavior.[23]

Ess and I are talking on a hot, sunny day, behind some buildings on one of UJ's campuses. She isn't old in years, but her manner resembles that of an esteemed speaker giving a plenary address—measured and weighty—in such a way that invites me to focus on her every word. Her voice is quiet, steady, and confident. She describes the feeling of empowerment in the face of repression in more detail, recalling a subsequent action. During a nighttime protest march that included parents and other community members, the police suddenly opened fire and dispersed the demonstration:

The police start firing rubber bullets at us.... People have
been shot in the back, they're lying there, and people are
hiding out, the cops are walking around with their guns ...
like a warzone. And it's so intense, and we are so broken. It
feels like there's no hope. So at that point a bus shelter was
burnt. And we all thought it was beautiful, to see the fire.
Because it's what Fanon mentions, it's kind of like a therapy
for us. We needed it in that moment. We needed the roads
to be blocked and we needed the stones.

At no point here does Ess discuss throwing stones or setting fires in terms of their tactical efficacy in beating back the
police, but rather describes these actions in terms of the feeling
and meaning derived from them. As symbols, these actions are
not just for participants either—their application can rouse students who were impartial or hesitant to join the struggle. But Ess
challenges the appropriateness of the word "violence" for these
actions, abruptly correcting herself midsentence, her voice con-
taining a frustration with the lack of better words for what she is
describing: "So there was also an attempt to use violence to—not
violence; it's termed violence, but certain actions or tactics, let's
put it that way—to be able to then trigger people, to wake them
up." The frustration does not come from a belief that actions
like rock-throwing are not physically confrontational, but rather
from that fact that the word violence for actions like rock-throwing obscures the systemic and structural violence that precedes
and necessitates them.

***

Ardee, an outsourced worker at Wits who was active in the OMF
campaign and was an ally to students in FMF, framed the word
"violence" in terms of who was ultimately to blame. To him, if the
students were responding to provocations from security, then
their actions were not violent even if they were not nonviolent,
because they would not have happened in the first place if they
had not been provoked. "They say the students are violent," he

tells me, leaning in with shoulders squared, the air of a man about to set the record straight. "But I can confess that was not true. Because I was involved in those things, I was always with the students. What we have is that the university just decided to bring outside securities and the police, and those people kept on provoking the students." He goes on to discuss confrontations that frequently escalated around a large concourse in a centrally located campus building.[24]

> For example, at Wits, the place the students want to go when there are actions or big meetings, they use that concourse. So, if you block the way of the students to go there, surely there will be a fight. Because whatever they do, they make sure they have to reach that point. It's what they do. If you don't need violence, don't stop them from going there! Because if they go there they don't do anything wrong. They don't have any violence. They just go there and sit and relax and talk about whatever they need to talk about. What will happen if you block the entrance for the students? You know what will happen. They can't just say, "No, the entrance is blocked, we will go out." No! They can't. They'll keep on saying, "We need to go in there!" So, when the students were trying to push hard to come in there, the securities decided to push the students out. So then the students tried to force in. So that's how the problem got started. So, if you block the entrance of the students, what do you expect? So, in fact I can say for me, I think they were provoking the students.

All this in response to a question about his experience in actions that became violent. He initially took my question in a defensive posture, the assumption being that violent actions are negative. But in his response, we also see that the baseline understanding of violence is not tethered to the action itself, but to its cause. When it is framed that way, it sounds like common sense. It is normalized to assume that whatever police or security forces do is legitimate, and that protesters must always react with deference—that no matter what authorities are doing, we should judge what activists do on their own terms, as though they are not happening in relationship to repression. In this case, the violence would be easy to frame as the students' fault for escalating when security closed Solomon Mahlangu House. Instead, Ardee sees it as security escalating by unnecessarily closing the building in the first place; student reactions to that unjustifiable denial of access then become justifiable. In this view, to paraphrase Sartre from the preface to *The Wretched of the Earth*, protester violence is just police violence on the rebound.

✳✳✳

A Wits undergraduate student, Abee, uses the terms, "big violence" and "little violence" to describe the difference between structural, epistemic violence on one hand and violent protest tactics in response on the other. This solution is a sort of rhetorical compromise, prioritizing the understanding that structural violence is the real problem while also acknowledging that throwing rocks is technically violent. Others insist on the altogether incomparability of protester "violence" to systemic violence, and therefore do not accept the same singular word for both, a position summed up by Fallist activist Moshibudi Motimele, who writes: "Violence has nothing to do with throwing stones."[25]

One way or another, Fallists frequently challenge the term "violence" when discussing protester actions, typically re-framing in terms of the systemic violence that the protests were fighting back against. Others—sometimes at the very same time as they critique the use of words like "violence" and "riots" to describe protests—argue for reclaiming these terms as well. For example, explaining the title of a Fallist-written book on the struggle, *Rioting and Writing*, a contributor and member of the editorial collective had this to say: "The word 'rioting' was a way of responding to the dominant narrative, which was that the students were just hooligans rioting. So, we're saying yes, we are rioting, but we're also writing, documenting our struggle. It is expropriating the term."[26] The tension between descriptors for movement actions and hegemonic political rhetoric is present throughout activists' accounts.

Returning to Ess's description of using forceful tactics intentionally to raise consciousness among students who have not yet taken a side in the university struggle, we can recall again Sorel's prescription of strategic violence to shake the apathetic class out of complacency and force them to take a side in the revolution. And, as in the black bloc case, Ess's remarks invert Sorel, speaking to violent tactics being applied to rouse the agnostic or meek student constituencies to action on her side.[27] Fallist activists speak of low-level violence in many of the ways that nonviolentists speak of nonviolent direct action—as building confidence and empowerment, mobilizing supporters to their side, and provoking retaliation that exposes the realities of the system they are fighting. Again, however, the type of "violence" being applied is extraordinarily minimal, pointing us back to the difficulty inherent in the language of violence versus nonviolence, which is especially challenging when trying to make meaning of actions that appear to straddle the line between the two, and most of all for participants who reject both terms.

Feeling defeated in the face of repressive police violence, Fallists describe a physically assertive response as therapeutic and rejuvenating in a way that a nonviolent response lacked the capability to be in the moment. Protester violence here does not reflect the "quest for political meaning" that Seferiades and Johnston propose, but rather the *production and communication of political meaning*—perhaps to opponents and onlookers, but most of all *to participants themselves*.[28]

Political sociologist Karl von Holdt and coauthors suggest that the ordinary deployment of low-level violent tactics in South African protest repertoires, most commonly in the form of stone-throwing and burning street barricades, functions primarily as a signal to authorities to take grievances seriously—a phenomenon they term, "the smoke that calls."[29] In my discussions with Fallists, participants discuss "burning it down" as signaling, but more as signaling to protesters themselves and potential allies than to the state. The difference relates to an underlying, perhaps at times unconscious ideological difference between reformism and revolutionary politics. While it is tempting to view riots as inherently radical due to their deployment of violent means, if their manifest objective is to bring about increased state attention to a social problem so that the state (or capital) will pay attention and solve that problem, then the underlying theory of change is fundamentally reformist, despite the direct action tactics. In this view, the problems justifying the riot can theoretically be solved by the authorities, who perhaps need a fire lit under them to get it done.

*✳✳

On my most recent trip to Johannesburg, I was staying with a friend of a friend. I had never met my host in person, but we had connected online, having been mutually vouched for by a comrade. I arrived at his home after a grueling thirty-something hour trip to discover that the water in the whole neighborhood had been shut off. It was not due to a breakage or construction or a public health concern, but in the opinion of my host and many of his neighbors, it was due to corruption—someone had not paid someone else off, and the water shut-off was the result. Days went by, and residents grew more and more agitated. Observing people piling loose bricks on sidewalks, I was told that the neighborhood was openly planning to riot—there were even ultimatums Tweeted at the mayor. My host, as angry as the rest, told me bluntly: "You know, we're going out there," letting me know that sitting the riot out would not be an option. As the ultimatum approached and I weighed, on various hands, the potential to so quickly experience first hand the type of action I was in-country to research, with how I would explain this "participant observation" to my dissertation committee, with my desire for a shower, the water service was suddenly restored. This almost-riot, the threat of civil unrest to leverage the city government into sorting out the service disruption, is an example of what we might call a reformist riot.

When the violence of the riot is directed against the forces of the state (and capital) in order to clear momentary space in which to exist outside its control, or to signal to rioters and allies that there exists resistance to domination, then the riot has a revolutionary character. The reformist riot then still bears more radical potential, since the act of rebelling itself easily leads from one to the other. It is this type of riot that Alain Badiou theorizes has at its far horizon the commune, as in the Paris Commune.[30] For some, the smoke of a riot may be meant to call authorities' attention to the site of protest in order to address a grievance; for others, this smoke is meant to call participants to their side of the barricades in order to ultimately, if not immediately, solve the problem themselves. Both elements appear among Fallist activists, and in fact this ambiguous relationship to regime and repertoire appears to be a primary characteristic of that movement.

One particularly notable instance of such a radical deployment of violence aimed at ally rather than opponent was when radicals raided a student government election site and destroyed the ballots. As Bede, a graduate student activist at UJ, told it:

> Management was very worried that this Wits thing [the FMF campus occupation] would spread. Of course, some of us were working very hard to make it spread, but without any success because the main student organizations were caught up in the Student Representative Council (SRC) elections at that time. They were kind of like, "No, we've got to do this first." And nobody was brave enough to risk the elections, because if only one group pulls out, then their opponents would win, so no one was really brave enough to give up the elections in favor of trying to win the struggle. They were all at that stage too tied up in getting power through getting onto the SRC, which at UJ is quite in with the management. So, this is a theme of the FeesMustFall experience at UJ, the kind of way management tried to manipulate student organizations and how it failed at some point when, finally, some students disrupted the elections... just went and tore down the tent where the ballots were and threw all the ballot boxes around and tore them up. And at that point one group, the independent ticket if you like,

abandoned the elections. They were abandoned already, you understand, but at least at that point they said it. Then we could focus on the struggle, because at that point Wits was already escalating.

Bede saw the elections as a waste of energy when the focus ought to have been more militant actions. She also refers to the *de facto* reality of everyone already knowing that the elections were irrelevant. However, it took someone materially destroying the ballots to disrupt the focus on the electoral process. Ess had described that disruption in a similar way, since even if they did not agree with that particular direct action itself, many students knew that SRC elections were somehow manipulated by management. "The university seems to have its way of getting its own people in there," she explained. And, in the frustration Bede expressed about the wasted energy of trying to win elections, which themselves do not produce more people power, this action perhaps contained a larger metaphor for discontent with the parameters of electoral democracy in South Africa, and with liberal democracy in general. (The attitude described here fundamentally relates to the U.S. as well, where national elections become the focus of political struggle contained within the most limited parameters, on which society has been teetering between cynical liberalism and fascism.)

Anyway, it is not uncommon for "democratic" governing officials and movements to consider each other illegitimate.[31] Here, the complex dynamic between Fallist movements and university SRCs—antagonistic in some ways and in other ways allied—is imbedded within a movement that overall contains similar dynamics *vis-à-vis* the state. The ANC government, which had been victorious in a contest sealed by the poster victory of electoral democracy in modern history, had come to represent the calcification of that very system, in this case represented by funding student leaders to cool the revolutionary politics of the movement.

***

For those who spoke affirmatively of violence, or forceful tactics that get called violent, many cited Fanon's discussion of the importance of violence by the colonized against the colonizer. However, when I spoke to white South African activists—some descendants of colonizers—several reported a similar subjective reaction to throwing stones. Abee, a white student activist at Wits, described how he typically refrained from throwing rocks himself due to "race and gender issues," by which he meant it would have been frowned upon by comrades because of his race and gender. He would, however, try to support "as a body" by positioning himself as a human shield between rock-throwers and police lines. During the interview, he generally described throwing rocks as "an important emotional release" for Black students in many of the same terms as the Black students I spoke with—that "it reclaims dignity that you are fighting"—indicating that this collective understanding is common in activist scenes. However, Abee describes one occasion during when he *did* engage in rock-throwing:

> It was after a long march around campus when we went to meet at Solomon House, and security blocked the doors and beat us away from the steps. We were tired, hot, and just wanted to meet and relax and talk together in our place.[32] And they blocked us for no reason. We just wanted to meet, you know, and the university was closed, so it wasn't getting in anyone's way. So that was one time I picked up rocks and threw them with everyone... It was an emotional release and it was a way of registering that they are doing something we don't accept. For them and also for ourselves. It didn't get us into Solomon House that day, but the goal also shifted. When something happens that isn't right, you have to show your discontent, you have to *show* them, and, you know, show yourself that you are not okay with this. Rock-throwing does a great job of registering your discontent.

Abee describes the direct motivation for throwing rocks here as frustration, which broke through the physical and legal risks associated with violent protest and, in this case, also his otherwise questionable eligibility to participate. He went on to paraphrase a sentiment that resonated with him, which had been related by a Palestinian comrade of his who had studied in South Africa. Speaking about throwing rocks at Israeli tanks at home, the friend had said: "We know it's not likely to hurt anyone, but all the hurt, pain, frustration, anger, you have to release it somehow. And sometimes yelling isn't good enough. Rock-throwing humanizes you in the face of a dehumanizing situation." Here Abee draws from the experience of a comrade from a colonized society in making meaning of rock-throwing, but nevertheless he also describes a similar feeling when he engaged in that action himself.

In the preface to *The Wretched of the Earth*, French philosopher Jean-Paul Sartre makes it clear he believes colonial Europe needs to reckon with decolonization as much as, though in a different way than, colonized Africa. Fanon himself discusses particular insecurity complexes developed by colonizer and colonized alike, complexes that must be overcome through action if a just future involving people from both groups is possible. In this case, however, the experience of a white protester in South Africa throwing rocks with Black comrades at Black security guards is especially noteworthy. Without knowing precisely what was going through his head at that moment, Abee's sensory reaction of catharsis as an aggrieved party substantially aligns with experiences of Black protesters engaged in the same action. This does not contradict the acute and particular importance of anti-colonial violence for historically oppressed peoples, but it does indicate that the collective engagement in violent protest against repressive authority to an extent contains its own experiential power dynamics.

Fallists of all backgrounds whom I interviewed from Wits, UJ, and UCT were aware of their universities' proximity to whiteness, including the differences between these universities and the ways those perceived differences impacted their mobilizations. UJ students framed Wits as the more prestigious university— which is intertwined with whiteness—in a way that was significant in their conditions of struggle. For example, Ess explained the difference between the two university spaces with a story: "We were trying to create another space apart from SRC and calling for an assembly. That was one of our major demands. And the vice chancellor said"—she straightens her shoulders and puts on a mockingly gruff, masculine voice, bobbing her head side-to-side as she impersonates the vice chancellor—"'This is not Wits, there will be no assembly!' So, it was very clear." She chuckles momentarily at her imitation, and then the humor disappears. "But you see, that's also profound to say, 'This is not Wits.' So, he recognizes that this space is a different kind of space, meant for a different kind of people."

Wits students were acutely aware of their university's prestige both in terms of capital and historical association with white colonial power structures. However, Wits, UJ, and UCT all stand apart from technical colleges and historically Black educational institutions. FMF at Wits drew media attention because of that institution's prestige, just as RMF at UCT had. But according to students, protests over fee increases had long originated in the technical colleges, specifically Tshwane University of Technology (TUT). Activists from TUT and elsewhere regularly protest and riot over fee increases with little or no media attention. In FMF, most of these students were boxed out of international and even many domestic narratives, and were even largely excluded from the organizing itself. For example, activists describe coordinating across campuses using SMS message groups (text groups). In South Africa, as in most places, phone plans are pay-as-you-go, and messaging costs money. Poorer students from poorer institutions without networked access to wealth were unable to participate for long. Even in the case of a thoroughly intersectional decolonial struggle, class and social capital continued to play significant material roles in whose stories were elevated.

***

The actions of TUT students appear prominently in the accounts from students at other schools. Aye, a student from Wits, who was a high-ranking member of the SRC during the FMF uprising, recounts the evolution of a distinctly contentious relationship between Wits and TUT activists. "When we occupied, the VC [Vice Chancellor] at Wits didn't call the police at first. I guess he was afraid of escalation and how it would look for him. At TUT the police come right away. It is a pattern. The students are more radical as a consequence." The police response at TUT is another reflection of the legacy of colonialism, and, according to Aye, it contributes to radicalizing the students, who have become used to fighting police in their campus spaces. TUT students protesting and being repressed was a pattern, but when Wits rose up, that drew attention. Bede explained it this way: "TUT and other colleges have won small things through their annual protests— lower fees, registration with debt, and that. The university system was on a collision course with students, but the state, media, and even South African society didn't care until it exploded at prestigious and historically white universities."

Students from poorer institutions who had been at it for years were understandably frustrated with the "Cinderella" students at Wits and UCT who received attention the moment they rose up—at least that is how some students I spoke with framed it. At the climactic 2015 protest in Pretoria, when then-president Zuma announced the zero percent fee increase, students from Wits and TUT were both present, and the groups reacted differently to the news of their apparent campaign success. When the fee reversal was announced, Wits students declared victory and moved to depart the rally, but TUT students intervened, in one instance even setting vehicles on fire to prevent Wits activists from leaving. As a non-student activist who was present that day put it to me, with a laugh, "The TUT students were like, 'Okay Wits kids, you wanted to be part of this, now we're here, let's do this.'"

TUT students directed arson attacks at more privileged students in precisely the way Ess had described using property destruction at UJ—to forcefully encourage would-be-allies to stand with them. I was unable to speak with activists from TUT— one of the most significant limitations of this study—but I did get a description from the other side of that dynamic. Aye was in one of the vehicles that was set on fire. Not surprisingly, she did not appreciate it.

Aye had told me to meet her at an espresso joint that turned out to be in a mall so pristine and shiny I felt like I was in a science fiction movie. We sat at a small table in a roped-off area of tables designating the seating as only for that café. It felt like we were outside due to the massively high ceiling of the mall. As well as her displeasure about nearly being set on fire, Aye had a number of negative things to say about the "rock-throwing brigade," including that the people who escalated to violence were usually drunk and were enacting toxic masculinity. Aye was the only activist I interviewed in South Africa who used nonviolence framing around protests in the way I'm used to in the U.S.—rioters are macho hooligans, not organizers; they invite repression; they turn off popular support; and so forth. This indicates that this rhetoric is alive and relevant in the South African context as well. Whether it was a coincidence that she had been an ANC-backed SRC member and mentioned that she was considering a career in formal politics, I cannot say.

Aye's disposition toward rock-throwers does not imply she was not committed to the struggle—as she saw it, it was just the opposite. She had organized with the student movement for years and took organizing strategy seriously. She had been shot with rubber bullets on multiple occasions, including at point blank range, and had spent time in the hospital for it. While her framing was one of strategic nonviolence, Aye's view of what constituted nonviolence was not as strict as the typical U.S. version. For example, Aye proudly described the discipline and planning that had gone into shutting down Wits's campus, including the crucial work of the "night brigade" who would jam small objects in the door locks of lecture halls overnight and engage in other vandalism to forcefully prevent the school from functioning.

Aye spent most of our interview speaking to the importance of strategic nonviolence, but after a tirade against rock-throwers, she paused for a long moment, and amazingly, finally blurted out: "Okay, maybe I even picked up a rock once or twice—but it was because I was angry!" This acknowledgment first of all demonstrates the comparative familiarity of rock-throwing in South African protest repertoires. But, more importantly, Aye's comments in opposition to the "rock-throwers" were not entirely from an outside perspective. After this comment, she began discussing those who engaged in violent actions with more empathy, now qualifying her earlier blanket statement that the rock-throwing brigade comprised a bunch of drunk hooligans: "I mean, people know how police will respond, yeah? So they show up drunk to deal with the fear and the pain." She paused again, sighed, and shook her head, then murmured, almost to herself: "It's amazing how police influence the direction protests take." Aye went on to explain that protests never began with any violence on the part of activists, but once security would attack, people would hit back out of frustration and rage. This was overall one of the most common dynamics relayed to me, and is consistent with experience and research that shows police violence to be a primary trigger of urban uprisings around the world. In any case, the car fires did not get Aye to join the riot the day the zero percent was announced, but it also did not *de*mobilize her, and she was active during the following year's wave of FMF protests.

* * *

If decolonization requires incoherence, and academic research requires coherence, then academic research about decolonization has a problem. A ones-and-zeros analysis for which types of actions are more successful than others has little chance of capturing the most important aspects of this type of civil resistance. Like the previous one, this chapter presents interviews that speak to a number of issues and topics that cannot be wrapped into a neat theoretical package. Some of the clearest take-aways are apparently contradictory. For example, physically confrontational protests are important for decolonization movements, but such actions usually take place only as a reaction to repressive violence by security forces. And a number of activists quoted Fanon in defense of violent resistance in nearly the same breath as they rejected the term "violence" for acts of resistance. I do not attempt to impose coherence in an effort to theoretically reconcile these positions. Instead, I aim to bring out some of the powerful and nuanced aspects of rioting in movements through the experiences of participants in contribution to a larger understanding of the dynamics of contentious resistance. A little theoretical coherence, however, does not require much imposition.

How does one distinguish contemporary revolutionary politics from dusty revolutionary rhetoric in a society that is a quarter-century removed from a democratic movement that toppled a fascist regime, living in a stalled revolution amidst conditions of racial inequality and colonial institutions that remain shockingly unaltered? One method is by declaring "burn it down," and doing it often enough to animate that slogan with reality. The "violence" of the riot, again, is most impactful in its implications, not its immediate material results.

So-called violent protest acts themselves—that is, setting fires, destroying property, and throwing stones—as well as the spaces they take place in, come with particular subjective experiences for participants. For many, the limited application of forceful and physically confrontational action was therapeutic and humanizing in the face of dehumanizing and disempowering police repression. Many activists pushed back against the characterization of rock-throwing and even arson as "violent" based on political and social positionality, but again, there is something viscerally different about protest spaces that are open to these types of actions and those in which protesters enforce nonviolent discipline.

In his study of Southern U.S. farmers' movements, sociologist Michael Schwartz distinguishes between *institutional* power, which relies on state or on institutional authority, and *noninstitutional* power, or people power.[33] In the introduction, I used this framework to distinguish between the institutional violence of police brutality and pogroms, and the anti-institutional violence of riots and street rebellion. Likewise, we might follow Fanon's theory and Fallists' accounts and distinguish between *dehumanizing* violence, enacted by authorities in defense of oppressive institutions, and the *humanizing* violence of resistance. Here, dehumanizing violence relies on institutional power and ultimately on the state, while humanizing violence relies on anti-institutional power.[34] Humanizing violence is distinguished by its primarily symbolic quality; in other words, the fight involves real violence and people *can* get hurt, but partisans are not necessarily aiming to physically hurt or kill an opponent. At a deeper level they are trying to register appropriately embodied opposition to dehumanizing violence. Humanizing violence reminds people that they are agents in a fight against the forces of domination— reminds activists that they are indeed *active*—and through this, in some circumstances, reveals a vision of a future world in which the fight would not be necessary.

For Fanon, decolonization is about remaking oneself and one's people through struggle, and violence is a crucial component. Violence here is not ultimately a tool to achieve a concrete goal, but the experience of physically fighting back against colonial forces is what Fanon argues is a necessary experience for the colonized person to become a liberated subject—a transformation that itself is necessary for long-term change. Some have attempted to interpret physical violence out of Fanon's account. For example, Barbara Deming argued that when assessing Fanon's work, references to "violence" could simply be replaced with nonviolent "radical and uncompromising action."[35] Indeed, the actions described by participants in this study are minimal with respect to a spectrum of political violence, and are entirely civilian based, incomparable to the scale or strategic organization of violence in armed warfare. But the collective willingness to engage in actions that physically destroy property and physically resist security forces are both materially and subjectively different from those that promise nonviolence.

The symbolic qualities of riotous resistance do not exist in opposition to the materiality of those actions, but in fact are precisely due to the measure of physicality involved. Vandalizing a statue is about getting rid of the statue, yes, but it is really about bringing to the surface the suppressed histories of injustice that forged today's institutions. Burning student election ballots might forestall the election, but at a deeper level it is about acknowledging that the elections are not representative of collective decision making. Throwing stones at security forces might be an impulsive reaction of immediate outrage, but under the surface it is about rejecting imposed power dynamics and the structures they uphold.

The most dehumanizing social conditions are those in which there is no visible rage in response to systemic violence.[36] Collectively registering resistance in a way that is viscerally understood by all is an insistence on our shared humanity. And that humanity demands the material struggle for justice. Activists I spoke to did not report getting the same kind of heightened sensations of exhilaration, catharsis, and empowerment from avowedly nonviolent action. Again, that is not to say nonviolent actions are not important or cannot be tactically effective, or even that they cannot contain their own kind of effervescent atmosphere. But the experiential effects of collective actions that physically confront property and police point toward a distinct semiotic and communicative power of riotous resistance. When people feel powerless in the face of gross historical injustice and overwhelming systemic violence, and where conventional protest strays into performativity and ineffectualness, riots keep hearts and minds squarely in the realm of resistance.

7.

A Revolution Is Not a Peaceful Protest

"I remember when someone threw a Molotov cocktail, I thought, 'My god, the revolution is here. The revolution is finally here!'"
—SYLVIA RIVERA

One night during my research in South Africa, I found myself at the house party of a well-connected activist in Johannesburg. The friend who had extended the invitation thoughtfully introduced me to a group of Wits graduate students, letting them know I was a U.S.-based sociologist studying riots, then after a time left me to schmooze. At some point in the conversation, one of them remarked that, "The line between violence and nonviolence is precisely the place where politics happens." I listened intently, asked her permission to use that quote, then stole away to the bathroom at the earliest polite convenience to record it verbatim. What an elegant introduction, I thought, to the idea that the language of violence and nonviolence is really about power. To most people, violence is wrong, so the ability to designate which actions are violent is really about the doing of power, or in other words, politics. The following morning, when my friend asked me if I had enjoyed the party and made good contacts for my research, I enthusiastically relayed that quote. She rolled her eyes and told me that hearing that line had been the reason she'd walked away from the conversation, adding, "That is the kind of meaningless bullshit that makes academics impossible to talk to."

Sometimes it feels like the best sociologists can do is to articulate in academic terms that which most people already know.

Unfortunately, this can still be necessary in service of undoing the damage that misleading theories have done to people's common sense. In the final analysis, much of this book points out the obvious: riots happen; riots are part of uprisings from below; riots can be empowering for rioters; riots send a message to onlookers and authorities about the seriousness of resistance; riots can spark broader rebellion. But if these statements feel self-evident, it is not for lack of opinions to the contrary.

When I initially wrote this conclusion, the U.S. was embroiled in another popular uprising over the racist brutality of the police and the persistent politics of white supremacy that pervade our society. The outpouring of rage was sparked by the deaths of George Floyd and Breonna Taylor—two horrifying examples of Black people callously murdered by police. In one case, an officer casually kneeling on a person who posed no threat for almost nine full minutes until he died; in the other, a woman shot to death in her home in the middle of the night by police supposedly looking for someone else entirely. Communities erupted in defiance of the agents of the state who committed these murders and so many others in this country's histories of racist atrocity and genocide. But even in that moment, media, talking heads, and activists were tied in knots over what to do about someone spray-painting a building during a protest, breaking a window, throwing a brick.

After several police cruisers were burned in a local protest that summer, Bill Peduto, then the mayor of Pittsburgh—the city where I wrote most of this book—re-Tweeted a statement by a prominent local activist organization implying that the arson had been the work of an outside agitator, who was white, in an act that unnecessarily put Black bodies at risk.[1] Peduto attached his own message to the organization's, promising to arrest the agitator who had ruined an otherwise legitimate and peaceful protest. The rhetorical maneuver allowed the mayor to appear the ally of the racial justice movement as he moved to solve its problems by deploying the very same police institution that was being protested. While a white activist did apparently use spray paint and allegedly started a vehicle fire, there were many people attacking the unoccupied police cars in question, most of them young Black activists. In other words, the initial Tweet was not describing what happened as much as it was describing a story in which legitimate protests are nonviolent, and violent actions are the work of outsiders.

It was certainly not the organization's intention to arm the mayor with justification for further police repression against protesters, and they made as much very clear, but the stories we tell about protest actions have consequences. Days later, after a subsequent demonstration in which police once again attacked protesters, the same mayor initially denied that officers had deployed tear gas despite overwhelming evidence to the contrary. When the denial became untenable, the mayor doubled back to the narrative that a small, outside contingent had become violent, prompting the police response.[2] Once the "outside agitator" story was out there, it was all too easy for authorities to redeploy it. In one analysis, this confusion derives from organized movements' discomfort with the justified reality that people are hurting, people are furious, and they need the world to know it. Still, the activists who insist on nonviolent discipline are not wrong in their belief that protester violence will likely bring down even more police violence disproportionately targeting the most marginalized and vulnerable. One of the reasons that the violence-vs.-nonviolence argument around riots is intractable is that in many ways both sides are right.

Even now, most of us do not know what to do with riots. What is clear is that riots happen, they happen as part of popular uprisings against oppression and domination, and they are symbolically important events. Perhaps we should not have needed proof of this, but for those who did want empirical evidence, this book provides it. For as long as movements have been studied, people outraged by injustice have been gathering in public to break things and set things on fire, and people are going to continue to do so. Whether or not we like it, whether or not we would include them if we got to script the revolution from behind the scenes, riots will not be organized out of the real-life movement repertoire. That is not because riots are metaphysically inevitable, but because the kinds of resistance that get called riot-ing mean something important to people.

Putting rioting on a pedestal above all over forms of col-lective action, as though it is the sole key to bringing down all oppressive institutions, would be just as distorted as claiming rebellions must remain completely nonviolent to affect positive change. Likewise, as futile as it would be to try and erase riots from resistance, endeavoring to foment them everywhere and all the time is surely a path to despair. Insurrectionary theories that highlight the propaganda value of rioting get something right, but rioting alone cannot transform society any more than strategic nonviolence can. Understanding how street rebellion fuels and enables social change requires incorporating riotous moments and practices into actionable theories of movement building, leverage, and power.

Riots are an ongoing feature of resistance from below, their effects conflicted and potent, and in this sense the discourse around violence *is* a place where politics happens. If sociological analysis can be useful here, it must help us understand the numer-ous ways people resist and rebel, and that requires reckoning with political actions that span the constructed line between "vio-lent" and "nonviolent." We must integrate recurring moments of unarmed collective violence—or, more precisely, moments that are not decidedly nonviolent—into our frameworks for under-standing civil resistance where dominant tendencies have tried to insulate us from this kind of disorder. Academic bullshit notwith-standing, this is an area where I believe that grounded research can help us better orient ourselves and take action together for justice and liberation.

Riotous Resistance: An Analysis

How do people change society from below? And by "from below," I mean from a collective position without access to high-level decision making about the conditions that affect our lives. I mean those who are marginalized, disenfranchised, incarcerated, forgotten, and I mean people who hustle for a better life only to make profits for employers. In most societies, that is most people. Elections are the main legitimized form of civil participation in which regular people are supposed to be able to select political leaders and hold them accountable, thereby having a say in how society is run. But even in states that allow people to vote, the options are largely selected for us, and election processes, even when comprehensible, accessible, and reliable, are manipulated and gerrymandered. When the process works to the letter of the law, government decision making is still far more beholden to elites and their interests than to voters.[3] Put simply, voters cast ballots; we don't *decide* anything. Without a real seat at the decision-making table, regular people need leverage to create change on the scale that is needed. That is where movements come in.

Organizing movements is one thing; ridding ourselves of the state of mind that keeps us tethered to the status quo is another. In theory, movements and radical politicians can mutually reinforce each other's power to agitate for a more just society. But more often than not, the needs and priorities of elected representatives and the funders, contractors, consultants, and non-profits that surround them, overwhelm and drown out the will for self-organization and direct action. There remains a tension over who the protagonist of struggle is—the people or our representatives in the State. *Stepping beyond the boundary of nonviolent discipline marks the will toward a decisive break with the current system.* In this mode, civilian mobilizations can become powerful weapons of political conflict. Some uprisings spark and catch fire so quickly they can topple seemingly stable regimes in a matter of weeks. For others, uprisings will ebb and flow for generations, rocking the state back and forth before the real push. Governments around the world know well that mass mobilizations from within are the state's Achilles' heel. State leaders who had forgotten this certainly remembered after the uprisings of 2011. That is leverage.

Those who advocate for strategic nonviolent uprisings imagine a revolt in which huge numbers of people peaceably refuse to participate in the goings on of everyday life, bringing society to a standstill and authorities to their knees without lifting a hand against anyone. The authorities will be violent, they say, but this violence only unites society against their oppressors, as the sight of police harming peaceful protesters horrifies conscientious onlookers. More and more people turn away from the government and toward the movement, and more and more regime officials defect until victory is ours. Advocates for nonviolence often speak as though they have found the video game cheat code to politics, the loophole that would enable masses of people to build power by breaking just the right number of rules, no more and no less, such that our moves advance our position and authorities' moves backfire. It is an attractive story, but it has little to do with the dynamics of real-world struggle.

When someone tells the story of strategic nonviolent rebellion, we must ask: Are they really concerned with reality? After all, the presence of riots, sabotage, community defense, and other forms of physical confrontation in just about every "primarily nonviolent" struggle is clear for anyone to see. Why ignore these events in resistance narratives? In the book, *On Bullshit*, philosopher Harry Frankfurt asks us to consider "a Fourth of July orator, who goes on bombastically about 'our great and blessed country, whose Founding Fathers under divine guidance created a new beginning for mankind.'"[4] As Frankfurt points out, "This is surely humbug… the orator does not really care what his audience thinks about the Founding Fathers, or about the role of deity in our country's history, or the like." At the same time, this orator is not trying to deceive anyone about these things either: "What he cares about is what people think of *him*."[5] I will refrain from further comment, but I hope that those still committed to reproducing the narrative of nonviolent rebellion at least pause to consider the question: What is the point of continuing to tell this story?

Moments of uprising are riotous. The ultimate civilian sanction against the state is the vision of masses storming the halls of power through sheer force of numbers. It is a vision because we all can picture it—authorities and elites can too. In the years following Occupy, self-described "plutocrat" Nick Hanauer, an early Amazon investor, published an open letter to "fellow zillionaires" in *Politico Magazine*. In it, he argued that society's inequality would lead us back to pre-revolution France, warning that "the pitchforks are coming...for us."[6] Speaking to the same constituency in 2022, the liberal group Patriotic Millionaires put it bluntly: "It's taxes or pitchforks." The pitchforks that these elites see coming are abstract, but not hypothetical. While rioters were setting the 3rd Precinct in Minneapolis on fire in June 2020, police in the next precinct over were frantically destroying their case files.[7] The type of mass revolt that could balance the scales of justice rarely materializes, but the key is, *sometimes it does*. Each riotous protest moment reveals a slightly more vivid picture of the Bastille, the fortress and prison stormed by crowds in 1789 in the defining moments of the French Revolution, and in that image lies the leverage of the riot. The riot contains so much potential energy that it informs the entire history of nonviolent struggle.

Beneath and behind any mass demonstration or march of consequence is the possibility that those consequences will materialize. Even when we are joyful, playful, or somber, we are *demonstrating* that we exist and we are many. Returning to the two underlying approaches to mass movements—petitions or disruption—we ask: Do our numbers signal the amount of signatures marching on an embodied petition, asking to be recognized? Or do our numbers symbolize a material threat to elites via our ability to take action? Ultimately, it is the latter. At the root, gathering masses of people together for a political demonstration is a show of force. In the back of everyone's mind is the possibility that the crowd will use its power in numbers and this is what makes mass political gatherings potent. Riots are that possibility. Even avowedly nonviolent demonstrations are therefore leveraging the possibility of violence by claiming they will abstain from it. The rhetorical power of refusal to fight back, whether it is personal or political, is derived from the mutual acknowledgment of the potential violence of fighting back. The nonviolent resistor is implicitly saying, *we can, but we choose not to*. In certain circumstances, this refusal can constitute a formidable force. For one who is unable or unwilling to physically resist, however, the claimed refusal to do so is essentially meaningless. The "we can" part of the message is real because people really have.

If I say at the outset of an argument that I will commit to not punching my adversary, I am invoking the possibility by refusing it. In congenial discussions and most social interactions, it does not need to be said that you won't punch someone, because it shouldn't be a relevant possibility. If the potential for physical force is raised even to assure its non-use, those involved implicitly understand that they are already in the arena of a fight. Moreover, it would be a meaningless statement if my arms were tied behind my back or if I was otherwise unable to throw a punch.[8] And the harder my adversary knows I can punch, the weightier my refusal to punch becomes. The possibility that we will take forceful action together connects all types of political demonstrations, explicitly nonviolent or otherwise, in their underlying political meaning. But that meaning requires the credible possibility— sometimes people do riot.

✷✷✷

Civil resistance scholars have made strides in identifying useful dynamics of unarmed conflict that can create material leverage against governments: Regimes require the active participation of society, and by organizing mass refusal to participate, civilians can exert leverage against authorities, change the balance of material considerations for rulers, and even topple governments. That is all correct and good, but on the ground, things are gritty and messy. People who desire change must agitate and organize masses of people in such a way that the machine grinds to a halt and collapses, all while building possibilities for something new from within. In doing so, we contend with multitudes of collective and individual interests, dynamics, and pressures. Imposing strict coherence to this process is ultimately part of the problem. This is why riots are most offensive of all to the agents of the non-profit industrial complex, who seek to bring social movements under control and maximize the imagery of disruption while managing actual disruptive capacity. Say what you will about riots, but they resist neoliberal cooptation as well as any action can. The symbol of people collectively burning public and private property in particular is manifestly a deep cut into neoliberal capitalist ideology.

Coherence and incoherence are not a hard binary either. We can embrace the reality of incoherence in manifestations of social struggle, like the riot, while building a program for organized political change. Riots can thus constitute all kinds of possibilities for movements. They signal the seriousness of dissent around a flashpoint issue or over the status quo in general, and they charge the political landscape with kinetic energy. They remind everyone that the rules of society are constructed by those who rule, and that they can be broken. And they produce partisans with new experiences of embodied resistance. Yet so many organizations and commentators rush to distance themselves from rioting, to tell the people who are rising up that they're doing it wrong. This move reinforces the gulf between non-profit advocacy organizations and everyday people who are fed up and frustrated and hurting, ironically reproducing the types of unorganized and sometimes violent outbursts that the professional class fears.[9]

The blanket declaration that "riots work" is meant to capture an important and under-emphasized productive quality of riotous resistance, but discussing the riot using this type of strategic language also misses the mark. Ironically, those who say that riots work are treating rioting the way strategic nonviolentists treat nonviolent action—by attempting to impose coherence on their preferred tactics through a selective picture of revolt, in this case by glossing over everything that happens between setting a squad car on fire and a liberated society. Riots are difficult to see through a strategic lens because they are usually not tactics planned and directed by an authority as part of a plan to achieve a specific goal.

In the most constrained and controlled circumstances, such as prison riots, the "chaos" of the riot can be directly transformed into a new regime. For example, in the Attica Uprising of 1971, as soon as the rebelling inmates achieved control of a cell block they reorganized, took guards hostage, drew up a set of demands, and began negotiating with authorities for improved prison conditions and fair treatment. Dehumanizing and racist prison conditions were the cause of the rebellion, but the riot that started it was spontaneous, in the sense that it had been sparked by a specific and unexceptional altercation between guards and inmates. In other words, the strategic element of this struggle commenced only after its opportunity was opened by the riotous rebellion. In this case, the degree of organization displayed by inmates and the demand that they receive amnesty for all actions associated with the rebellion led the New York governor to choose to order in assault teams to retake the prison by force, in a brutal, indiscriminate attack that killed dozens of prisoners and ten hostages. The governor had agreed to demands to improve prison conditions, but to grant amnesty for the uprising would have risked validating the strategic use of rioting as a means for prisoners to win the dignity to bargain with authorities as equals—something the ruling authority saw as intolerable.[10] But prison is a hyper controlled institution and closed physical architecture. Riots that take place in cities only begin the direct transition to organized strategy if they are successful in liberating an entire area, which is to say, if they are successful in ending the riot component of the rebellion—a rare achievement.

Burning the police station in Minneapolis did not physically drive the police out of the city for good, and it is unlikely any participants thought it would. Such a policy-level notion may not have even occurred to many participants as they were setting fire to the 3rd Precinct. Those actions did help a lot of people around the world see the problem of policing for what it is and had a major role in launching the largest mass movement for racial justice in U.S. history. That movement made possible the national conversation about the degree to which we should change the nature of policing, from reform to abolition. Locally, that riot led the city council to vote unanimously to disband the Minneapolis Police Department.[11] Years and years of organizing in communities and counter-hegemonic intellectual work made the idea of abolishing the police possible, but a riot put it on the political agenda. Since then, the agents of control have of course attempted to recoup this loss, and at this writing, Minneapolis still has a police department. In fact, no sooner had the city council voted to defund the police than the Minneapolis and Minnesota governments moved to reverse course, minimizing budget cuts and undermining a ballot initiative that would have replaced the police department with a social service–oriented department of safety.[12] Indeed, persistent organizing and perhaps more riotous action may be required to finish the job.

The 2011 Egyptian revolution revealed how riots can open physical space to create for a moment the feeling of a new society in public space while building the popular momentum capable of bringing down a government.[13] However, though that revolt ultimately ousted a president, it did not expand public control of space or reorganize society. As with Minneapolis, Egypt today is far from liberated. Riots as collective formations are brief and typically fade within hours or, at most, days. The riot in and of itself, just like mass nonviolent protest alone—and even the two together—is, in the final analysis, far from sufficient. But both and everything in between are probably necessary in the process of social transformation. For their part, riots reveal the reality of social struggle in a way that few other kinds of actions can. Riots do not create per se, but they can improve our vision of society's contradictions, and at least in some circumstances, open us to visions of a liberated future that we *can* create.

Our understanding of revolutionary social change can aspire to clarity even as we—in fact, *only if* we—incorporate the fact that there will be messiness. Rioting is rarely "on message," but it does send a message. Riots are not only feared for their direct physical destructiveness, but for forcing us to confront reality. It can be hard to speak the most difficult truths out loud—it makes them real.

Riots ground the incoherence of social conflict in the coherent lineage of struggle by the many at the bottom against the social order of the few at the top. In this way, riots can connect struggles across time and space. We can see this in riot imagery in popular art and propaganda. Take, for example, the music video to Keny Arkana's 2006 song, *La Rage*, a prime example of what some call "riot porn."[14] Looking at the images, we immediately recognize the characters in each scenario. We don't even need to know where in the world each confrontation is taking place. There are always armored cops with weapons—batons, shields, tear gas, water cannons, tanks, guns—and there are always angry crowds marching, chanting, throwing bricks or rocks or bottles, ripping down fences, setting things on fire. Even without context, we look at an image of a riot and we immediately understand that there are authorities trying to impose order, and there are masses resisting. What is that order? It is dispossession, the control of the many by the few, the ability to exploit, to hoard riches while others starve, to profit from the destruction of the planet, to steal land and resources, destroy cultures, rewrite history. In the simplest analysis, riots pronounce this order unacceptable.

The kinds of radical and uncompromising action that today get called violent are not the opposite of, but rather are intertwined with more formal organizing efforts in the social-political processes and currents of resistance. But it is not simply a matter of adding physically confrontational actions into the long list of civil resistance tactics, alongside peaceful marches and demonstrations and sit-ins and walk-outs and guerrilla theater and the rest. It is also about integrating the possibility for physical contention into the understanding of what it means for a movement to challenge power. It is about understanding that the violence of control and the counter-violence of resistance lurks somewhere beneath every political action. Every action does not need to be physically destructive or to explicitly threaten physical action, but there must exist the possibility, the collective readiness to cross that boundary if and when the time comes. Movements must signal a willingness to fight, even if a given struggle never comes to that. In other words, there must at some level be mutual recognition that we the people understand we are in political conflict, and it is serious, and we are willing to throw hands or bricks about it if necessary. Each movement or organization needn't send that signal themselves. The signal is palpable in the air around any space and time when a riot has happened in recent memory, and it is open source, available to all. It is for precisely this reason that many organizations and individuals brandish images of Molotov cocktails and burning police cars on signs and banners and social media graphics. Those images are powerful, but only because people sometimes actually do it.

This vision of civil resistance is not as clean or elegant as the nonviolence version, but neither are real-world politics. Riots can hold contentious space in moments of abeyance, when movement organizing feels weak, reminding us that the will to resist persists. We saw this in the U.S. at the 1999 "Battle of Seattle," when the mass unarmed assault on the meeting of the WTO shattered the notion that history had ended with neoliberalism. Movements for equality and justice were back.

Riots can fortify us when we are feeling the overwhelming weight of structural violence and defeat. We saw this in the response to Donald Trump's 2017 inauguration, which was greeted with thousands of activists blockading entrances to the ceremony as others marched, fought with police, broke windows, and set fires. The feeling in Washington, DC that day resembled a state of emergency, as National Guard and police vehicles attempted to lock down the streets, the air thick with smoke and the sound of rubber bullets and stun grenades. The following day saw perhaps the largest day of mass protest in U.S. history up to that point. The combination spoke loud and clear: the country would not descend to fascism without a fight.

Riots can rouse us to action, producing movements that grow beyond the need for rioting. We saw this in 2019 in Puerto Rico, when government scandals brought protesters to the streets in fiery demonstrations and fights with riot cops, demanding the resignation of the island's then-governor, Ricardo "Ricky" Rosselló.[15] The riots would catalyze mass protests that lasted for weeks, escalating to a general strike in which up to one-third of Puerto Rico's population took part, forcing Rosselló to step down.[16] In this case, civil resistance mobilized toward political victory precisely as nonviolence theories say it can—and it was sparked by rioting. And from these moments, new political subjects emerge who will go on to struggle in ways that perhaps would not have been possible otherwise. We hear in the accounts of rioters, voiced by many of the people interviewed for this book, how participation in physically transgressive acts has powerful subjective effects, elevating people's consciousness, clarifying political conflict, empowering partisans of social struggle, and fortifying resolve.

The experiences of rioters reveal direct insights into social struggle that can be difficult to access from times and places that are not in acute conflict. Based on his experiences in Tahrir Square in 2011, social theorist Mohammed Bamyeh writes of the "anarchist enlightenment" that develops in a revolutionary moment as an ordinary person, through collective action, reacts differently to their oppression one day than the ways they previously had. "No revolution was ever predicted and nothing in a previous oppression prepares one for revolution by any force of necessity," he writes. "The fact that one is oppressed or has great grievances does not in itself lead to a revolution," rather, it takes a series of decisions by individuals and collectives.[17] Once a person, together with others, reacts to an oppressive event in a way they understand to be *extraordinary*, the focus shifts from the oppression to the collective resistance, and to the revolutionary possibilities that resistance opens up. In other words, resistance becomes revolutionary. Through the experience of extraordinary resistance, and through revolutionary decision making, Bamyeh witnessed how the Tahrir participant "experienced herself *directly* as the agent of a grand moment in history."[18] It is in this way that Badiou and Clover see the *commune*—as in Cairo or Barcelona in 2011, or Shanghai or Paris in 1967-68—as the horizon of the riot.[19] However, a crucial aspect of this revolutionary knowledge-creation is its temporality, its *movement in the moment*. The instant that grand moment in history is institutionalized, it becomes something else.

For the riot to be liberatory as such it must necessarily be a liminal condition, both in terms of the individual experience and the movement's collective struggle. In her work *On Violence*, Arendt argues that "under certain circumstances violence—acting without argument or speech and without counting the consequences—is the only way to set the scales of justice right again."[20] However, she qualifies this statement with a paradox: violent resistance risks becoming irrational the moment its agents begin to rationalize its organized use. The emotionality of the riot in its collective reaction to injustice is a major part of what makes it so human. But we must resist the urge to juxtapose this emotional response with rational strategic thinking.

Fanon points to the importance of disorder, as in the need to disorder the oppressive order of things such that they can be re-ordered. Here we see that the disordering and the re-ordering, while connected and mutually dependent, operate on different logics, on different emotional-cognitive processes. The riot belongs to disorder. Yet it contains the productive potential of decolonial violence without providing the organized threat of institutionalizing that violence. The riot's apparent chaos, its anarchy—which is always seen as a flaw to those seeking to control movements—ultimately also means that as a form of struggle it lacks the capacity to become institutionalized. Of course, institutions can coopt the imagery and sentiment behind riots and can capitalize on their aftermath. But the disorder of rioting can contribute positively to social re-order, especially if we want the new order to look fundamentally different from the old, not least via the new ways of seeing the world unleashed by people who have glimpsed it first hand in the riot. This glimpse, described by many rioters as *empowering* and *beautiful*, or in the words of one, as *sensory practices of freedom*, begets "a *gnosis* of a new type," a new way of knowing the world that can, when strung together by revolutionary decisions, constitute the birth of a revolution.[21] In this way it becomes clear that rioting is not at odds with organizing. On the contrary, distance from rioting only cuts off a primary source of knowledge and practice of rebellion.

To understand the contentious dynamics of revolutionary change from below, we must understand riots. There might always be a tension between the disorder of rioting and the order of political strategizing (as well as the order of analyzing both), but pretending that riots do not exist, or that they are not part of movements for justice, or that they are random and mindless events only hurts our comprehension of social change. Violent protest is not some alien parasite attaching itself to otherwise organic nonviolent struggle, nor is it an aberration, nor is it proof of humanity's chaotic and antisocial nature. The standard repertoire of actions that get labeled riots are integral components to the uprisings of our time, as they have been to uprisings in previous eras.

Riots are part of civil resistance movements. More than that, moments when crowds collectively experiment with violence—which is only to say, when people collectively move beyond the bounds of strict nonviolence—have distinct and significant impacts on participants and audiences. By rejecting the use of "violence" as a catch-all category for everything that is not nonviolent, we can demystify riotous actions and allow them to be returned to reality. But wordplay is not enough; there *is* something violent about forceful resistance to violent authority. We might maintain the use of the terms "violence" and "nonviolence," but we must move beyond approaching them as a holistic dualism if we are to accurately analyze the types of struggle that populate both categories, with the steepest learning curve for those actions that cross the line that has been drawn in between.

***

We return at last to the dictionary definition of a riot, derived from the seminal Riot Act: *a violent disturbance of the peace by a crowd*. This often involves a particular and age-old repertoire of action including fires and barricades in the street, thrown projectiles, damaged property, and physical altercations with authorities, but these only constitute the most iconic manifestation of the riot. Riotous resistance really means to fiercely and forcefully and publicly disrupt the façade of normality that hides the violently enforced status quo. Herein lies the essence of street rebellion. Resistance must actually *resist*, it must disrupt, it must disorder. The riot embodies and symbolizes sheer, unadulterated resistance. Each act of collective resistance does not need to be riotous in the sense of throwing bricks and bottles and Molotov cocktails. Many organized actions will not be so raw, and an effective strategy always involves less risky and more polished actions as well, but the moment we attempt to impose a universal boundary on the ways people fight back against oppression is the moment we drain resistance of its riotous quality.

Riotous resistance disrupts the routines of civic and economic life upon which systemic domination relies; rioting can be an empowering experience; riots can spark uprisings and rouse movements for justice. Can riots themselves be the centerpiece of strategy? For me, this is the wrong question. Disruptive collective action is essential movement strategy, and riots have their place among such actions. Rioting might in a sense be viewed as a tactic, but a chaotic tactic that is frequently (though not always) unorganized and spontaneous. Rioting might be viewed as a strategy itself, but only in the broadest sense possible, in which we might envision the commune or liberated zone as the far horizon of the anti-police riot.

Incorporating riotous street rebellion into our frameworks for resistance is necessary, but in doing so we must approach violent actions—like nonviolent actions—as a set of real-world practices and meanings, not as an ideal type. Better yet, we should think beyond the boundaries of these terms as defined from without. Ultimately, in these discussions "violence" and "nonviolence" are just words we use to describe resistance. Let us not begin with the terms for struggle we have been given and proceed from there, but instead craft analyses and strategies based on conditions, terrain, capacity, resources, and values, then apply the terms that make the most sense in context.

In the late 1960s, when Barbara Deming proposed that we replace in Fanon's work the word "violence" with "radical and uncompromising action," she was intervening in a Left that often assumed the need for global armed struggle as a starting point. Deming argued against this assumption from the standpoint of an ally, even using examples from revolutionary warfare to make her case. Deming points to the ways in which acts of generosity toward captured state troops by communist Chinese and Cuban guerrillas often resulted in widespread recruitment for revolutionaries.[22] Deming did not condemn the purpose of these armed campaigns nor the mentality that leads oppressed people to take up arms. Rather, she highlighted the ways that kindness could at times fulfill strategic as well as moral aims within revolutionary struggle, pushing back against dominant assumptions that nonviolence was a fool's errand. Times have changed. Today we face both states and structures of institutional violence that are far more consolidated than ever before, and we face a Left that too often assumes that strict nonviolence is the only way out. In these times, I want to make an inverse proposition: What if, when we are tempted to envision *nonviolent* resistance, we instead substitute in our minds: "radical and uncompromising action."

Concluding Thoughts

Strategy-minded organizers look for the ways we can mobilize large numbers of people in a sustained way, and those who say riots can make this task more difficult are not necessarily wrong. Then again, no one said it would be easy. There are undoubtedly risks and costs for organized movements associated with riots, and of course for rioters themselves. But in times of uprising, outbursts of riots are associated with overall increased mobilizations, at times leading to wholesale revolts.

There are major opportunities we forfeit if we aren't willing to set things on fire. As with the Fallists, "burning it down" can be metaphorical, representing a break with the established order, but it is also sometimes literal. Riots are a consistent element of the civil resistance repertoire, and they happen regardless of whether those who organize movements want them to. It is not really viable to encourage people to riot on this basis, and even if it were, people do not riot because a book tells them to; people riot because they are fed up, frustrated, outraged, heartbroken. Riots have been going on as long as there have been states that defend the theft of the commons for the sake of the few, and there are no signs they are going away. If anything, they are on the rise. So, regardless of whether we are masking up and breaking bricks in half or not, the questions become: How do we understand the power dynamics at play when masses confront authorities? When do we incorporate riotous elements into our practices of resistance? And how do we respond when people inevitably do riot?

The things that make riots cathartic and emotionally empowering are the same things that make them messy, unpredictable, and uncontrollable. Or, as a South African activist put it, incoherent. The tensions at play in riotous spaces can make them difficult to situate in a broad view of social change. For critics and supporters alike, the easiest way to approach their incoherence is to imagine riots as subject-less, as crowd hysteria or mob mentality, as a background condition, a sign of the times, a bellwether of the political landscape, a political opportunity. Even many of those who theorize the connection between what appears to be mass civil destruction and the opening of generative revolutionary space—for example Badiou, who articulates the connection between what he calls the "immediate riot" (the riot) and the "historical riot" (the commune)—miss the experiential importance of the immediate riot. The riot's position in the long struggle for liberation can only be properly understood if we are willing to acknowledge the rioter as a subject—before, during, and after the riot. A non-static, transforming subject.

In considering the experiences that were shared with me over the course of my research for this book, and in considering my own, I'm reminded of the three metamorphoses of the spirit that Nietzsche proposes in *Thus Spoke Zarathustra.* The first is a load-bearing spirit, represented by a camel, which carries the weight of the past. Then a rebel, represented by a lion, which fights back and destroys the old ways. And finally, innocence, represented by a child, embodying the birth of a new system that does not exist in reaction to the old, but is fully its own. In this allegory of cycles, Nietzsche describes essentially the same process as Fanon—revolution. When it comes to the riot, we are dealing with the second metamorphosis, that of the lion. Nietzsche describes the lion's defining struggle as against a great dragon named "Thou shalt." On every scale of the dragon is inscribed the words, "Thou shalt!" Where the camel had long carried what it was told to, the spirit finally responds—in Rage Against the Machine's words, *fuck you I won't do what you tell me*—and transforms into a lion. The lion *becomes* in the process of a fight, a vulgar process, and the spirit is thus molded by the fight, designed to hunt and destroy its opponent. The lion is required for the struggle against "Thou shalt," but is also limited by it; this hunter spirit's *raison d'être* is its prey, what it fights, what it struggles *against*. Its success necessarily requires another transformation, one which moves beyond the fight *against*, and fully into the creation of something new.

Nietzsche does not describe the defeat of the dragon; it is implied in the lion's subsequent transition to the spirit of the child. Physical victory is not part of the story. Riots are not a place where "overcoming is possible."[23] The point of the riot is the fight itself. Like *Zarathustra*'s lion, the violence of the riot is not meant purely in the instrumental sense; it is not in a realistic way about militarily destroying the forces of the enemy for decisive victory, but rather is part of a psycho-social process of destroying the values of present-day society within the collective and individual self. The will to violence in the rioter reveals a rebellious experience of living in the moment, a reminder of our humanity amidst anti-human systems of domination and exploitation. And, where capitalism and state authority both depend on predictability and control, it is a specifically anti-capitalist, anti-authoritarian experience too. In and of itself, the actions of the riot may not be creative, but the experience can create the conditions for "a new type of political being."[24] Riots in one sense are reacting, resisting something, rebelling against something, but in another sense, they experientially open the door to the next metamorphosis, the possibility of moving from resistance to revolution to liberation.

In itself, the riot is temporary and always in movement, and thus can only open a portal to other places and times. Here we can see how analyses that attempt to ascertain the short-term ability of riots to achieve specific goals are missing the point. The old adage that violence never solves anything is not necessarily wrong. The idea of the riot's violence is not to solve the problem, *it is to clarify the problem.* And clarifying the problem can be a step to solutions.

It is important that we return to rioters' full subjectivity. The riot only exists in the minutes between when the riot starts and when the riot ends, but people who participate in riots continue to exist in the world after the smoke clears. Those I interviewed are not only rioters, they are also teachers, students, medical professionals, service workers, sex workers, poets, farmers, athletic trainers, blue collar mechanics, white collar non-profit staffers, landscapers, lawyers, artists, therapists, and even policymakers. They are family members and neighbors, friends and acquaintances, regulars at the bodega, the café, and the bar. Rioters are all around us, meaning that the experiential effects of rioting are all around us.

We can and should challenge the rhetorical use of the word "violence" to describe the actions that rioters take when the same term is applied to systemic violence, to state repression, and to warfare. Yet the nonviolence theorists get something right about the connection between riots and more extreme forms of violent action. Whether or not participants are actually prepared to, the willingness to break things and burn things and throw things at authorities signals a psychic preparedness to possibly do more. The specter of the Haitian Revolution lives in every anti-police riot—in the wreckage of every torched police car, a glimpse of the world in which the last shall be first and the first shall be last. And not only for the rioter. From Fanon and other decolonial thinkers we learn that deep down, colonizers know that their position is illegitimate, that it is based on violence. Somewhere more or less consciously in the mind of the oppressor lingers the fear that, in the end, all the violence that has been forced upon the oppressed for the sake of hoarding profits and privilege will be returned with interest.

This anxiety was formative for the nascent United States. In 1797, just following the Haitian Revolution, Thomas Jefferson wrote: "But if something is not done and soon done, we shall be the murderers of our own children ... the revolutionary storm now sweeping the globe will be upon us, and happy if we make timely provision to give it an easy passage over our land. From the present state of things in Europe and America the day which begins our combustion must be near at hand, and only a single spark is wanting to make that day tomorrow."[25]

That spark is visible, in a flashing moment, in the flames of a riot, its smoke perceptible in every protest that refuses to proclaim itself nonviolent; the dread that the oppressed will finally declare, to paraphrase James Baldwin: *no more marches, the fire next time*. This emotion-soaked sensation does not imply that the kind of violent inversion that haunts the colonizer's nightmares is inevitable or desirable. Even for rioters themselves, who in actuality tend to display far more generosity toward their targets in the moment than police or military forces do. But the willingness to signal that we are all aware of the possibility is a crucial element of leverage from below. The potential for violent tactics thus charges resistance with revolutionary energy. It does not necessarily lead to any immediate material victories, and physical confrontation with police or property can have significant costs for movements and participants, but even when rioters are not sacking the government in the endgame, they remind those on all sides of the barricades that politics is still a fight. They remind us that Margaret Thatcher's famous slogan for the neoliberal world order—*There Is No Alternative*—is still aspirational for them. The forces of domination are winning, but they have not won; there are still alternatives, and people willing to fight for them. The advocates of nonviolence are also correct that violent tactics are likely to bring greater repression as conflict intensifies. Riots represent a clear and present danger to the status quo, and in certain moments they touch a collective nerve in a way that nonviolent disruption, however widespread, simply does not.

This is why it is crucial that we are able to examine riots and rioters themselves. Between condemnations of rioters as outside agitators, or criminals destroying neighborhoods, or the break down of the social contract, and the romanticization of riots in reproduced images of burning police cars and Molotov cocktails—lost in all that noise are those actual riotous moments in the streets, the thick air of possibility between police lines and protesters, or between protesters and each other when someone throws a rock, breaks a window, lights a fire, jumps on a squad car. These moments are precious sites of struggle.

Time is getting short. To the extent that rioting adds urgency to the compounding crises we face, and adds sparks of radical consciousness, rioting is a necessary component of movements for justice and liberation. Regardless of whether or not we have the opportunity or disposition to feel those moments ourselves—and there are many ways to encounter the rioter in each of us—we can look to them for knowledge and inspiration in the struggle to build a better world.

Appendix

A Discussion of Riotology

The purpose of social inquiry is to better understand the world around us. Knowledge is power, and there is no apolitical approach to power. I study social change from the position of a long-time organizer who believes that radical collective action from below is required to build anything approximating a just society. Social investigation that is both grounded in real-world struggle and based on rigorous social scientific research practice should hone and deepen knowledge that enables people to better organize and take action for a more humane world. This project came about after years of witnessing the violence/nonviolence debate impede movements' capacity to build power in the U.S., at times seeming to serve as a self-destruct mechanism. The deeper I dug, the more it became clear that this debate was fueled in large part by misconception and misunderstanding.

The research and analyses in this book unpack the weaknesses in dominant theories of strategic nonviolent resistance and advance arguments for integrating rioting and other forms of non-nonviolent action into our understandings of social change from below. Civil resistance studies has in many ways innovated the use of robust research to catalogue resistance techniques and use them to inform, train, and guide practitioners. However, that field remains stuck in misguided obsession with a purist notion of nonviolence, and is intertwined with a nonviolence industrial complex that is more concerned with controlling resistance than unleashing it. The study of riotous resistance is meant to develop on useful aspects of this tradition by incorporating the full range of real-life civil-resistance practices and experiences. There remains much to learn. There are case studies to dig into, datasets to improve upon, and lived wisdom to incorporate, and I look forward to seeing where the study of riotous collective action takes us. My hope is for this book to help open the way.

Studying riotous resistance presents the researcher with a number of challenges. First, as I have argued, there is a tension between the embodied radicality of riotous action in the moment and the removed, deliberate reflection of analyzing and writing about it. Second, as Michael Loadenthal puts it in his study of insurrectionary anarchism: "It is important that those partaking in research on and for social movements engage in the process of knowledge construction in a way that does not make ... repurposing easy for state forces seeking to extract actionable intelligence from research meant to exist in solidarity with the subject."[1] Knowledge production generates information without being able to control how it is used, but there are ways we can mitigate potential misuse of research while maximizing its constructive potential. Some forms of knowledge regarding resistance practices are particularly susceptible to being deployed by authorities to suppress movements. At the very least, responsible research must be designed to insulate participants from direct harm, but additionally research on contentious political actions can provide information and knowledge that is generative for the forces of justice. Finally, my research and analysis are to some degree molded and limited by my own experiences, perspectives, and context—something I do my best to account for, but nonetheless should be stated here.

With this all in mind, this appendix explains the research methods I used and addresses some important issues that warrant further reflection.

Quantitative Research

Statistics is about simplifying the world into a set of numbers in such a way that important patterns and tendencies stand out. There are two components to the quantitative research in this study. In the first, I establish that riots are common in the types of uprisings that get called nonviolent. In the second, I demonstrate that riots are correlated with increased nonviolent mobilizations. Together, these interventions are meant to refute the arguments that major nonviolent campaigns do not involve riotous action, and that riots have demobilizing effects on nonviolent protest.

In the first intervention, presented in chapter three, I read through the NAVCO 1.3 dataset and interpolate riots from the CNTS dataset into NAVCO's nonviolent campaigns. This involves dropping a number of cases (thirty-five) due to missing data in CNTS or coding differences in country name between the two datasets, resulting in 285 cases. I first recorded the number of riots that took place between the year prior to campaign onset and the year of campaign conclusion; I then created a binary variable for whether or not there was at least one riot recorded in CNTS during the relevant campaign time period recorded in NAVCO. I analyze descriptive statistics and report the results.

There are several distinct limitations to this research. First, as I detail in chapter three, both datasets have their own limitations. CNTS data collection methods make it highly likely to undercount riots, especially in countries that are further from *The New York Times*'s gaze, while working with NAVCO as a baseline involves accepting its list of unarmed campaigns as accurate. Technically, my finding is not that 82 percent of maximalist nonviolent campaigns involved riots, but that 82 percent of maximalist nonviolent campaigns as catalogued *in NAVCO* involved riots based on the data available in CNTS. This is primarily a conservative limitation, since there is good reason to believe that the real number of social movements that threaten to overthrow a government and involve protester violence is significantly higher than that. That NAVCO limits itself to maximalist campaigns also means that this component of the research is also limited to maximalist campaigns. However, as discussed in chapter three, there are some nonviolent cases that do not appear to fit based on maximalist criteria—often ones with no data on riots associated with them.

Another limitation is that CNTS data collection on relevant political events only includes major riots and relies on U.S.-based news coverage. Again, these parameters likely lead to under-reporting errors—there is high likelihood that these data fail to include riots that happened, but it is far less likely that they include major riots that did not happen. If data on riots included those involving less than a hundred people and less than significant material damage, or riotous elements within otherwise nonviolent demonstrations, then the number of riots would increase dramatically. In other words, I take a conservative approach that likely overcounts maximalist campaigns and undercounts riots, leading me to a high degree of confidence in the results as a reliable minimum. *At least* 82 percent of nonviolent maximalist campaigns occur with or alongside major rioting.

The second component of the quantitative study, presented in chapter four, comprises statistical analyses of CNTS data on riots and nonviolent demonstrations for ten countries: the United States, South Africa, Philippines, Mexico, Iran, Britain, France, Ethiopia, China, and Brazil. I select these countries in part because they all have data on protests events in CNTS going back to 1946, which is the longest uninterrupted stretch in that dataset. I also apply qualitative criteria to arrive at ten countries that span five continents and represent different political structures, cultures, economic systems, and histories of struggle to get a wide view of how riots impact nonviolent demonstrations in a variety of country contexts. I also exclude countries where I am less confident that spikes in riots and nonviolent demonstrations in the same year relate to the same issues or collective action frames.

CNTS data contains variables for both major riots and large anti-government demonstrations that are nonviolent. I do not include a measure for specific campaigns or for success or failure. While it might be appropriate for some purposes, when it comes to this analysis I am skeptical of framing all movements as campaigns and using binary variables for movement success, as I think these approaches simplify the reality of political struggle in such a way that obscures some of the most important aspects. Instead, I use only the number of mobilizations, which is in any case close to the main explanatory variable in Chenoweth and Stephan's research—mass participation. I therefore test the relationship between riots and nonviolent protest and find that riots are associated with increased nonviolent protest within the same year and in many cases also in the following year, making them efficacious elements of civil resistance by Chenoweth and Stephan's standards.

The CNTS dataset catalogues events annually and nationally, and thus is a blunt tool with which to measure interaction between types of collective action. This also makes the impact of one type of protest on another within the same time period a reasonable measure of the way these types of actions interact during moments of uprising. In addition, I use a regression model and a time-series model to account for the effects of actions from the previous year. In terms of the national scope, it is no more imprecise than NAVCO in this regard, but still quite imprecise. One further avenue of study could be to analyze daily data for particular cities or regions. However, while this level of granularity would add a great deal, it would also lose something without a national-level study alongside it. For example, following 2015's Baltimore uprising, sparked by the police murder of Freddie Gray and subsequent repression, mobilizations of all sorts in that city were muted for a time, but nonviolent solidarity actions associated with the Black Lives Matter movement exploded nationwide. The national scope of data captures this type of diffusion, which we have reason to believe is increasingly common in the era of mass communication, but nevertheless it lacks the ability to see more precise local mobilization patterns.

Additionally, I include only one exogenous variable: GDP per capita. The most updated version of the CNTS dataset also included GDP measures only through 2016; I supplemented for years 2017–2020 using publicly available data from the World Bank.[2] GDP per capita is the most comparable and most likely to be relevant, but there certainly could be others that might add to the robustness of these statistical tests, and there are innumerable variables that we might consider. For example, some experts I have consulted have insisted that it would be necessary to include season fluctuations in weather patterns in order to be confident of these results. Nevertheless the Adjusted R-Squared values indicate that these models perform quite well for most countries, which means that the variables that are included explain a lot of the variance in the dependent variable.

Two of the three models I use are OLS regressions, a rudimentary but trusty statistical analysis tool that describes the relationship between a number of independent explanatory variables and a dependent variable. Including the lagged variables in model 2 can lead to biased standard errors (although for the purposes of this study, this should be negligible concerning the findings), but model 3 should give us a more accurate result, as it is designed to handle time-series datasets like CNTS. I use an autoregressive moving average (ARMA) model with multiple independent variables, sometimes called an ARIMAX model, with a first order autoregressive term, or an ARIMAX (1,0,0) model. ARIMAX modeling is often used for predictive econometrics but is also useful for studying the relationship between social phenomena over time.[3] The first order auto-correlation is the closest ARMA model to the OLS regression with lagged variables I used in model 2, and therefore the best choice to supplement and ensure the results are accurate. Diagnostic examination of correlograms, auto-correlation function (ACF), and partial auto-correlation function (PACF) plots also indicate a first order auto-correlation function, and the residuals for the ARIMAX (1,0,0) model generally conform to white noise. For the sake of overfitting, I tested a first order moving average model as well as experimented with differencing, and while the results of these models are similar, the diagnostics perform less well.

What do we learn from these methods? Riots are positively correlated with increased nonviolent demonstrations within the same year. The effects of actions from previous years, both violent and nonviolent, have mixed but generally small impacts. This tells us that uprisings often rise and fall within the span of a year, but also can last longer, with prior actions likely having different effects depending on context. These models are sufficient to tell us this much, but not a whole lot more. In the aggregate, on a national level, riots in these ten countries are associated with increased nonviolent demonstrations in the same year, and sometimes in the following year. Investigating further will require more granular levels of data and more detailed methods, providing a fertile direction for further research.

Qualitative Research

What kinds of knowledge about rioting can be most informative and beneficial to movements, while providing the least useful interventions for security forces? Focus on the subjective experiences of rioters fits this call.

Interviewing activists about violent protest is tricky, especially considering increased repression of such activities and surveillance of *milieus* within movements considered likely to engage in them. I initially contacted interlocutors in both cases based on personal references within activist scenes and proceeded to make contacts through snowball sampling or based on chance encounter in activist spaces. Charges of rioting can carry heavy penalties in most countries, as can related crimes of arson, sabotage, vandalism, and assault. Anonymization of sources, use of encrypted storage, and diligence around publishing sensitive information were all important for this study. Out of an abundance of caution, I encouraged interviewees to refrain from telling me what they or others specifically did during relevant actions but rather to focus on how those moments felt, resulting in the focus on more affective sides of participation in chapters five and six. I was sure to remind people not to share any incriminating details like specific locations, names, or acts that might identify an individual and expose them to prosecution. It is also the burden of researchers in this area that we sometimes learn things that, no matter how interesting or juicy, are foreseeably harmful to movements, and we must take responsibility for withholding these aspects in ways that do not detract from the veracity of the research.

Interviewees not only described their activist experiences but were also highly reflexive about their political engagement and discussed protest experiences alongside theoretical analyses, making them closer to co-researchers than interview subjects. Since anonymization was a crucial element of this work, I am unable to credit interviewees by name for their contributions; my hope is that the results, which were only made possible by firm security protocols, make the sacrifice worth it. I likewise approach this study as a trained researcher but am informed by my own experiences of activism and contentious political engagement. In navigating these dynamics, I am guided both by formal sociological training from my doctoral work at the University of Pittsburgh, and by praxis of *partisan social science*.[4]

In the U.S. case, I conducted interviews between 2015 and 2020 with anarchists and activists who participated in black bloc tactics. In South Africa, I conducted interviews in 2017 with activists associated with Fallist student movements.[5] I used an in-depth, semi-structured interview format based on the method's particular benefits for social movement research, especially related to contentious activity.[6] While I did not seek out interviews based on prior knowledge of individuals' protest actions, there was an element of convenience to the U.S. sample, since black bloc formations are associated with physically confrontational tactics. Individuals who participate in acts of unarmed collective violence are a difficult to reach sub-population of protesters, and thus in many cases, are only reachable through purposive sampling techniques. All interviews were conducted in person, mostly in public locations such as cafés and parks, as well as in several people's homes or places of work, and ranged from forty-five minutes to two-and-a-half hours in length. Interviews were mostly with individuals, with four exceptions of groups who preferred to be interviewed together: two couples in the U.S., and one pair of activists and one group of three students in South Africa. I supplemented formal interviews with numerous informal interviews and interactions in activist spaces, attendance at relevant public talks and discussions, and activist-written literature.

I disclose overall demographics and some locations but obscure information that might identify an interviewee. The genders and pronouns I use in the text are accurate but names are artificial and randomized, based on spelled out letters in the English language. In the U.S., the twenty-seven participants interviewed were based in four cities in different geographic regions. Thirteen black bloc interlocuters were men, ten were women, and four identified as trans-nonbinary. The majority (twenty) identified as white (including several who were Jewish), three were Black, two were Latino/x, one was Asian-American, and one identified as multi-racial. In South Africa, the majority of the fifteen participants were based in Johannesburg, while four were based in Cape Town and one was based in Pretoria. Demographically, eight South African interlocuters were women and seven were men; eight were Black, four were white (including one who was Jewish), two identified as "Coloured" (mixed-race heritage), and one was of Asian descent (who was Muslim). I interviewed students and former students from University of the Witwatersrand, University of Johannesburg, and University of Cape Town, as well as one professor and one university worker at Wits who participated in FMF.

The two qualitative interview studies do not necessarily speak to any universal experience; they give us insight into how some activists in some countries and some movements have understood the violent protest actions they have been a part of. In the U.S. case, I interviewed anarchists, most of whom have directly participated in black bloc tactics. They represent an interesting case because members of a black bloc sometimes show up with the intention to riot, and many ascribe to an ideology that encourages it. In some cases, anarchists are falsely blamed for causing violence and chaos at otherwise peaceful protests. There are also occasions where those accusations are not inaccurate, where self-described anarchists do attempt to disrupt a more conventional action or trigger a riot in an otherwise peaceful demonstration. Either way, black bloc anarchists certainly do not speak for all rioters, and, as I'm sure many would insist, they do not speak for other anarchists either. That being said, there were remarkable similarities in the accounts that many activists shared about their contentious moments in the streets, leading to the analysis in chapter five.

In the South Africa case, my research has added limitations. I do not have the familiarity with South African movement scenes or norms of protest that I do in the U.S. from my own experience as an organizer and activist in that country, which undoubtedly alters my analytic capability. I attempted to compensate for this through added discussions and informal interviews with South African activists, and by spending as much time as possible in activist spaces and attending public events. I also had limited time in-country by comparison to the U.S. case, and interviewed fewer individuals as a result. My positionality in South Africa as a white U.S. American researcher also likely limited my access. In one case that I know of, a potential interviewee refused to meet with me when she discovered that I was based at a U.S. American university—if you want to know about violence, she told me via SMS, look at the way that American academics treat the world. It is possible that there were additional nonresponses that were related to this understandable perspective, but I cannot say for sure. Of the activists that I did talk to, I believe my awareness of movements from a practitioner standpoint and my association with mutual activist networks were able to convince most that I would do justice to their struggle in my work, and that they could speak openly with me without fear of their identity being compromised, or of me misrepresenting or taking credit for their ideas. Still, my positionality combined with my restricted time in South Africa likely limited the analysis in chapter six.

A word on counterexamples: While I did not hear activists who had participated in both violent and nonviolent actions speak about the empowering, consciousness-raising effects of the latter, this is not to say that nonviolent actions cannot have that effect. What is more dignified, to sit nonviolently while being beaten or to fight back? I can only venture that it may depend on what you believe. If you believe in nonviolence on a religious or spiritual level, then it might feel dignified to refrain from violence no matter what. That is a spiritual victory, and is thus politically empowering, and might well stimulate transcendent sensations. For others, fighting back, even against all odds, even if the "battle" cannot be won, even if you don't really want to hurt anyone, is important. Here, showing adversaries, comrades, and yourself that you still fight back is the spiritual victory, and is thus politically empowering. Either way, the visceral sense that opponents, no matter how powerful, cannot break your will to resist, that you are a subject and an agent in your own history, that strength contains within it something special. This study does not say that the only way to achieve this is through physical violence. It does, however, indicate that it is one important path that comes with particular social, psychological, and political dynamics.

In addition to direct limitations, there were topics that were raised in interviews and possibilities to pull on analytic strands that I chose not to pursue in the body of this work. Below I briefly discuss several, with an eye on fertile areas for future research on riots and resistance.

The Gendered Riot

It is difficult to speak for long about violence without gender coming to mind. When you search the keyword "violence" in a university library system, the majority of the results relate to gender: gendered violence, violence against women, domestic violence, and so forth. Gendered dynamics are necessarily embedded in social movements, as they are in just about everything, and specifically so around violence. The accusation of hypermasculinity is commonly levied against activists who breach nonviolent discipline, the assumption often being that the rioters are men. There are reasons to believe that movement spaces that lend themselves to violent actions might also be characterized by gendered violence. In research on anti-racist movement scenes in Japan, a recent study found that violent protest actions can create atmospheres in which gendered violence is overlooked, which can exacerbate gendered exclusion and sexual harassment.[7] Others, meanwhile, have pointed towards liberatory potential of gendered experiences of embodied resistance to violent authority.[8]

In my study, some interviewees spoke to the presence of toxic or aggressive masculinity in riots, but most associated this behavior with problematic individuals, and, according to some participants, possibly *agents provocateurs*. As one woman in the U.S. study put it: "Within an affinity group or collective, at least the groups I've been part of, there is a tremendous amount of work around gender equity, and it's never perfect, but I don't feel like action machismo is a problem we run into. But there are always a couple of people who are bloc-ed up who aren't accountable to anyone."

Like this account, some others spoke about the presence of toxically masculine individuals being empowered to even more problematic behavior in black bloc scenes, but the attitude toward them was usually closer to an eyeroll than a curse. The connection of the black bloc to movement affinity groups, communities, and alternative sub-cultures that are committed to gender equity, where individuals are un-masked apart from during actions (and often it isn't all that difficult to recognize someone you already know well when they have a mask on), is at least one safeguard against problematic behavior. There is no doubt though that the riotous space provides an avenue for some activists to justify hypermasculine behavior. In South Africa, it was sometimes connected to drunkenness and young men who wanted to fight but not organize, and also sometimes blamed on *agents provocateurs*.

Still, at least in the interviews I conducted, experiences during protests with toxic masculinity (from comrades) were in the vast minority, and only represented a significant point of discussion in one interview in each case—though a great deal more discussion in several interviews was devoted to problematic masculinity in organizing scenes in general and in repression by police or security forces. It is conceivable of course that my own positionality as a cis man with generally normative gender presentation influenced what interviewees shared with me, but the willingness and in fact eagerness with which some activists discussed violent patriarchy in movement scenes but *not* in their experiences of riots is some indication that the information I received was not entirely unreliable in this regard. And, as the quote above states, many of the activist scenes consistently involved in violent protest actions are aware of, intentional about, and practiced in internal discussions of gender equity.

Interviews do suggest a complicating story about protester violence and gender. While it was my goal to attempt a demographic balance in terms of interviewees, I operated via pre-existing radical networks, snowball sampling, and chance, and I did not have to go out of my way to interview women or people who were LGBTQ, all five letters of which are represented among participants. Focusing on the words of several queer women in the U.S. study was, in part, intended to mitigate hegemonic masculinity slipping into activist accounts, but also the experiences they shared did not differ greatly from those of cis men. (I did not specifically ask about people's sexuality, so I only knew if someone identified as queer or gay or straight if they told me. Likewise, I did not ask about gender identity, but several people chose to tell me they were trans and/or nonbinary.) Not only did women, trans, and nonbinary people speak openly about their experiences with violent protest, but in many cases those actions had significant positive impacts and associations for them on feminist bases, and several voiced a chip on their shoulder about the typical association of physically confrontational protest with masculinity and men.

My findings regarding empowering feelings around gender resulting from women's participation in riots are largely consistent with the previous few interview studies there are with rioters.[9] In the words of gender, feminist, and women's studies scholar Tammy Kovich: "Riots can present openings for the transgression of dominant gender ideologies and related expectations. As eruptions of innately volatile politics, they engender moments in which established social boundaries, political arrangements, and cultural customs become more malleable."[10] Nor are women newcomers to rioting; in previous eras, food riots in various countries have been closely tied to the participation and leadership of women.[11] Still, the overall majority of participants in many riots are men, usually young men, and my more balanced interview sample has the potential to understate hegemonic masculine experiences of those actions.

The gendered aspects of violent protest are an important area for continued study. Masculinity might be pronounced in spaces where violence is allowed or encouraged, and at the same time, this might depend heavily on definitions and types of both violence and masculinity. Many women, trans, and nonbinary activists reported feeling empowered by experiences with rioting, and some spoke to the avowedly feminist activist spaces associated with them. Hegemonic masculinity is everywhere—in my experience there is no shortage of toxic masculinity in groups committed to political nonviolence—and the ways in which it flows through violent protest is less straightforward than one might think. One way or another, the perception of protester violence as inherently and toxically masculine is itself a manifestation of normative gender logic and should be reconsidered.

Race and the White Riot

Race is a significant element of this study insofar as histories of racial violence are woven into the fabric of social movements for justice, contentious protest, and policing. In chapter six, race is particularly central to discussions of decolonization and movements in South Africa. But there is a great deal more that can and should be said about race as it relates to violent protest. As I discussed in the introduction, the "race riot" has become its own term, and one that has meant a variety of things in different contexts over time. In some senses, the riot itself has become a fundamentally *raced* concept.[12] In the black bloc study presented in chapter five, specific discussion of race is sparse, but that should not indicate that racial dynamics are absent. As sociologist George Weddington has pointed out, movement studies have often boxed race into its own category of analysis separate from otherwise "race-neutral" analyses, whereas in reality, race permeates the social fabric of the U.S.[13]

Especially considering recent instances of violence in Black-led racial justice protests being blamed on white anarchists, it is both highly relevant and also fraught to center a study of riots in the U.S. on mostly white anarchists. Part of the decision to focus there had to do with the political import of this perspective; another aspect had to do with my capabilities as a researcher and the possibilities of conducting robust qualitative research as someone with trusted connections in anarchist *milieus*. In South Africa, my outside position as a U.S. American may have enabled me to partially bypass intra-country racial tensions, while it probably created additional barriers in other ways. The decision to focus on student movements was in part due to my experiences as a graduate student labor organizer, who had in the past taken part in campus occupations in the U.S., which gave me some legible common ground with interviewees.

While the majority of U.S. interviewees were white, several were not, which kept me from digging into a deeper racialized analysis of the "white riot," as Joe Strummer and AK Thompson have put it—that is, the will on the part of some middle-class white people to riot alongside Black uprisings—since I did not want to erase the experiences of non-white interviewees. At the same time, there were not enough non-white interviewees to merit comparison groups. In the South African case, the overall sample of interviews was fairly small, and I did not have the background there to venture in-depth racial analyses. Nevertheless, there were differences along racial lines in both U.S. and South Africa studies that are worth mentioning.

Activists I spoke to in South Africa, most of whom are Black, tended to describe a euphoric sensation during violent protests less often and less centrally than did interviewees in the U.S., most of whom were white, instead speaking more to feelings of humanization and catharsis in the face of repression. At the same time, feelings of humanization and catharsis were also present in U.S. interview responses. In the U.S., only three interviewees are Black, which is an extremely small sample, but of those three activists, two of them described heightened effervescent feelings in substantially similar ways as white participants in the black bloc, while the third was more matter-of-fact about their experiences and affectively less heightened when discussing riotous moments. Two white interviewees were also emotively nonchalant about their experiences with riots.

While there were differences within groups, it seemed the difference between nationality came into play more than did race within each national study. The heightened and cathartic experiences relayed by white South African student activists who had participated in protests that included rock-throwing and fighting with police resonated closely with the experiences of Black and Coloured South African Fallists, just as the experiences of Black U.S. anarchists was in many ways similar to that of white anarchists when it came to the heightened sensation of the riotous space. Still, each sample was far too small to say more, and the study was not designed to answer comparative questions like this. While there has been a wealth of research into "race riots" and urban rebellions against racial violence, research specifically on racial composition and experiences within contemporary protests and riots is an important area for further study.

Of course, in the face of resurgent fascism, "white riot" can also take on a very different meaning. The far-right insurrection at the U.S. Capitol on January 6, 2021 was often referred to in the media as a riot, and groups like the Proud Boys have been increasingly engaged in aggressive public demonstrations and pogrom-like attacks. Precisely these sorts of demonstrations have been significant to the rise of political fascism in the past. Counter-violence confronting the far-right from antifascists or "antifa" groups has also been a source of some unarmed street violence in protests in recent years, as well as entrenched arguments over these actions' legitimacy and effect.[14] In the introduction, I distinguish between pogroms and riots based on the direction of social power and violence flowing through a crowd. That the police nearly always take sides *against* the antifascists and in some cases even collaborate directly with fascist protesters in such encounters clearly demonstrates the *institutional violence* behind rightwing demonstrations and the *anti-institutional violence* behind those who confront them.[15] But the January 6 attack admittedly bears elements of both. The studies in this book are not designed to examine the experiences of racial or religious supremacists and fascists during riots. Those groups' political ideology, violence targeting the marginalized and vulnerable, and disposition towards the concept of authority—all of which are starkly different from those I interviewed—makes me hesitant to comment further based on this research, though it is conceivable that some of the findings apply.

The Class Struggle

Economic class background is another area that many interviewees spoke to which I chose not to make a central part of this analysis. There were many discussions of class among Fallists, both in terms of individual class and the class association of university spaces, which I discuss in chapter six. But there was significantly more to it than I felt able to speak to, especially given my position as a foreign researcher. One of the most significant limitations of that study in particular was my inability to interview activists from Tshwane University of Technology and other technical colleges, who activists almost universally named as the originators of the student movement, and whose protest actions were consistently the most physically contentious. There was a stark class difference in engagement with the official Fallist movements between activists at the institutions from which I interviewed people—the ones that received media attention and thus the ones I as an outsider had been aware of—and the activists at less prestigious and poorer institutions, who typically come from poorer backgrounds, and in many cases were restricted from participating in physical or virtual organizing with the former group on that basis.

The application of Fanon's theories to class in black blocs is a central theme in one of the most prominent works on black bloc rioting, AK Thompson's 2010 book, *Black Bloc, White Riot*. Thompson focuses of the cultural alienation of white middle-class suburban life—the ways in which "the category 'white middle-class political being' is experienced ... as a contradiction in terms."[16] I had been aware of Thompson's analysis, and class did indeed emerge as a topic in some of my interviews with black bloc participants—mostly as interviewees relayed their personal histories. After analyzing interview responses, I chose not to follow these threads in this study. Among the interlocutors in the U.S. case, many interviewees were not from middle-class backgrounds (some were from working-class and poor backgrounds, and at least one grew up wealthy). Although I had some stories and reflections that related to class positionality, and there is certainly analytical hay to be made there—riots are most frightening for those of us with something to lose, and black bloc anarchists are perhaps an exception, since those among them with something to lose are often trying to lose having something to lose—I did not feel as though the subject had enough qualitative data for inclusion as a main focus.

Class struggle is another area that does not get much treatment this book. It shows up in chapter five in the discussion of alienation, through the connection between workers' struggles and student struggles in chapter six, and implicitly through many of the theorists I deploy and because everyone I interviewed to a person identified as an anti-capitalist. It is also implied in the critical discussion of the role that professionalized non-profit movement organizations can play in moderating and attempting to govern resistance. And in the broadest view, this study shares with Marx attention to what Arendt calls "the very basis of leftist humanism," namely the idea that people can create themselves.[17] However, I do not utilize a historical or materialist frame to understand riots and violent protest—for something closer to that, I encourage readers to see Joshua Clover's 2016 book, *Riot. Strike. Riot.*

Repression

"It's amazing how police influence the direction protests take." That quote had been relayed by the South African activist I interviewed who was most critical of violent protest actions. She was lamenting how many protests that could have—and in her view, should have—remained nonviolent turned violent as a direct result of police violence. Among South African activists who were more enthusiastic about their experiences with confrontational tactics, the overwhelming sentiment was still that in most cases protests escalate to riots because of actions taken by police or security forces. In the U.S., where most interviewees discussed actions in which they showed up ready to escalate, in some cases with the explicit intention of rioting, many still described initially coming to black bloc tactics following experiences of being assaulted by police during peaceful demonstrations. As one interviewee put it: "I was very aware that nonviolent protest, if you're doing anything actually disruptive, it gets met with violence if they want, and the narrative will become that the protests were violent no matter what you do." Research on this phenomenon has demonstrated that the best predictor of police repression is how threatening a protest is deemed to be by authorities.[18] Historian and law professor Elizabeth Hinton, meanwhile, has shown that racist police violence is a direct precursor to Black rebellions in the U.S.[19] And, in the quote above we see how nonviolent protest is often treated as though it were violent when it is sufficiently disruptive, and then called violent by authorities after the fact in order to justify the repression; a sort of reverse backfiring mechanism, if such a term makes any sense.

A comrade of mine during Occupy Wall Street once remarked to me that nothing radicalizes a person quite like getting cracked over the head by a riot cop. Qualitative interviews in this study indicate that police repression is variously responsible for: 1) the escalation of many protests into riots, and 2) the radicalization of activists who experience police violence during nonviolent protest. How the police behave is responsible for a great deal of what happens in protests at a granular level too, from march routes and duration to tone, affect, and physical escalation. Broad research exists in this area, mainly focusing on categorizing and describing types of repression, and outlining the militarization of police forces in recent decades.[20]

Sociologists Jennifer Earl and Sarah Soule identify two main factors that predict police violence against protests: first, the police anxiety around maintaining control, and second, fear of getting hurt.[21] While this is a useful starting point, many anecdotal counter examples do not appear to fit, specifically when police initiate violence against non-confrontational crowds, which if anything raises the chances both of police losing control of a situation and their getting hurt. In addition to their social role as internal defenders of a political and economic regime, police training has been increasingly oriented toward a "warrior mentality" that encourages and glorifies the use of violence.[22] One study found that police in India learn to orient their moral compass toward violence to such a degree that they can torture detainees while believing they are ultimately upholding human rights.[23] And, of course, Michelle Alexander's 2010 book, *The New Jim Crow* teaches us that the police and the criminal justice system are through one lens simply contemporary enforcers of a racial caste system, which clarifies a great deal about how police forces—institutions that in the U.S. evolved from Southern slave patrols—view social justice protests today.[24]

There remains a great deal we do not know about how police strategize and experience what movement scholars call repression. Police and military forces study riots in order to hone suppression techniques and improve command and control capabilities during popular unrest, but much of this material is not publicly available.[25] There are obvious barriers to researching police tactics in protests, and much of what the public learns comes via direct experience or leaked documents.[26] There also exist activist manuals and training materials designed to help participants understand and prepare for riotous protests.[27] An interesting area for future study may be to approach demonstrators and authorities as both separate forces and as an interconnected dynamic. In a recent foray into this type of research, sociologist Chloe Haimson examined interactive engagements between Black Lives Matter protests and police regimes, focusing on how authorities try to enforce control and the ways protesters evade and push boundaries.[28]

***

As for opportunities for future research on the dynamics of riot-ous resistance, for better or worse, there is no reason to believe there will be a shortage of emergent case studies in the near future. When the COVID-19 pandemic hit in 2020, police departments rushed to stock up on riot gear. When storefronts began boarding up their windows, it wasn't to keep the coronavi-rus out.[29] One of the few economists who predicted the collapse of the housing market in the early 2000s recently advised that we are headed for food riots in major U.S. cities.[30] As inequal-ity worsens and the ecologies that sustain life are consumed for profit, the wealthiest people see pitchforks on the horizon. War games at the Pentagon now include training exercises for a youth-led civil rebellion.[31] Street rebellion is a part of our politi-cal moment. We would do well to take seriously its full range of possibilities.

Notes

Riots and Resistance

1. Samuel J. Brannen, Christian S. Haig, and Katherine Schmidt, *The Age of Mass Protests: Understanding an Escalating Global Trend* (Washington, DC: Center for Strategic and International Studies, 2020).

2. Lee Fang, "Federal Government Buys Riot Gear, Increases Security Funding, Citing Coronavirus Pandemic," *The Intercept*, May 17, 2020, https://theintercept.com/2020/05/17/veterans-affairs-coronavirus-security-police.

3. Paul Gilje, *The Road to Mobocracy: Popular Disorder in New York City, 1763–1834* (Chapel Hill: University of North Carolina Press, 1987), 17.

4. Devorah Manekin and Tamar Mitts, "Effective for Whom? Identity and Nonviolent Resistance," *American Political Science Review* 116, no. 1 (2022): 161–80.

5. In this case, in addition to "violent," local newspaper headlines would call the incident a "skirmish" and a "clash." Dillon Carr and Michael Divittorio, "20 Arrested as Protests Turn Violent in East Liberty, Shadyside," *Pittsburgh Tribune*, June 1, 2020, https://triblive.com/local/pittsburgh-allegheny/hundreds-of-george-floyd-protesters-march-through-east-liberty; Ryan Deto, "Residents Who Filmed East Liberty Skirmish Charged with Allegedly Throwing Water Bottles at Police, Both Deny Accusations," *Pittsburgh City Paper*, June 5, 2020, https://www.pghcitypaper.com/pittsburgh/residents-who-filmed-east-liberty-skirmish-say-they-were-accosted-by-pittsburgh-police-and-deny-that-any-objects-were-thrown-at-police-from-b/Content?oid=17398748; Andrew Goldstein, Lauren Lee, and Nick Trombola, "Protesters, Police Clash in East Liberty; 20 Arrested, 9 Officers Injured," *Post-Gazette*, June 1, 2020, https://www.post-gazette.com/news/crime-courts/2020/06/01/Protesters-police-clash-East-Liberty-Pittsburgh-tear-gas-riots/stories/202006010115.

6. Matthew Impelli, "54 Percent of Americans Think Burning

Down Minneapolis Police Precinct Was Justified After George Floyd's Death," *Newsweek*, June 3, 2020, https://www.newsweek.com/54-americans-think-burning-down-minneapolis-police-precinct-was-justified-after-george-floyds-1508452.

7. See for example Mark Engler and Paul Engler, *This Is an Uprising: How Nonviolent Revolt Is Shaping the Twenty-First Century* (New York: Nation Books, 2016); Sharon Erickson Nepstad, *Nonviolent Struggle: Theories, Strategies, and Dynamics* (New York: Oxford University Press, 2015).

8. Erica Chenoweth and Maria J. Stephan, *Why Civil Resistance Works: The Strategic Logic of Nonviolent Conflict* (New York: Columbia University Press, 2011).

9. Robert D. Benford and David A. Snow, "Framing Processes and Social Movements: An Overview and Assessment," *Annual Review of Sociology* 26 (2000): 618.

10. Seraphim Seferiades and Hank Johnston, eds. *Violent Protest, Contentious Politics, and the Neoliberal State* (Burlington: Ashgate, 2012), 4 (emphasis theirs).

11. Benjamin S. Case, "Riots as Civil Resistance: Rethinking the Terms of 'Nonviolent' Struggle," *Journal of Resistance Studies* 4, no. 1 (2018): 9–44. This paper would evolve into chapters three and four of this book.

12. There are of course exceptions, which include Alain Badiou, *The Rebirth of History: Times of Riots and Uprisings*, trans. Gregory Elliott (Brooklyn: Verso, 2012); Joshua Clover, *Riot. Strike. Riot.* (Brooklyn: Verso, 2016); Robert Connery, ed., *Urban Riots: Violence and Social Change* (New York: The Academy of Political Science, 1968); Paul Gilje, *Rioting in America* (Indianapolis: University of Indiana Press, 1996); Neil Ketchley, *Egypt in a Time of Revolution: Contentious Politics and the Arab Spring* (Cambridge: Cambridge University Press, 2017); Frances Fox Piven and Richard Cloward, *Poor People's Movements: Why They Succeed, How They Fail* (New York: Vintage, 1978); Seferiades and Johnston, *Violent Protest, Contentious Politics, and the Neoliberal State*; E. P. Thompson, *The Making of the English Working Class* (New York: Vintage, 1966); AK Thompson, *Black Block, White Riot: Anti-Globalization and the Genealogy of Dissent* (Oakland: AK Press, 2010); Karl von Holdt, Malose Langa, Sepetla Molapo, Nomfundo Mogapi, Kindiza Ngubeni, Jacob Dlamini, and Adèle Kirsten, *The Smoke that Calls: Insurgent Citizenship, Collective Violence, and the Struggle for a Place in the New South Africa* (Johannesburg: CSVR and SWOP, 2011).

13. See Michael Loadenthal, *The Politics of Attack: Communiqués and Insurrectionary Violence* (Manchester: Manchester University Press, 2017).

14. Carwil Bjork-James, "Unarmed Militancy: Tactical Victories, Subjectivity, and Legitimacy in Bolivian Street Protest," *American Anthropologist* 122 (2020): 514–27; Mohammad Ali Kadivar and Neil Ketchley, "Sticks, Stones, and Molotov Cocktails: Unarmed Collective Violence and Democratization," *Socius* 4 (2018): 1–16; Shon Meckfessel, *Nonviolence Ain't What It Used to Be: Unarmed Insurrection and the Rhetoric of Resistance* (Oakland: AK Press, 2016); Seferiades and Johnston, *Violent Protest, Contentious Politics, and the Neoliberal State*; *Revisiting the Riot: 10th Anniversary of AK Thompson's Black Bloc, White Riot* (Special Edition), ed. E. Colin Ruggero, *Theory in Action* 14, no. 1 (2021); Candice Delmas, *A Duty to Resist: When Disobedience Should Be Uncivil* (New York: Oxford University Press, 2018); Andreas Malm, *How to Blow Up a Pipeline* (New York: Verso 2021).

15. See in particular Crispen Chinguno, Morwa Kgoroba, Sello Mashibili, Bafana Nicolas Masilena, Boikhutso Maubane, Nhlanhla Moyo, Andile Mthombeni, and Hlengiwe Ndlovu, eds., *Rioting and Writing: Diaries and the Wits Fallists* (Johannesburg: University of Witwatersrand, 2017); Leigh-Ann Naidoo, Asher Gamedze, and Thato Magano, eds., *Publica[c]tion* (Johannesburg: Publica[c]tion Collective + NewText, 2017).

16. Clover, *Riot. Strike. Riot.*, 6–7; See also: "1714: 1 George 1 St.2 c.5: The Riot Act," *The Statutes Project*, http://statutes.org.uk/site/the-statutes/eighteenth-century/1714-1-geo-1-st-2-c-5-the-riot-act. The Riot Act's definition, including its arbitrary choice of the number twelve, has stuck around in scholarly research on riots; Gilje defines a riot as "any group of twelve or more people attempting to assert their will immediately through the use of force outside the normal bounds of the law," though he admits this definition is imperfect. Gilje, *Rioting in America*, 5–6. And, as many have noted, the number twelve associates riots with a trial jury, the number of apostles in Christianity, the number of months in the Gregorian calendar year, the signs of the zodiac, and many other things.

17. Charles Tilly, *Regimes and Repertoires* (Chicago: Chicago University Press, 2006), 190.

18. Tilly, *Regimes and Repertoires*, 46.

19. Barbara Alpern Engel, "Not by Bread Alone: Subsistence Riots in Russia during World War I," *The Journal of Modern History* 69, no. 4 (1997): 696–721; Lynne Taylor, "Food Riots Revisited," *Journal of Social History* 30, no. 2 (1997): 483–96.

20. There is conceptual slippage regarding the meaning of riots across cultural contexts as well. See Beth Roy, *Some Trouble with Cows: Making Sense of Social Conflict* (Berkeley: University of California Press, 1994).

21. For example, Elizabeth Hinton, *America on Fire: The Untold Story of Political Violence and Black Rebellion Since the 1960s* (New York: Liveright, 2021).

22. See John D. Klier and Shlomo Lambroza, eds., *Pogroms: Anti-Jewish Violence in Modern Russian History* (New York: Cambridge University Press, 1992).

23. Paul Gilje, *The Road to Mobocracy: Popular Disorder in New York City, 1763-1834* (Chapel Hill: University of North Carolina Press, 1987), 17.

24. Thompson, *Black Bloc, White Riot*, 25; Vicky Osterweil uses "not-non-violent" for substantially similar purposes. See Vicky Osterweil, *In Defense of Looting: A Riotous History of Uncivil Action* (New York: Bold Type Books, 2020).

25. See Clark McPhail, *The Myth of the Maddening Crowd* (Piscataway, NJ: Transaction Publishers, 1991).

26. Gustave Le Bon, *The Crowd: A Study of the Popular Mind* (Mineola, NY: Dover Publications, [1895] 2002).

27. Christian Borch, *The Politics of Crowds: An Alternative History of Sociology* (New York: Cambridge University Press, 2012), 48.

28. Émile Durkheim, *Suicide: A Study in Sociology*, trans. John A. Spaulding and George Simpson (New York: Free Press, [1897] 1951), 142.

29. See for example Borch, *The Politics of Crowds*; and Sergio Tonkoff, "A New Social Psychic: The Sociology of Gabriel Tarde and Its Legacy," *Current Sociology* 61, no. 3 (2013).

30. See Hobbes's *Leviathan*: "Hereby it is manifest, that during the time men live without a common power to keep them all in awe, they are in that condition which is called war, as is of every man against every man." Needless to say, this notion has nothing to do with how societies actually looked prior to the state, nor does it resemble those societies that escape the state today. Thomas Hobbes, *Leviathan*, in *Classics of Moral and Political Theory*, ed. Michael L. Morgan (Indianapolis: Hackett Publishing Company, [1651] 2001), 532.

31. Elias Canetti, *Crowds and Power*, trans. Carol Stewart (New York: Farrar, Straus, and Giroux, 1962), 20.

32. Frances Fox Piven, "Protest Movements and Violence," in *Violent Protest, Contentious Politics, and the Neoliberal State*, eds. Seferiades and Johnston (Burlington: Ashgate, 2012), 20.

33. Sociologists generally understand movements as contentious politics that involve collective claims and sustained campaigns, typically aimed at authorities, and employing public displays and repertoires of contention in pursuit of those claims. See Suzanne Staggenborg, *Social Movements* (New York: Oxford University Press, 2007); Charles Tilly, *Social Movements, 1768-2004* (Boulder: Paradigm Publishers, 2004); Charles Tilly and Sidney Tarrow, *Contentious Politics*

(Boulder: Paradigm Publishers, 2007). Social movements can also be approached on cultural, moral, and relational bases, and their actions do not always target authorities: Marcy Darnovsky, Barbara Epstein, and Richard Flacks, eds. *Cultural Politics and Social Movements* (Philadelphia: Temple University Press, 1995); James Jasper, *The Art of Moral Protest: Culture, Biography, and Creativity in Social Movements* (Chicago: University of Chicago Press, 1997); Seraphim and Johnston, *Violent Protest, Contentious Politics, and the Neoliberal State.*

34. George Rudé, *The Crowd in the French Revolution* (London: Oxford University Press, 1959).

35. The "collective behavior" approach fueled this fire as it understood social movements in terms of their irrationality, while the "resource mobilization" approach stoked the same flames from the opposite angle by judging movements by the ability of rational "movement entrepreneurs" to gather and leverage resources in support of their grievances. And Tilly's famous conceptualization of social movements as being composed of activists who seek to display their worthiness, unity, numerous members, and commitment ("WUNC") to authorities and to the public at large essentially excludes riots from the field of social movement studies by definition. See Suzanne Staggenborg, *Social Movements* (New York: Oxford University Press, 2007); John D. McCarthy and Mayer Zald, "Resource Mobilization and Social Movements: A Partial Theory," *American Journal of Sociology* 82, no. 6 (1977): 1212–41; Charles Tilly, *Social Movements, 1768–2004* (Boulder: Paradigm Publishers, 2004).

36. William A. Gamson, *The Strategy of Social Protest* (Belmont: Wadsworth Publishers, [1975] 1990); Seferiades and Johnston, *Violent Protest, Contentious Politics, and the Neoliberal State*; and Meckfessel, *Nonviolence Ain't What It Used to Be.*

37. Sharon Erickson Nepstad, "Nonviolent Resistance Research" *Mobilization* 20, no. 4 (2015): 415.

38. John Markoff, "Opposing Authoritarian Rule with Nonviolent Civil Resistance," *Australian Journal of Political Science* 48, no. 2 (2013): 235.

39. Ward Churchill (with Michael Ryan), *Pacifism as Pathology: Reflections on the Role of Armed Struggle in North America* (Oakland: PM Press, 2017); Peter Gelderloos, *How Nonviolence Protects the State* (Cambridge: South End Press, 2007) and *The Failure of Nonviolence* (Seattle: Left Bank Books, 2013); and Osterweil, *In Defense of Looting.*

40. Gelderloos, *The Failure of Nonviolence*, 40.

41. CrimethInc. is an anarchist publishing group most famous for high-quality prints of situationist-inspired insurrectionary propaganda, such as *Days of War, Nights of Love* (2001) and *Expect Resistance* (2008). On the subject of this book, CrimethInc. has an excellent

pamphlet on the concept of violence in movements, "The Illegitimacy of Violence, the Violence of Illegitimacy," https://crimethinc.com/2012/03/27/the-illegitimacy-of-violence-the-violence-of-legitimacy.

42. Lorenzo Bosi and Marco Giugni, "The Outcomes of Political Violence: Ethical, Theoretical, and Methodological Challenges," in *Violent Protest, Contentious Politics, and the State*, eds. Seraphim Seferiades and Hank Johnston (Burlington: Ashgate, 2012), 34.

43. Charles Tilly, *The Politics of Collective Violence* (Cambridge: Cambridge University Press, 2003), 3.

44. Paolo Friere, *Pedagogy of the Oppressed*, trans. Myra Bergman Ramos (New York: Continuum, [1968] 2000), 8.

45. James Baldwin and *Esquire* editors, "James Baldwin: How to Cool It," *Esquire*, July 1968.

46. Pierre Bourdieu, *Pascalian Meditations*, trans. Richard Nice (Stanford: Stanford University Press, 2000), 170.

47. Karl von Holdt, "The Violence of Order, Orders of Violence: Between Fanon and Bourdieu," *Current Sociology* 61, no. 2 (2012): 127.

48. Michael Schwartz, *Radical Protest and Social Structure: The Southern Farmers' Alliance and Cotton Tenancy, 1880–1890* (Chicago: University of Chicago Press, 1976), 130.

49. Nicole Gallucci, "Photos Show Stark Contrast in Police Responses to Capitol Riot vs. Black Lives Matter Protests," *Mashable*, January 6, 2021, https://mashable.com/article/capitol-police-trump-riot-black-lives-matter-protest.

50. As Hannah Arendt once noted, Fanon's views on violence are often discussed as though commentators stopped reading *The Wretched of the Earth* after the first chapter. Hannah Arendt, *On Violence* (New York: Harcourt, Inc., 1970), 14.

51. Franz Fanon, *The Wretched of the Earth*, trans. Richard Philcox (New York: Grove Press, [1961] 2004), 103.

52. Arendt, *On Violence*, 8.

53. Interviews are presented using pseudonyms to protect the identity of interviewees. For more detail on these studies, see relevant sections in the Appendix.

54. These works include: Benjamin S. Case, "Toward Riotous Resistance," *Theory in Action* 15, no. 2 (2022): 90-103; Benjamin S. Case, "Contentious Effervescence: The Subjective Experience of Rioting," *Mobilization* 26, no. 2 (2021): 179-96; Benjamin S. Case, "Molotov Cocktails to Mass Marches: Strategic Nonviolence and the Mobilizing Effect of Riots," *Theory in Action* 14, no. 1 (2021): 18-38; Benjamin S. Case, "Nonviolent Civil Resistance: Beyond Violence and Nonviolence in the Age of Street Rebellion," *Social Movements, Nonviolent Resistance, and the State*, ed. Hank Johnston (New York:

Routledge, 2019), 190–210; Benjamin S. Case, "Riots as Civil Resistance: Rethinking the Terms of 'Nonviolent' Struggle," *Journal of Resistance Studies* 4, no. 1 (2018).

A Sharp Critique of Strategic Nonviolence

1. Brian Martin, "Gene Sharp's Theory of Power," *Journal of Peace Research* 26, no. 2 (1989): 213–22.
2. This distinction is sometimes alliteratively worded as *pragmatic* versus *principled* nonviolence. It is also worth noting that Sharp himself would later claim that strategic and principled nonviolence were connected and that one could not truly have one without the other. Gene Sharp, *Gandhi as a Political Strategist* (Boston: Porter Sargent, 1979), 252. This is perhaps important for understanding the theorist, but one could be forgiven for missing this qualification, as it was buried in a less-read text and was rarely emphasized by Sharp, his Albert Einstein Institution, or the most vocal proponents of his theory.
3. Gene Sharp, *The Politics of Nonviolent Action* 2 (Boston: Porter Sargent, 1973), also here: https://www.aeinstein.org/nonviolentaction/198-methods-of-nonviolent-action.
4. I refer here to Gandhi's philosophy as written, his political strategy for India, and his movement legacy via the work of nonviolence practitioners and theorists he influenced. See Mohandas Gandhi, *An Autobiography, Or the Story of My Experiments with Truth*, trans. M. Desai (Ahmedaban: Navajivan Publishing House, 1927). But referencing his legacy in this way does not imply that we should ignore Gandhi's behavior toward his wife and nieces, his openly racist views during his life in South Africa, his British colonial military service, or his amicable 1940 letter to Hitler, to name but a few apparent deviations from pacifism and moral enlightenment.
5. Gene Sharp, *The Politics of Nonviolent Action* (Boston: Porter Sargent, 1973), 19–44.
6. Quoted in *The Black Power Mixtape 1967–1975*, directed by Göran Olsson (Sundance Selects, 2011). Ture's dismissal of King's nonviolence in this speech is a good encapsulation of the way many radicals have dismissed nonviolence. It is worth noting, however, that it is not necessarily an accurate description of King's nonviolence; King himself appears to have been at least as concerned with stopping material violence against Black people and improving the conditions of the poor as he was with changing his opponents' hearts.
7. Sharp, *The Politics of Nonviolent Action*, 610.
8. Sharp, *The Politics of Nonviolent Action*, 64.

9. Sharp, *The Politics of Nonviolent Action*, 608; A common rebuttal I have received from nonviolentists is that property destruction isn't violence. Fair enough. However, that is not how the term is treated on the ground, as anyone who has been to an avowedly nonviolent action where someone throws a rock through a window can attest. Anecdotally, I was once part of a campus occupation where we spent an interminable meeting debating whether or not someone picking a lock to access a balcony (thus enabling us to communicate directly with activists outside) constituted violence. So, in real-life movements, at least in the U.S., the line for what gets considered violence is typically drawn as close to the nonviolent extreme as possible.

10. Sharp, *The Politics of Nonviolent Action*, 34.

11. Sharp, *The Politics of Nonviolent Action*, 698.

12. Shon Meckfessel, *Nonviolence Ain't What It Used to Be: Unarmed Insurrection and the Rhetoric of Resistance* (Oakland: AK Press, 2016), 57.

13. Sharp, *The Politics of Nonviolent Action*, 77.

14. Voltairine de Cleyre, "Direct Action," *Selected Works of Voltairine de Cleyre*, ed. Alexander Berkman (New York: Mother Earth Publishing, 1914), 235–36.

15. Sharp, *The Politics of Nonviolent Action*, 71.

16. See Mao Zedong, *On Guerrilla Warfare*, trans. Samuel Griffith (New York: Anchor Press, [1937] 1978); Vo Nguyen Giap, *People's War, People's Army: The Viet Cong Insurrection Manual for Underdeveloped Countries* (Honolulu: University Press of the Pacific, [1961] 2001); Ernesto "Che" Guevara, *Guerrilla Warfare* (New York: Ocean Press, [1963] 2006). As with Gandhi, here I am discussing these revolutionaries based on their written and practiced guerrilla war strategies, and not commenting on other aspects of their lives or legacies.

17. See for example: Ruaridh Arrow, "Gene Sharp: Author of the Nonviolent Revolution Rulebook," *BBC*, February 2, 2011, https://www.bbc.com/news/world-middle-east-12522848.

18. Brian Martin, "Gene Sharp's Theory of Power," *Journal of Peace Research* 26, no. 2 (1989): 217.

19. Sharp, *The Politics of Nonviolent Action*, 29–30.

20. Sharp cites Max Weber in passing for his typology of ruling authority. He does not, however, engage with Weber's classic definition of the state as the institution with a monopoly on the use of violence. Sharp also cites in passing Georg Simmel for his insight into the complex nature of the speaker-audience relationship, which Simmel says is not unidirectional but rather involves the participation of the audience in performing their role, which in turn allows the speaker to perform theirs. Sharp makes a direct analogy to the state—i.e., not unidirectionally powerful but requiring the consent of the public. As with Weber, Sharp does not engage with Simmel's

extensive work on society and power. Even the example Sharp cites has complicating implications for his own conclusions if engaged with beyond a superficial analogy. Audiences, like "the people" in a society, are not unified blocs, but are composed of individuals and groups with different backgrounds, goals, and motivations. In addition to push-back by the speaker and perhaps security, audience members who disrupt an event might find themselves supported or confronted by other audience members for various reasons based on the content and style of the disruption, local norms for such events, social-political context, and so forth.

21. Sharp, *The Politics of Nonviolent Action*, 78–79.

22. Sharp, *The Politics of Nonviolent Action*, 94.

23. Gene Sharp, *Social Power and Political Freedom* (Boston: Porter Sargent, 1980); Hannah Arendt, *Eichmann in Jerusalem: A Report on the Banality of Evil* (New York: Viking Press, 1963).

24. I'm leaving aside here comment on the self-satisfaction that I so often detect when someone, who does not descend from the peoples targeted for extermination, finds a way of using the Holocaust to justify whatever unrelated point they are trying to make.

25. See WGBH radio interview with Barbara Deming after returning from Hanoi, January 24, 1967, https://americanarchive.org/catalog/cpb-aacip-15-33rv1fsw.

26. Anna Johansson and Stellan Vinthagen, *Conceptualizing "Everyday Resistance": A Transdisciplinary Approach* (New York: Routledge, 2020).

27. Frances Fox Piven, *Challenging Authority: How Ordinary People Change America* (Lanham, MD: Rowman & Littlefield, 2006), 37.

28. See interview with Marcie Smith on Doug Henwood's WBAI radio show *Behind the News,* February 22, 2018 (31:21).

29. Project Camelot's official name was "Methods for Predicting and Influencing Social Change and Internal War Potential."

30. Joy Rohde, "Grey Matters: Social Scientists, Military Patronage, and Democracy in the Cold War," *Journal of American History* 96, no. 1 (2009): 99–122; Marcie Smith, "Change Agent: Gene Sharp's Neoliberal Nonviolence," *NonSite*, May 10, 2019, https://nonsite.org/change-agent-gene-sharps-neoliberal-nonviolence-part-one/. See also the publicly available lectures regarding the use of nonviolent warfare for U.S. political interests, for example: "Nonviolent Resistance and Expanding the Unconventional Warfare Toolkit" by a think tank called NSI, featuring speakers from the U.S. Army Special Operations Command, https://nsiteam.com/nonviolent-resistance-and-expanding-the-unconventional-warfare-uw-toolkit.

31. Ruaridh Arrow, "Gene Sharp: The Academic Who Wrote the Playbook for Nonviolent Revolution," *Politico*, December 30, 2018,

https://www.politico.com/magazine/story/2018/12/30/gene-sharp -obituary-academic-nonviolent-revolution-223555; Sam Roberts, "Gene Sharp: Global Guru of Nonviolent Resistance, Dies at 90," *The New York Times*, February 2, 2018, https://www.nytimes. com/2018/02/02/obituaries/gene-sharp-global-guru-of-nonviolent-resistance-dies-at-90.html; Paul Engler, "The Machiavelli of Nonviolence: Gene Sharp and the Battle Against Corporate Rule," *Dissent,* Fall 2013, https://www.dissentmagazine.org/article/the -machiavelli-of-nonviolence-gene-sharp-and-the-battle-against -corporate-rule.

32. See "Open Letter in Support of Gene Sharp and Strategic Nonviolent Action," http://stephenzunes.org/wp-content/ uploads/2010/12/Open-Letter_Academics_Zunes.pdf.

33. Albert Einstein Institution, *Annual Report on Activities* 2000–2004, https://www.aeinstein.org/wp-content/uploads/2014/04/2000 -04rpt.pdf.

34. Albert Einstein Institution, 21.

35. Luke McKenna, "The Fabulous Life of Secretive Investor, Peter Ackerman," *Business Insider*, January 6, 2012, https://www.businessinsider.com/peter-ackerman-2012-1.

36. George Ciccariello-Maher, "Einstein Turns in His Grave," *CounterPunch*, April 16, 2008, https://www.counterpunch.org/2008/ 04/16/einstein-turns-in-his-grave.

37. Craig Brown, "Gene Sharp: More Anarchist than Neoliberal," *Journal of Resistance Studies* 6, no. 1 (2020): 69–104.

38. Brian Martin, "Gene Sharp's Theory of Power," *Journal of Peace Research* 26, no. 2 (1989): 220.

39. For example, the Momentum training program. See Tyler Kingkade, "These Activists Are Training Every Movement that Matters," *Vice*, November 18, 2019, https://www.vice.com/en_us/article/8xw3ba/these-activists-are-training-every-movement-that-mattersv26n4. See also Paul Engler and Sophie Lasoff, "Resistance Guide: How to Sustain the Movement to Win," 2018, http://www.guidingtheresistance.org.

40. Hannah Arendt, *On Violence* (New York: Harcourt, 1970), 48.

41. This view of movement building is not solely an issue for nonviolence studies; it has been a hallmark of many strands of Marxism as well.

42. See Chenoweth's 2013 TedxTalk: "The Success of Nonviolent Civil Resistance," November 3, 2013, https://www.youtube.com/ watch?v=YJSehRlU34w.

43. See, respectively: Daniel Robson, "The 3.5% Rule: How a Small Minority Can Change the World," *BBC*, May 13, 2019, https://www.bbc.com/future/article/20190513-it-only-takes-35

-of-people-to-change-the-world; and Darian Woods, "The Magic Number Behind Protests," *NPR*, June 25, 2019, https://www.npr .org/sections/money/2019/06/25/735536434/the-magic-number -behind-protests.

44. Doug McAdam, Robert Sampson, Simon Weffer, and Heather Mac-Indoe, "'There Will Be Fighting in the Streets': The Distorting Lens of Social Movement Theory," *Mobilization* 10, no. 1 (2005): 1–18.

45. Noam Chomsky, *The Common Good* (Berkeley: Odonian Press, 1998), 43.

Why Civil Resistance Works with the Wrong Data

1. Chenoweth and Stephan first introduced NAVCO 1 in 2008 in the security policy journal *International Security*, and updated it to NAVCO 1.1 for publication in *Why Civil Resistance Works: The Strategic Logic of Nonviolent Conflict* (New York: Columbia University Press, 2011). Since 2011, the dataset has been updated two more times, most recently in 2020, to NAVCO 1.3, which is the dataset I use here. Chenoweth and other researchers have introduced several other datasets, including the time-recurring NAVCO 2.0 dataset (Erica Chenoweth and Orion Lewis, "Unpacking nonviolent campaigns: Introducing the NAVCO 2.0 dataset," *Journal of Peace Research* 50, no. 3 [2013]: 415–423), and a geographically limited event-level NAVCO 3.0 dataset, but NAVCO 1 continues to be the main source for both academic and popular audience publications on this data.

2. See Erica Chenoweth, "Online Methodological Appendix Accompanying 'Why Civil Resistance Works,'" July 17, 2019, https://www. ericachenoweth.com/wp-content/uploads/2019/07/WCRW-Appendix.pdf. Accessed May 12, 2022.

3. For example, NAVCO 1.3 lists the anti-Trump movement as a maximalist campaign aimed at regime change even though there was no central organization and, as far as I am aware, zero explicit attempts at extra-legal overthrow of government via mass mobilization. The 2019 #RickyRenuncia uprising in Puerto Rico, however, is not included, presumably because Puerto Rico is not a sovereign state and the movement was not directly calling for secession. But by all measures the Puerto Rican uprising was far more similar to classic civil resistance movements than the sporadic hodgepodge of public statements and sub-maximalist protest actions that got labeled #Resistance to Trump.

4. Chenoweth and Stephan, *Why Civil Resistance Works*, 13; Meredith Reed Sarkees, "The COW Typology of War: Defining and

Categorizing Wars (Version 4 of the Data)," The Correlates of War Project, 2010, http://cow.dss.ucdavis.edu/data-sets/COW-war/non -state-wars-codebook-1. Chenoweth and Lewis have discussed reducing this threshold from one thousand to twenty-five battle-related casualties—a significant difference. Nevertheless, twenty-five battle related deaths between two armed parties can be clearly distinguished from the types of property destruction and bodily injury resulting from civilian violence. See Chenoweth and Lewis, "Unpacking nonviolent campaigns: Introducing the NAVCO 2.0 dataset."

5. Amitai Etzioni, "Notes for Antifa From a Former 'Terrorist,'" *Boston Review*, November 29, 2017, https://bostonreview.net/forum/etzi-oni-notes-antifa-former-terrorist.

6. Erica Chenoweth, "Violence Will Only Hurt the Trump Resistance," *New Republic*, February 7, 2017, https://newrepublic.com/article/140474/violence-will-hurt-trump-resistance.

7. Chenoweth and Stephan, *Why Civil Resistance Works*, 14.

8. Chenoweth and Stephan, *Why Civil Resistance Works*, 12.

9. Marilena Simiti, "The Volatility of Urban Riots," in *Violent Protest, Contentious Politics, and the Neoliberal State,* Seferiades and Johnston, eds. (Burlington: Ashgate, 2012): 133–45.

10. See Fabrice Lehoucq, "Does Nonviolence Work?" *Comparative Politics* 48, no. 2 (2016): 269–87.

11. Appendix entries are from Erica Chenoweth, "Online Methodological Appendix Accompanying 'Why Civil Resistance Works,'" July 17, 2019, https://www.ericachenoweth.com/wp-content/uploads/2019/07/WCRW-Appendix.pdf.

12. Chenoweth, "Online Methodological Appendix Accompanying 'Why Civil Resistance Works,'" 53–54.

13. Deborah Norden, "The Rise of the Lieutenant Colonels: Rebellion in Argentina and Venezuela," *Latin American Perspectives* 23, no. 3 (1996): 77.

14. Chenoweth, "Online Methodological Appendix Accompanying 'Why Civil Resistance Works,'" 48.

15. Simon Romero, "Desmond Hoyte, 73, Former President of Guyana, Dies," *The New York Times*, December 29, 2002, https://www.nytimes.com/2002/12/29/world/desmond-hoyte-73-former-president-of-guyana-dies.html.

16. Chenoweth, "Online Methodological Appendix Accompanying 'Why Civil Resistance Works,'" 81–82.

17. Daniel Smith, "Consolidating Democracy? The Structural Underpinnings of Ghana's 2000 Elections," *Journal of Modern African Studies* 40, no. 4 (2002): 622.

18. Chenoweth, "Online Methodological Appendix Accompanying 'Why Civil Resistance Works,'" 63–64.

19. Victor Peskin and Mieczysław P. Boduszyński, "International Justice and Domestic Politics: Post-Tudjman Croatia and the International Criminal Tribunal for the Former Yugoslavia," *Europe-Asia Studies* 55, no. 7 (2003): 1130.

20. Chenoweth, "Online Methodological Appendix Accompanying 'Why Civil Resistance Works,'" 98.

21. Solofo Randrianja, "'Be Not Afraid, Only Believe': Madagascar 2002," *African Affairs* 102, no. 407 (2003): 320.

22. Randrianja, "'Be Not Afraid, Only Believe,'" 317, 319.

23. Randrianja, "'Be Not Afraid, Only Believe,'" 324.

24. Lewis Abedi Asante and Ilse Helbrecht, "Seeing through African protest logics: A longitudinal review of continuity and change in protests in Ghana," *Canadian Journal of African Studies* 52, no. 2 (2018): 159–81.

25. For example, *Why Civil Resistance Works* won the American Political Science Association's Woodrow Wilson Foundation Award in 2012 for the best book on government, politics, or international relations; the 2013 Grawemeyer Award for Ideas Changing the World; and was named a 2011 book of the year by *The Guardian*.

26. See "User's Manual for Cross-National Time Series Archive," Databanks International, March 15, 2021, https://manuals.plus/cross-national/cross-national-time-series-data-archive-user-s-manual#axzz7Ud1XEbSh.

27. Of the 320 cases of nonviolent campaigns listed in NAVCO 1.3, thirty-five had to be dropped due to missing data in CNTS or due to coding differences between the two datasets. NAVCO codes by non-state territory names such as Tibet and Papua New Guinea, and also uses the names of states prior to their political independence. CNTS codes by formal country name, so political events in the previously mentioned countries would be coded under China and Indonesia, respectively, while many nations are unaccounted for prior to their emancipation. Because it is not immediately clear in the data if, for example, the riots in Indonesia in 1989 were associated with West Papua, I omitted these cases.

28. Alexei Anisin, "Debunking the Myths Behind Nonviolent Civil Resistance," *Critical Sociology* 46, nos. 7–8 (2020): 1121–39.

29. Wilson, "User's Manual for Cross-National Time Series Archive," 18.

30. For example, the BBC reported rioters storming a police headquarters, beating up officers, and parading them around on horseback, "Protests Force Kyrgyz Poll Review," March 21, 2005, http://news.bbc.co.uk/2/hi/asia-pacific/4369065.stm.

31. Jonathan Pinckney, *Making or Breaking Nonviolent Discipline in Civil Resistance Movements* (Washington, DC: International Center for Nonviolent Conflict Press, 2016), 57.

32. Chenoweth and Stephan, *Why Civil Resistance Works*; Erica Chenoweth and Kurt Schock, "Do Contemporaneous Armed Challenges Affect the Outcomes of Mass Nonviolent Campaigns?," *Mobilization* 24, no. 4 (2015): 427–51.

33. Peter Ackerman and Christopher Kruegler, *Strategic Nonviolent Conflict: The Dynamics of People Power in the Twentieth Century* (Westport: Praeger, 1994), 9.

34. Figure 1 taken from Pinckney, *Making or Breaking Nonviolent Discipline in Civil Resistance Movements*, 17.

35. Chenoweth and Stephan, *Why Civil Resistance Works*, 16.

36. Mohammad Ali Kadivar and Neil Ketchley, "Sticks, Stones, and Molotov Cocktails: Unarmed Collective Violence and Democratization," *Socius* 4 (2018): 1–16.

37. Lincoln A. Mitchell, *The Color Revolution* (Philadelphia: University of Pennsylvania Press, 2012); Joshua Paulson, "Case Study: Serbia, 1996–2000," ed. Gene Sharp, *Dictionary of Power and Struggle: Language of Civil Resistance in Conflicts* (Oxford: Oxford University Press, 2012), 10–33.

Molotov Cocktails and Mass Marches

1. Gene Sharp, *The Politics of Nonviolent Action* (Boston: Porter Sargent Publishers, 1973), 70.

2. See "User's Manual for Cross-National Time Series Archive," Databanks International, March 15, 2021, https://manuals.plus/cross-national/cross-national-time-series-data-archive-user-s-manual#axzz7Ud1XEbSh.

3. User's Manual for Cross-National Time Series Archive, 2021: n.p.

4. For further discussion of my methods, see the relevant section in the Appendix.

5. Luke Abbs and Kristian Gleditsch, "Ticked Off but Scared Off? Riots and the Fate of Nonviolent Campaigns," *Mobilization* 26, no. 1 (2021): 21–39.

6. Abbs and Gleditsch, "Ticked Off but Scared Off? Riots and the Fate of Nonviolent Campaigns," 33.

7. Not shown in table.

8. "Diversity of tactics" is a term used by activists for the symbiotic use of different types of tactics, often specifically relating to more and less violent forms of resistance.

9. See Appendix for further discussion of methods and limitations.

10. Kurt Schock, "The Practice and Study of Civil Resistance," *Journal of Peace Research* 50, no. 3 (2013): 277–90.

11. Erica Chenoweth and Maria J. Stephan, *Why Civil Resistance Works*

(New York: Columbia University Press, 2011), 39–40; Erica Chenoweth, "It May Only Take 3.5 Percent of the Population to Topple a Dictator—with Civil Resistance," *The Guardian*, February 1, 2017, https://www.theguardian.com/commentisfree/2017/feb/01/worried-american-democracy-study-activist-techniques.

12. Chenoweth and Stephan, *Why Civil Resistance Works*, 30.

13. Chenoweth and Stephan, *Why Civil Resistance Works*, 36–37.

14. Karen Rasler, "Concessions, Repression, and Political Protest in the Iranian Revolution," *American Sociological Review* 61, no. 1 (1996): 137.

15. Charles Kurzman, *The Unthinkable Revolution in Iran* (Cambridge: Harvard University Press, 2004), 121.

16. Seraphim Seferiades and Hank Johnston, eds., *Violent Protest, Contentious Politics, and the Neoliberal State* (Burlington: Ashgate, 2012), 7–8.

17. Javier Auyero, *Contentious Lives: Two Argentine Women, Two Protests, and the Quest for Recognition* (Durham: Duke University Press, 2003), 170.

18. Doug McAdam, Robert Sampson, Simon Weffer, and Heather MacIndoe, "'There Will Be Fighting in the Streets': The Distorting Lens of Social Movement Theory," *Mobilization* 10, no. 1 (2005): 1–18.

19. Shon Meckfessel, *Nonviolence Ain't What It Used to Be: Unarmed Insurrection and the Rhetoric of Resistance* (Oakland: AK Press, 2016), 16–17.

20. Seferiades and Johnston, *Violent Protest, Contentious Politics, and the Neoliberal State*, 5.

21. Seferiades and Johnston, *Violent Protest, Contentious Politics, and the Neoliberal State*, 5.

22. Seferiades and Johnston, *Violent Protest, Contentious Politics, and the Neoliberal State*, 6.

23. Guest lecture in the Sociology Department of the University of Pittsburgh, March 26, 2015.

24. Sharp, *The Politics of Nonviolent Action*, 657.

25. Meckfessel, *Nonviolence Ain't What It Used to Be*, 190–93.

26. See Erica Chenoweth, "Violence Will Only Hurt the Trump Resistance," *New Republic*, February 7, 2017, https://newrepublic.com/article/140474/violence-will-hurt-trump-resistance.

27. George Lakey, "Understanding Trump's game plan in Portland could be the key to preventing a coup in November," *Waging Violence*, July 25, 2020. Lakey backs up his usage of Wasow's findings with a deep mischaracterization of an essay by Keeanga-Yamahtta Taylor, citing Taylor as saying that the 1992 LA riots led Democrats to pivot to a "law and order" agenda. Taylor's essay—one of the sharpest and most nuanced political assessments to come out during the George Floyd Uprising—does talk about how politicians used the Los Angeles riots as an excuse to gut welfare

programs, and how the Democrats in particular exploited the moment to expand policing and entrench the prison-industrial complex. Her point is not that riots caused this backlash whereas an alternative history in which people did not riot would have had different results. Instead, Taylor situated the George Floyd Uprising, including its riotous elements, within a long history of radical Black-led resistance to racist violence and inequality in the U.S. She argues the 2020 rebellion could lead to more radical change than preceding uprisings had if organizers learned lessons from previous struggles, expanded demands and vision for social transformation beyond minor reforms, and intersectionally incorporated class struggle into the movement against racist police violence. See Keeanga-Yamahtta Taylor, "How Do We Change America?," *The New Yorker*, June 8, 2020, https://www.newyorker.com/news/our-columnists/how-do-we-change-america.

28. Omar Wasow, "Agenda Seeding: How 1960s Black Protests Moved Elites, Public Opinion, and Voting," *American Political Science Review* 114, no. 3 (2020): 649.

29. Ryan D. Enos, Aaron R. Kaufman, and Melissa L. Sands, "Can Violent Protest Change Local Policy Support? Evidence from the Aftermath of the 1992 Los Angeles Riot," *American Political Science Review* 113, no. 4 (2019): 1012–28; Daniel Gillion, *The Loud Minority: Protests Matter in American Democracy* (Princeton: Princeton University Press, 2020).

30. Rasler, "Concessions, Repression, and Political Protest in the Iranian Revolution."

31. Chenoweth and Stephan, *Why Civil Resistance Works*, 103.

32. Matthew Impelli, "54 Percent of Americans Think Burning Down Minneapolis Police Precinct Was Justified After George Floyd's Death," *Newsweek*, June 3, 2020, https://www.newsweek.com/54-americans-think-burning-down-minneapolis-police-precinct-was-justified-after-george-floyds-1508452.

33. See for example Steve Chase, *How Agent Provocateurs Harm Our Movements* (Washington, DC: ICNC Press, 2021). Incidentally, this monograph misquotes and misrepresents my own arguments on the subject at length.

34. Charles Tilly, *Social Movements, 1768–2004* (Boulder: Paradigm Publishers, 2004), 222.

35. John Markoff, "Violence, Emancipation, and Democracy: The Countryside and the French Revolution," *The American Historical Review* 100, no. 2 (1995): 379.

36. This was not always as it is today. In previous eras, a riotous crowd could possess weapons approximating those held by soldiers and potentially pose a military threat to state forces, even when not

organized in a martial formation. This can still be so in some places through sheer force of numbers. However, the possibility has faded as weapons technology and state control have expanded. See William Robinson, *Global Capitalism and the Crisis of Humanity* (New York: Cambridge University Press, 2014).

37. Cathy Schneider, *Police Power and Race Riots: Urban Unrest in Paris and New York* (Philadelphia: University of Pennsylvania Press, 2014).

38. Chenoweth and Stephan, *Why Civil Resistance Works*, 58.

39. Sharon Erickson Nepstad, "Defections or Disobedience? Assessing the Consequences of Security Force Collaboration or Disengagement in Nonviolent Movements," in *Social Movements, Nonviolent Resistance, and the State*, ed. Hank Johnston (Waldham: Routledge, 2019), 79–97.

40. William Gamson, *The Strategy of Social Protest* (Homewood, IL: The Dorsey Press, 1975), 81.

41. See Alexander L. George and Andrew Bennett, *Case Studies and Theory Development in the Social Sciences* (Cambridge, MA: MIT Press, 2005).

42. See Erica Chenoweth and Maria Stephan, "Drop Your Weapons: When and Why Civil Resistance Works," *Foreign Affairs,* July/August 2014; Mark Engler and Paul Engler, *This Is an Uprising: How Nonviolent Revolt Is Shaping the Twenty-First Century* (New York: Nation Books, 2016).

43. Like the Egyptian revolution, unarmed violence played a substantial role in the Tunisian revolt. See Craig Brown, "Riots in the 2010/11 Tunisian Revolution: A Response to Case's Article in JRS Vol. 4 Issue 1," *Journal of Resistance Studies* 4, no. 2 (2018): 112–31; Asef Bayat, *Revolution without Revolutionaries: Making Sense of the Arab Spring* (Stanford: Stanford University Press, 2017), 9.

44. Mona El-Ghobashy, "The Praxis of the Egyptian Revolution," in *The Journey to Tahrir*, eds. Jeannie Sowers and Chris Toensing (London: Verso, 2012), 31.

45. Engler and Engler, *This Is an Uprising*, 252; Erica Chenoweth and Kathleen G. Cunningham, "Understanding Nonviolent Resistance: An Introduction," *Journal of Peace Research* 50, no. 3 (2013): 272.

46. Salwa Ismail, "The Egyptian Revolution Against the Police," *Social Research* 79, no. 2 (2012): 446.

47. El-Ghobashy, "The Praxis of the Egyptian Revolution," 22.

48. In addition to riots, popular committees involving neighborhood defense were an important social aspect of the January 25 revolution. See Hatem M. Hassan, "Extraordinary Politics of Ordinary People: Explaining the Microdynamics of Popular Committees in Revolutionary Cairo," *International Sociology* 30, no. 4 (2015): 383–400.

49. Ismail, "The Egyptian Revolution Against the Police," 446; Neil Ketchley, *Egypt in a Time of Revolution: Contentious Politics and the Arab Spring* (Cambridge: Cambridge University Press, 2017), 38.

50. Ketchley, *Egypt in a Time of Revolution*, 21.

51. Ketchley, *Egypt in a Time of Revolution*, 37.

52. Ketchley, *Egypt in a Time of Revolution*, 19.

53. Rabab El-Mahdi, "Orientalizing the Egyptian Revolution," *Jadaliyya*, April 11, 2011, http://www.jadaliyya.com/pages/index/1214/orientalising-the-egyptian-uprising.

54. Chenoweth and Stephan, "Drop Your Weapons: When and Why Civil Resistance Works."

The U.S. Black Bloc: Anarchy and the Effervescent Riot

1. Edward Avery-Natale, "'We're Here, We're Queer, We're Anarchists': The Nature of Identification and Subjectivity Among Black Blocs," *Anarchist Developments in Cultural Studies* 1 (2010): 105.

2. On the "anarchist turn," see Jacob Blumenfeld, Chiara Bottici, and Simon Critchley, eds., *The Anarchist Turn* (London: Pluto Press, 2013).

3. Mark Bray, *Antifa: The Anti-Fascist Handbook* (Brooklyn: Melville House, 2017).

4. Quoted from Kim Kelly's 2020 op-ed "Stop blaming everything bad on anarchists," *The Washington Post*, June 4, 2020, https://www.washingtonpost.com/outlook/2020/06/04/stop-blaming-everything-bad-anarchists.

5. Quoted from Farah Stockman's 2020 op-ed, "The Truth About Today's Anarchists," *The New York Times*, September 30, 2020, https://www.nytimes.com/2020/09/30/opinion/anarchists-protests-black-lives-matter.html.

6. Chris Hedges, "The Cancer in Occupy," *TruthDig*, February 6, 2012, https://www.truthdig.com/articles/the-cancer-in-occupy.

7. Charles Marino, "Putting Antifa and Black Lives Matter on Notice," *The Hill*, February 23, 2021, https://thehill.com/opinion/national-security/539903-putting-antifa-and-black-lives-matter-on-notice.

8. John Horgan, "Dear Anti-Trump Protestors: Please Renounce Violence," *Scientific American*, January 22, 2017, https://blogs.scientificamerican.com/cross-check/dear-anti-trump-protestors-please-renounce-violence; George Lakey, "Understanding Trump's Game Plan in Portland Could Be the Key to Preventing a Coup in November," *Waging Nonviolence*, July 25, 2020, https://wagingnonviolence.org/2020/07/portland-trump-federal-agents-law-order-preventing-coup.

9. For a few recent examples, see the *Batman* film, *The Dark Knight* (2008); the *Mission: Impossible* movies, *Rogue Nation* (2015) and *Fallout* (2018); James Bond films, *The World Is Not Enough* (1999) and *No Time to Die* (2020); and *XXX* (2002).

10. Francis Dupuis-Déri, *Who's Afraid of the Black Blocs?: Anarchy in Action Around the World*, trans. Lazer Lederhendler (Oakland: PM Press, 2014); David Graeber, *Direct Action: An Ethnography* (Oakland: AK Press, 2009); AK Thompson, *Black Bloc, White Riot: Anti-Globalization and the Genealogy of Dissent* (Oakland: AK Press, 2010).

11. Cindy Milstein, *Anarchism and Its Aspirations* (Oakland: AK Press, 2010).

12. All interviewee names are artificial in order to protect their identities. Pronouns, however, are accurate so as to preserve the speaker's gendered standpoint in his, her, or their context.

13. An affinity group is an autonomous cluster of activists with trusted personal ties who operate together during an action.

14. Seraphim Seferiades and Hank Johnston, eds., *Violent Protest, Contentious Politics, and the Neoliberal State* (Burlington: Ashgate, 2012), 6.

15. Hannah Arendt, *On Violence* (New York: Harcourt, 1970), 46.

16. William Gamson, *The Strategy of Social Protest* (Homewood, IL: The Dorsey Press, 1975), 81.

17. Also called "de-arresting," this is the act of physically intervening to liberate a fellow protester from the police during an arrest. Though there are still many instances of successful unarrests, especially among those who are masked, this practice has become increasingly symbolic due to police cameras, social media tracking, and facial recognition software.

18. See Laura Bassett, "Why Violent Protests Work," *GQ*, June 2, 2020, https://www.gq.com/story/why-violent-protests-work.

19. CrimethInc., *The Ex-Worker Podcast*, Episode 9, 2013: 13:29, https://crimethinc.com/podcasts/the-ex-worker/episodes/9.

20. CrimethInc., *The Ex-Worker Podcast*, Episode 9: 8:30.

21. Georges Sorel, *Reflections on Violence*, trans. T. E. Hulme and J. Roth (Glencoe, IL: The Free Press, [1950] 2004).

22. See for example: The Invisible Committee, *The Coming Insurrection* (Los Angeles: Semiotext(e), 2007).

23. Georges Sorel, *Reflections on Violence*, 90.

24. AK Thompson, *Black Bloc, White Riot*, 5.

25. Here, Em is referring to a participant in the Battle of Seattle who is quoted in the 2000 documentary, *This Is What Democracy Looks Like*, dir. Jill Friedberg and Rick Rowley (Big Noise Films, 2000). In that film, the activist quotes himself as having said: "That's really not fear in your gut or in your throat, that's really your first taste of freedom" (26:45).

26. "Dumpster," short for "dumpster dive," is a term used for the prac-
    tice of rescuing edible food from the garbage for consumption,
    often from the dumpsters of grocery stores or restaurants, as she
    had referenced doing with the pizza from the bar we were sitting in.

27. Émile Durkheim, *The Elementary Forms of Religious Life*, trans. J. W.
    Swain (New York: The Free Press, [1915] 1965), 246–50.

28. Durkheim, *The Elementary Forms of Religious Life*, 247; Gustave Le
    Bon, *The Crowd: A Study of the Popular Mind* (New York: Dover Pub-
    lications, [1895] 2002).

29. Randall Collins, *Violence: A Micro-Sociological Theory* (Princeton:
    Princeton University Press, 2008), 94.

30. Collins, *Violence*, 98.

31. See Benjamin S. Case, "Contentious Effervescence: The Subjective
    Experience of Rioting," *Mobilization* 26, no. 2 (2021): 179–96.

32. See also Matthew Kearney, "Totally Alive: The Wisconsin Uprising
    and the Source of Collective Effervescence, *Theory and Society* 47, no.
    2 (2018): 233–54.

33. James Baldwin and *Esquire* editors, "James Baldwin: How to Cool
    It," *Esquire*, July 1968.

34. See NAACP, "The Origins of Modern Day Policing," n.d., https://
    naacp.org/find-resources/history-explained/origins-mod-
    ern-day-policing; Sam Levin, "White supremacists and militias
    have infiltrated police across US, report says," *The Guardian*, August
    27, 2020, https://www.theguardian.com/us-news/2020/aug/27/
    white-supremacists-militias-infiltrate-us-police-report.

35. Erik Ortiz, "'Disturbing texts between police and far-right group
    prompt investigation," *NBC News*, February 5, 2019, https://www
    .nbcnews.com/news/us-news/disturbing-texts-between-oregon
    -police-far-right-group-prompts-investigation-n972161; See also:
    Mark Bray, *Antifa*.

36. Anyone who lived through the COVID-19 pandemic likely encoun-
    tered the ways that masks make it difficult to recognize people in
    some instances and really don't in others.

37. Edward Avery-Natale, "'We're Here, We're Queer, We're Anar-
    chists'"; Dupuis-Déri, *Who's Afraid of the Black Blocs?*; Claryn Spies,
    "Reading Black Bloc Aesthetically," *Theory in Action* 14, no. 1 (2021):
    39–62.

38. Incite! Women of Color Against Violence, *The Revolution Will Not be
    Funded: Beyond the Non-profit Industrial Complex* (Boston: South End
    Press, 2007).

South African Fallists: Decolonization and Humanizing Violence

1. On the Haitian Revolution, see C. L. R. James, *The Black Jacobins: Toussaint L'Ouverture and the San Domingo Revolution* (New York: Random House, 1963).

2. Frantz Fanon, *The Wretched of the Earth*, trans. Richard Philcox (New York: Grove, [1961] 2004), 1.

3. Ngũgĩ wa Thiong'o, *Decolonizing the Mind: The Politics of Language in African Literature* (Portsmouth, NH: Heinemann Educational Books, 1986).

4. What U.S. Americans call university *administrations*, South Africans call *management*—a practice that university labor movements in the U.S. might do well to adopt.

5. Roseanne Chantiluke, Brian Kwoba, and Athinangamso Nkopo, eds., *Rhodes Must Fall: The Struggle to Decolonize the Racist Heart of an Empire* (London: Zed Books, 2018).

6. As an identifiable movement, FeesMustFall began at Wits, a prestigious and historically white institution, and quickly spread to other schools. However, protests and riots against tuition (and other issues) are common at historically Black technical colleges, most prominently at Tshwane University of Technology (TUT). While a deeper discussion of the relationship between activists at these different universities is important, it is outside the scope of this research.

7. Chantiluke, Kwoba, and Nkopo, eds., *Rhodes Must Fall: The Struggle to Decolonize the Racist Heart of an Empire* (London: Zed Books, 2018).

8. Hibist Kassa, "A Reflection on the Student-Worker Alliance," in *Publica[c]tion,* ed. Leigh-Ann Naidoo, Asher Gamedze, and Thato Magano (Johannesburg: Publica[c]tion Collective + NewText, 2017): 18–19; Morwa Kgoroba, "The #EndOutsourcing Protest: Outsourced Workers and Students vs. Wits University," in *Rioting and Writing*, ed. Chinguno, Crispen, Morwa Kgoroba, Sello Mashibili, Bafana Nicolas Masilena, Boikhutso Maubane, Nhlanhla Moyo, Andile Mthombeni, and Hlengiwe Ndlovu (Johannesburg: Society, Work and Politics Institute, 2017): 126–34.

9. *Intersectionality* is a term credited to legal scholar Kimberlé Crenshaw and is associated with other Black Feminist scholars like Patricia Hill Collins. The original intervention challenged the idea of "single-issue" politics, pointing to the ways Black women in the U.S. faced both racism as Black people and sexism as women in an *intersectional* dynamic that altered and multiplied the effect of both forms of oppression. The genealogy of the intersectional idea is often traced to the 1977 Combahee River Collective statement. *Intersectionality* has come to mean a variety of things but is often associated with the

ways that multiple forms of systemic oppression create differently oppressed identities. See Kimberlé Crenshaw, "Demarginalizing the Intersection of Race and Sex: A Black Feminist Critique of Antidiscrimination Doctrine, Feminist Theory and Antiracist Politics," *University of Chicago Legal Forum* 1 (1989): 139–67; Kimberlé Crenshaw, "Mapping the Margins: Intersectionality, Identity Politics, and Violence against Women of Color," *Stanford Law Review* 43, no. 6 (1991): 1241–99; Patricia Hill Collins, *Intersectionality as Critical Social Theory* (Durham: Duke University Press, 2019); and Patricia Hill Collins, *Black Feminist Thought: Knowledge, Consciousness, and the Politics of Empowerment* (New York: Routledge, 2000). On intersectionality in the Fallist movements, see Danai S. Mupotsa, "Intersectionality Is, or Perhaps Intersectionality As," in *Publica[c]tion*, ed. Naidoo et al. (Johannesburg: Publica[c]tion Collective + NewText, 2017), 54.

10. The will to (self-)critique that I observed in Fallist scenes was exceptional, if at times appearing to me to border on excessive. In activist publications, public talks, and personal interactions, many Fallists were determined to center the marginalized, prioritize praxis, and to foreground collective failures in these regards.

11. Student activist publications regarding the Fallist movements demonstrate extraordinary theoretical depth and analytic sharpness. I highly recommend *Publica[c]tion*, eds. Naidoo, Gamedze, and Magano (Johannesburg: Publica[c]tion Collective + NewText, 2017), *Rioting and Writing: Diaries and the Wits Fallistseds*, eds. Crispen Chinguno, Morwa Kgoroba, Sello Mashibili, Bafana Nicolas Masilena, Boikhutso Maubane, Nhlanhla Moyo, Andile Mthombeni, and Hlengiwe Ndlovu (Johannesburg: Society, Work and Politics Institute, University of Witwatersrand, 2017), as well as the publication *Chimurenga*, which is not specifically related to student activists but involves some, and published pan-African material that is influential and related to the overall politics of the Fallist movements.

12. Nhlanhla Moyo, "The Gates," in *Rioting and Writing*, eds. Chinguno et al. (Johannesburg: Society, Work and Politics Institute, University of Witwatersrand, 2017), 51.

13. "Historically white" meaning in the apartheid period; the student population has been majority Black for years, while the colonial culture of the university persists in many ways.

14. Richard Ballard, Adam Habib, and Imraan Valodia, eds., *Voices of Protest: Social Movements in Post-Apartheid South Africa* (Pietermaritzburg: University of Kwazulu Natal Press, 2006). One of the editors of this volume, Adam Habib, was Vice Chancellor of Wits during the FMF uprising, and, according to students and workers I spoke with, was a personified target of protests at that university. Student activists described at one point essentially holding Habib hostage

in a campus general assembly, forcing him to call university board members on the phone to relate student grievances. Habib himself publicly said of this event he was not held but elected to remain at the general assembly. In any event, Habib is an academic authority on protest in post-apartheid South Africa and also was the target of one of the defining post-apartheid movements, and that should not go unmentioned. On this, see Bandile Bertrand Leopeng, "A Response to Habib," in *Rioting and Writing*, eds. Chinguno et al. (Johannesburg: Society, Work and Politics Institute, University of Witwatersrand, 2017).

15. Is Fallism a civil resistance movement or is it a post-civil resistance movement? In the connection and the antagonism between the ANC revolution and the Fallist uprising, the limitations of the campaign-oriented frame of civil resistance studies is apparent. Both Sharp's theory and Chenoweth's data would endeavor to characterize these as discreet campaigns, analyzable on their own terms based purely on their tactical repertoires. The reality of Fallism as a movement of its own and also an outcome of the outcomes of the ANC movement simultaneously challenges the notion of the campaign as a unit of analysis and highlights the failure of civil resistance literature to take seriously the outcomes of campaigns.

16. See Greg Nicolson, "#FeesMustFall: UJ's continuing use of violent private security—a dangerous move in dangerous times," *Daily Maverick*, September 30, 2016, https://www.dailymaverick.co.za/article/2016-09-30-feesmustfall-ujs-continuing-use-of-violent-private-security-a-dangerous-move-in-dangerous-times.

17. Other major tensions within the movement included gender, leadership, and representation in the struggle (see *Rioting and Writing*, eds. Chinguno et al.).

18. Hannah Arendt, *On Violence* (New York: Harcourt, 1970), 14.

19. Karl Von Holdt, "The Violence of Order, Orders of Violence: Between Fanon and Bourdieu," *Current Sociology* 61, no. 2 (2012): 112–31.

20. In perhaps the most extreme example, a campus law library was burned down during the 2016 wave of the movement. Reuters Staff, "South African university library torched, 32 students arrested," *Reuters*, September 7, 2016, https://www.reuters.com/article/us-safrica-protests/south-african-university-library-torched-32-students-arrested-idUSKCN11D1YZ. See also Xola Mehlolakulu, "Burning Buildings," in *Publica[c]tion,* ed. Naidoo et al. (Johannesburg: Publica[c]tion Collective + NewText): 33.

21. Recorded in handwritten notes from the book release event for *Rioting and Writing: Diaries of the Wits Fallists*, University of Witwatersrand, July 27, 2017.

22. Publica[c]tion Collective, "This Here Collection is Incoherent...,"
    Publica[c]tion, ed. Naidoo et al. (Johannesburg: Publica[c]tion Col-
    lective + NewText, 2017), 3.

23. Marilena Simiti, "The Volatility of Urban Riots," in *Violent Protest,
    Contentious Politics, and the Neoliberal State*, ed. Seferiades and John-
    ston (Burlington: Ashgate, 2012).

24. Specifically, he is referring to the concourse in Solomon Mahlangu
    House, a large indoor space in a main campus building where stu-
    dent meetings typically took place. It had previously been called
    "Senate House" and following the FMF uprising was officially
    renamed for Mahlangu, a martyr from Umkhonto we Sizwe (Spear
    of the Nation), the militant wing of the ANC during the anti-
    apartheid struggle.

25. Moshibudi Motimele, "Violence Has Nothing to Do with Throw-
    ing Stones," in *Publica[c]tion*, ed. Naidoo et al. (Johannesburg: Publi-
    ca[c]tion Collective + NewText, 2017), 5.

26. Recorded in handwritten notes from the book release event for
    Rioting and Writing: Diaries of the Wits Fallists, University of Witwa-
    tersrand, July 27, 2017.

27. Counter-intuitive as in might sound, this strategy has parallels in
    military combat as well. Historians say that in a famous battle in feu-
    dal Japan, a general fired on a contingent of troops from a clan that
    was present at the battlefield but had yet to engage, as if to say, "Time
    to choose sides." Shaken and reminded of what was at stake, the pre-
    viously undecided general joined the fight on the side that had fired
    at him, taking a flanking maneuver that would end up being decisive
    for the outcome. See "Battle of Sekigahara," *Encyclopedia Britannica*,
    https://www.britannica.com/event/Battle-of-Sekigahara.

28. Seraphim Seferiades and Hank Johnston, eds. *Violent Protest, Conten-
    tious Politics, and the Neoliberal State* (Burlington: Ashgate, 2012), 6.

29. Karl von Holdt, Malose Langa, Sepetla Molapo, Nomfundo
    Mogapi, Kindiza Ngubeni, Jacob Dlamini, and Adèle Kirsten,
    *The Smoke That Calls: Insurgent Citizenship, Collective Violence, and the
    Struggle for a Place in the New South Africa* (Johannesburg: CSVR and
    SWOP, 2012).

30. Alain Badiou, *The Rebirth of History: Times of Riots and Uprisings*, trans.
    Gregory Elliott (New York: Verso, 2012).

31. John Markoff, *Waves of Democracy: Social Movements and Political
    Change* (Boulder: Paradigm Publishers, 2015), 136.

32. He is referring to the concourse in Solomon Mahlangu House, the
    same location referenced by Ardee above.

33. Michael Schwartz, *Radical Protest and Social Structure: The Southern
    Farmers' Alliance and Cotton Tenancy, 1880–1890* (Chicago: University
    of Chicago Press, 1976), 130.

34. If the anti-police riot relies on anti-institutional power, and the pogrom relies on institutional power, we might say that the sports riot represents noninstitutional power—not inherently institutional or anti-institutional, but with the potential to go either way.

35. Barbara Deming, *Revolution and Equilibrium* (New York: Grossman Publishers, 1971), 197.

36. Arendt, *On Violence*, 63.

A Revolution Is Not a Peaceful Protest

1. Bill Peduto, @billpeduto, Twitter, May 30, 2020, https://twitter.com/billpeduto/status/1266857104259899392. The original Tweet by @1Hood reads: "Dear allies, it is imperative that you listen to organizers. These young Black organizers had a clear plan and message that was disregarded. If you fight for Black lives, you don't unnecessarily place Black bodies in jeopardy." Peduto's re-Tweet adds: "To those vandalizing Downtown. You will be arrested. You have turned on the very mission, and more importantly—the people, you supposedly marched for 2 hours ago. You have turned their peaceful march for justice into your self-centered, violent act of attention."

2. Bill Peduto, @billpeduto, Twitter, June 2, 2020, "East Liberty protest's violence spurred by small 'splinter group' of outsiders," https://twitter.com/billpeduto/status/1267786041999704071.

3. See Kevin Young, Tarun Banerjee, and Michael Schwartz, *Levers of Power: How the 1% Rules and What the 99% Can Do about It* (New York: Verso, 2020).

4. Harry G. Frankfurt, *On Bullshit* (Princeton: Princeton University Press, 2005), 16.

5. Frankfurt, *On Bullshit*, 16–18.

6. Nick Hanauer, "The Pitchforks are Coming… For Us Plutocrats," *Politico Magazine*, July/August, 2014, https://www.politico.com/magazine/story/2014/06/the-pitchforks-are-coming-for-us-plutocrats-108014; Tweet by Patriotic Millionaires, January 1, 2022: https://twitter.com/PatrioticMills/status/1477327509016428545.

7. Andy Mannix, "As the Third Precinct Burned, Minneapolis Police Officers in Another Precinct Destroyed Case Files," *Star Tribune*, July 14, 2021, https://www.startribune.com/as-the-third-precinct-burned-minneapolis-police-officers-in-another-precinct-destroyed-case-files/600078074.

8. Let it not be misunderstood from my vulgar analogy that rioting is only for the able-bodied. On the contrary, the means of riotous

resistance are available to anyone with the will and creativity to jam the gears of the system when necessary.

9. Seraphim Seferiades and Hank Johnston, eds. *Violent Protest, Contentious Politics, and the Neoliberal State* (Burlington: Ashgate, 2012), 6.

10. See Dave Davies, "How the Attica prison uprising started—and why it still resonates today," *NPR* interview with Arthur Harrison and Stanley Nelson, October 27, 2021, https://www.npr.org/2021/10/27/1049295683/attica-prison-documentary-stanley-nelson.

11. Sam Levin, "Minneapolis Lawmakers Vow to Disband Police Department in Historic Move," *The Guardian*, June 7, 2020, https://www.theguardian.com/us-news/2020/jun/07/minneapolis-city-council-defund-police-george-floyd.

12. Akin Olla, "Minneapolis promised change after George Floyd. Instead it's geared up for war," *The Guardian*, March 11, 2021 https://www.theguardian.com/commentisfree/2021/mar/11/minneapolis-promised-change-after-george-floyd-instead-its-geared-up-for-war.

13. Neil Ketchley, *Egypt in a Time of Revolution: Contentious Politics and the Arab Spring* (Cambridge: Cambridge University Press, 2017).

14. Keny Arkana, "La Rage," YouTube, February 22, 2011, https://www.youtube.com/watch?v=oewRadlyrHo; On riot porn, see Maple John Razsa, "Beyond 'Riot Porn': Protest Video and the Production of Unruly Subjects," *Ethnos* 79, no. 4 (2014): 496–524.

15. Joshua Garcia Aponte, "Scenes of Fire and Tear Gas During Protests in Puerto Rico," *The New York Times*, July 16, 2019, https://www.nytimes.com/video/us/politics/100000006613786/protest-puerto-rico.html.

16. William Ramirez, "After the Power of Protest Ousts a Governor, Puerto Rico has a New Leader. For Now," ACLU, August 8, 2019, https://www.aclu.org/blog/free-speech/rights-protesters/after-power-protest-ousts-governor-puerto-rico-has-new-leader-now.

17. Mohammed A. Bamyeh, "Anarchist Method, Liberal Intention, Authoritarian Lesson: The Arab Spring Between Three Enlightenments," *Constellations* 20, no. 3 (2013): 189.

18. Bamyeh, "Anarchist Method, Liberal Intention, Authoritarian Lesson," 191.

19. Alain Badiou, *The Rebirth of History: Times of Riots and Uprisings*, trans. Gregory Elliott (Brooklyn: Verso, 2012); Joshua Clover, *Riot. Strike. Riot.* (Brooklyn: Verso, 2016).

20. Hannah Arendt, *On Violence* (New York: Harcourt, 1970), 64.

21. Bamyeh, "Anarchist Method, Liberal Intention, Authoritarian Lesson," 188.

22. Barbara Deming, *Revolution and Equilibrium* (New York: Grossman Publishers, 1971).

23. Clover, *Riot. Strike. Riot.*, 48.

24. AK Thompson, *Black Bloc, White Riot: Anti-Globalization and the Genealogy of Dissent* (Oakland: AK Press, 2010), 21.

25. Thomas Jefferson to St. George Tucker, August 28, 1797, https:// founders.archives.gov/documents/Jefferson/01-29-02-0405.

Appendix: A Discussion of Riotology

1. Michael Loadenthal, *The Politics of Attack: Communiqués and Insurrectionary Violence* (Manchester: Manchester University Press, 2017), 23.

2. See World Bank GDP per capita data: https://data.worldbank.org/ indicator/NY.GDP.PCAP.CD.

3. See Janet Box-Steffensmeir, John R. Freeman, Matthew P. Hitt, and Jon C. W. Pevehouse, *Time Series Analysis for the Social Sciences* (New York: Cambridge University Press, 2014).

4. CounterPower, *Organizing for Autonomy: History, Theory, and Strategy for Collective Liberation* (Brooklyn: Common Notions, 2020), 12–14.

5. My travel was made possible by the Stanley Prostrednik Memorial Scholarship for graduate students.

6. Kathleen Blee and Verta Taylor, "Semi-Structured Interviewing in Social Movement Research," in *Methods of Social Movement Research,* eds., Bert Klandermans and Suzanne Staggenborg (Minneapolis: University of Minnesota Press, 2002), 92–117.

7. Vivian Shaw, "'Extreme Pressure': Gendered Negotiations of Violence and Vulnerability in Japanese Anti-Racism Movements," *Critical Asian Studies* 52, no. 1 (2020): 109–26.

8. Tammy Kovich, "Gender at the Barricades: The Politics and Possibilities of the Riot," *Coils of the Serpent* 7 (2020): 113–45.

9. E.g., Javier Auyero, *Contentious Lives: Two Argentine Women, Two Protests, and the Quest for Recognition* (Durham: Duke University Press, 2003); Francis Dupuis-Déri, *Who's Afraid of the Black Bloc: Anarchy in Action Around the World,* trans. Lazer Lederhendler (Oakland: PM Press, 2014); Shon Meckfessel, *Nonviolence Ain't What It Used to Be: Unarmed Insurrection and the Rhetoric of Resistance* (Oakland: AK Press, 2016).

10. Kovich, "Gender at the Barricades," 138.

11. See Barbara Alpern Engel, "Not by Bread Alone: Subsistence Riots in Russia during World War I," *The Journal of Modern History* 69, no. 4 (1997): 696–721; Lynne Taylor, "Food Riots Revisited," *Journal of Social History* 30, no. 2 (1997): 483–96; E.P. Thompson, "The Moral Economy of the English Crowd in the Eighteenth Century," *Past and Present* 50 (1971): 76–136.

12. Raven Rakia, "Black Riot," *The New Inquiry,* November 14, 2013, https://thenewinquiry.com/black-riot.

13. George Weddington, "Political Ontology and Race Research: A Response to 'Critical Race Theory, Afro-pessimism, and Racial Progress Narratives,'" *Sociology of Race and Ethnicity* 5, no. 2 (2019): 278–88.

14. See Mark Bray, *Antifa: The Anti-Fascist Handbook* (Brooklyn: Melville House, 2017).

15. For example, see Erik Ortiz, "'Disturbing' texts between Oregon police and far-right group prompt investigation," *NBC News*, February 15, 2019, https://www.nbcnews.com/news/us-news/disturbing-texts-between-oregon-police-far-right-group-prompts-investigation-n972161.

16. AK Thompson, *Black Bloc, White Riot: Anti-Globalization and the Genealogy of Dissent* (Oakland: AK Press, 2010), 20.

17. Hannah Arendt, *On Violence* (New York: Harcourt, 1970), 12.

18. Jennifer Earl, Sarah A. Soule, and John D. McCarthy, "Protest Under Fire? Explaining the Policing of Protest," *American Sociological Review* 68, no. 4 (2003): 581–606.

19. Elizabeth Hinton, *America on Fire: The Untold History of Police Violence and Black Rebellion Since the 1960s* (New York: Liveright, 2021).

20. Christian Davenport, Hank Johnston, and Carol Mueller, eds. *Repression and Mobilization* (Minneapolis: University of Minnesota Press, 2005); Balko Radley, *Rise of the Warrior Cop: The Militarization of America's Police Forces* (New York: Public Affairs, 2014).

21. Jennifer Earl and Sarah A. Soule, "Seeing Blue: A Police Centered Explanation of Protest Policing," *Mobilization* 11, no. 2 (2006): 145–64.

22. See also the recent leak—broken by a high school newspaper—of Kentucky State Police training materials that quote Adolf Hitler repeatedly on the importance of consistent and ruthless use of violence: Nicholas Bogel-Burroughs, "Kentucky Police Training Quoted Hitler and Urged 'Ruthless' Violence," *The New York Times*, October 31, 2020, https://www.nytimes.com/2020/10/31/us/kentucky-state-police-hitler.html; Radley, *Rise of the Warrior Cop*.

23. Rachel Wahl, *Just Violence: Torture and Human Rights in the Eyes of the Police* (Stanford: Stanford University Press, 2017).

24. Ben Brucato, "Fabricating the Color Line in a White Democracy: From Slave Catchers to Petty Sovereigns," *Theoria* 61, no. 4 (2014): 30–54; Sally Hadden, *Slave Patrols: Law and Violence in Virginia and the Carolinas* (Cambridge: Harvard University Press, 2001).

25. Some is. See, for example, Christopher M. Schnaubelt, "Lessons on Command and Control From the Los Angeles Riots," *The U.S. Army War College Quarterly: Parameters* 27, no. 2 (1997): 88–109, https://press.armywarcollege.edu/cgi/viewcontent.cgi?article=1830&context=parameters; Nicholas Blasco, "The Hong Kong Protests:

A Case Study of Police and Military Use of Force," *War Room—U.S. Army War College*, October 17, 2019, https://warroom.armywar college.edu/articles/hong-kong-protests-a-case-study.

26. See, for example, the recently leaked Chicago Police Department manual for crowd control: https://www.documentcloud.org/documents/7279259-Crowd-Control-and-Behavior.html.

27. See, for example, Unity and Struggle, "Big Brick Energy: A Multi-City Study of the 2020 George Floyd Uprising," Common Notions, July 21, 2022, http://www.unityandstruggle.org/2022/07/big-brick -energy-a-multi-city-study-of-the-2020-george-floyd-uprising; Anonymous, "Lasers in the Tear Gas: A Guide to Tactics in Hong Kong," *It's Going Down*, August 13, 2019, https:/itsgoingdown .org/lasers-in-the-tear-gas; Anonymous, "Making the Best of Mass Arrests: 12 Lessons from the Kettle During the J20 Protests," CrimethInc., January 30, 2017, https:/crimethinc.com/2017/01/ 30/making-the-best-of-mass-arrests-12-lessons-from-the-kettle -during-the-j20-protests; Maple Razsa and Milton Guillén, *The Maribor Uprisings* (Slovenia: En Masse Films, 2017), http:/maribor uprisings.org.

28. Chloe Haimson, "Interactional Resistance During Black Lives Matter Protests: The Political Stakes of Rebelling Against the Public Order," *Mobilization* 25, no. 2 (2020): 185–200.

29. Lee Fang, "Federal Government Buys Riot Gear, Increases Security Funding, Citing Coronavirus Pandemic," *The Intercept*, May 17, 2020, https://theintercept.com/2020/05/17/veterans-affairs-coro navirus-security-police; Nathaniel Meyersohn, Alexis Benveniste and Chauncey Alcorn, "From Tiffany to Target, stores are boarding up windows in case of election unrest," *CNN*, November 3, 2020, https://www.cnn.com/2020/11/02/business/retail-election -security/index.html.

30. Mohamed Theron, "'Dr. Doom' Economist Nouriel Roubini Says He Predicted US Protests 'Months Ago,'" *Business Insider*, June 1, 2020, https://markets.businessinsider.com/news/stocks/nouriel-roubini -dr-doom-economist-predicted-riots-months-ago-protests -2020-6-1029268529.

31. Nick Turse, "Pentagon War Game Includes Scenario for Military Response to Domestic Gen Z Rebellion," *The Intercept*, June 5, 2020, https://theintercept.com/2020/06/05/pentagon-war-game -gen-z.

Index